KIDS RULE!

CONSOLE-ING PASSIONS

TELEVISION AND CULTURAL POWER

EDITED BY LYNN SPIGEL

KIDS RULE!

Nickelodeon and
Consumer Citizenship

SARAH BANET-WEISER

Duke University Press
Durham and London
2007

© 2007 Duke University Press
All rights reserved
Printed in the United States of
America on acid-free paper ∞
Designed by Amy Ruth Buchanan
Typeset in Minion by Keystone
Typesetting, Inc.
Library of Congress Cataloging-in-
Publication Data appear on the last
printed page of this book.

For my father,

Anthony George Banet

1937–2005

CONTENTS

ILLUSTRATIONS

ACKNOWLEDGMENTS

There are many people who helped make this book possible, and I am happy to have this opportunity to express my profound appreciation. *Kids Rule!* is a result of my thinking through ideas about children, media, and citizenship over the past several years, and I am fortunate to have had many different contexts in which to try out these ideas.

Colleagues and friends at the University of Southern California and elsewhere provided invaluable guidance and support at every stage of this project. Marita Sturken is an amazing colleague, mentor, and friend—she counseled me, read every word, and gave me sound advice and guidance. Her tenacious faith in me helped me get through many rough stages in both my personal and professional life. Dana Polan is, quite simply, the most generous person I know—intellectually, personally, professionally. I am tremendously grateful to him for his careful reading, constructive advice, and loving support. Val Hartouni is a wonderful friend and mentor; her unflagging support and last-hour advice made this a much better book. Larry Gross came into my life at a crucial time, and his encyclopedic knowledge, wise suggestions, and supportive friendship truly helped me finish this project. Abby Kaun is an important friend and colleague, and her perspective and reality checks throughout the past six years have been invaluable. George Sanchez is a true inspiration to me, and his faith in not only this project but also me personally has meant the world to me.

The Annenberg School for Communication at USC has been a wonderful environment in which to start and finish a book. My colleagues and friends at Annenberg offered me support from the moment I was hired as an assistant professor, guiding me through not only the initial stages of this project but also through the undeniably stressful experience of the tenure process. I am grateful to all at Annenberg, but in particular to Sandra Ball-Rokeach, Geoff Cowan, Patti Riley, Tom Hollihan, Peter Monge, Stacy Smith, Chris Smith, Rebecca Weintraub, François Bar, Hernan Galperin, Doug Thomas, Walter Fisher, Stephen O'Leary, Manuel Castells, and Josh Kun. I owe thanks to many other colleagues and friends, including Ruthie Gilmore, Nancy Lutkehaus, Michael Messner, Tony

Frietas, Susan Douglas, Eric Zinner, Herman Gray, Barbie Zelizer, Toby Miller, Lynn Spigel, Katherine Sender, Ishita Sinha Roy, and George Lipsitz. Billy Higgins provided needed expertise in retrieving frame-grabs from DVDs. The staff at Annenberg was incredibly helpful in figuring out the logistics of preparing a book for publication. I gained a tremendous amount from exchanging work with Alison Trope. Cynthia Chris read much of the manuscript, and her sage advice helped me immensely. Heather Hendershot read the manuscript several times, and her advice and her own work has been invaluable to my thinking about children and media. Ellen Seiter continues to be an inspiration—I am grateful for her support and friendship. Angela McRobbie's political and intellectual commitment to girls and media has made an immeasurable impact on my own work.

I am fortunate to have the support of many graduate students—this book could have never been finished without their tireless energy and willingness to help. They are a constant reminder to me of the importance of research and teaching. Cara Wallis and John Kephart provided crucial copyediting and suggestions to the manuscript. Becky Herr's enthusiasm for not only this project but for scholarship on children and media was always appreciated. Laura Portwood-Stacer was essential to this project—her organized work ethic, steadfast enthusiasm, and unbelievable attention to detail made this book possible. Daniela Baroffio-Bota offered a willing ear, sharp insights, and an important friendship. Jade Miller helped a great deal with last-minute changes.

Academic life can at times seem isolating, and it is only because I have a whole other life and community outside the university that I was able to complete this project. I am grateful to Joyce Campion, for her love and support, and her willingness to drop whatever she was doing to help me out, whether that be in the form of picking up my children, offering baby-sitting, or sitting down to share a glass of wine at the end of a long day. Tina Reyes helped me navigate through not only carpool issues but also through the ups and downs of being the parent of an adolescent. Claudia Dodson also was an expert navigator in the many complicated arenas of my life, and I am grateful for her friendship. Liz Sharzer, Scott Merrill, JoAnn Merrill, Kevin Reyes, Tiare Meegan, and many others added to the richness of my life, and provided the perspective I needed.

At Duke University Press, I could not have asked for a more conscientious, enthusiastic, and considerate editor than Ken Wissoker. His expert advice on all stages of this book was absolutely crucial, and I am profoundly thankful for his supportive friendship and faith in me. Anita Grisales answered all my questions in record time and guided this project through all the different stages of publishing. The copyeditor, Lynn Walterick, was a thorough and efficient fact-checker, for which I'm very grateful.

I want to acknowledge the industry professionals who shared their experience, their political commitments, and their conviction in quality children's media with me. Linda Simensky shared an incredible wealth of knowledge about the children's television industry. Donna Mitroff is a valued colleague and friend, and her insights into the industry have convinced me of the great need to have good, smart people making children's TV. I am also grateful to all the people I interviewed for this book, including the children who were willing to sit down with me and share their insights about Nickelodeon. Ellen Seiter shared with me interviews and conversations she and Vicki Mayer had with industry professionals, which added richness to my analysis.

My family has been supportive of every stage in my career, and I am indebted to all of them. My siblings, Suzannah and Sean Collins, Angela and Ron Reich, Genevieve and Cary Crank, Matt Banet, Candice Seti and Joseph and Jurima Banet have always been there for me, with support, laughter, and love. Kathy and Les Weiser, and Dan and Peg Weiser have been unfaltering in their love and support. My extended family, especially my aunt Dodie, have been a constant source of support (even from a great distance). My mother, Anne Banet, has been a true inspiration my entire life. I hope she knows that I am as proud of her as she is of me. My father, who died during the last stages of this project, gave me and continues to give me hope and faith in this world. This book is dedicated to him and his love of the written word.

I began this project because of an ongoing interest in the connections between national identity and the popular media, and my interest in kids' media culture emanates from a number of different places. Most importantly, I became interested in children's media as my own children became avid media participants—and specifically Nickelodeon watchers. Listening to them sing the "Nickelodeon Nation" theme song, seeing them watch *SpongeBob SquarePants* or *Hey Arnold!*, or hearing their commentary on which shows were interesting and which ones were silly or dumb forced my attention to children's television. Sam Weiser offered invaluable suggestions and commentaries about my interpretation of children's media—his intellect, wit, and willingness to take risks have thrilled and inspired me. The unconditional love of Luke Weiser made it possible to think that writing this book was worth it. He was an expert research assistant and was always willing to fill me in on the complicated terrain of kids' TV. Lily Weiser is the sheer embodiment of girl power—her tenacity, beauty, and intelligence are a constant reminder of what is good in this world. Finally, Bill Weiser, my husband

and great love, has shown me time and time again that there is more to life than being an academic. His patience, rationality, and common sense give me perspective; his integrity, commitment, and love give me hope.

A different version of chapter 4 was published as "Girls Rule! Gender, Feminism, and Nickelodeon," in *Critical Studies in Media Communication* 21, no. 2 (2004). A different version of chapter 1 was published as " 'We Pledge Allegiance to Kids': Nickelodeon and Citizenship," in *Nickelodeon Nation: The History, Politics, and Economics of America's Only TV Channel for Kids*, edited by Heather Hendershot (New York: New York University Press, 2004). Chapter 5 appears, in a slightly different form, as "What's Your Flava? Race and Postfeminism in Media Culture," in *Interrogating Postfeminism: Gender and the Politics of Popular Culture*, edited by Yvonne Tasker and Diane Negra (Durham, N.C.: Duke University Press, 2007).

1

"WE, THE PEOPLE OF NICKELODEON":
THEORIZING EMPOWERMENT AND
CONSUMER CITIZENSHIP

In January 2005, the popular Nickelodeon cartoon character Sponge-Bob SquarePants became a figure of controversy when he was featured in an educational video intended to promote tolerance and diversity. The video, called *We Are Family*, featured "lessons" on racial, ethnic, and sexual tolerance, including a short segment depicting a family with gay parents. The representation of same-sex parents prompted U.S. conservative religious groups to attack the video, focusing the assault on SpongeBob SquarePants and Nickelodeon. No stranger to sexual controversy, SpongeBob has been frequently identified as a gay character by both conservative organizations and gay fans and has consequently provoked homophobic organizations in the United States.[1] The latest controversy around the video (or, as conservative religious group Focus on the Family depicted it, the "vehicle for pro-gay propaganda") prompted Focus on the Family spokesperson Paul Batura to say, "We see the video as an insidious means by which the organization is manipulating and potentially brainwashing kids."[2]

Later that same year, Nickelodeon made headlines again, but for a very different reason. In October 2005, the U.S.-based Alliance for a Healthier Generation entered into a partnership with Nickelodeon and former President Bill Clinton to combat the spread of childhood obesity.[3] The aim of the partnership was to "provide the necessary tools to empower children and families to be agents of change in their communities through grassroots activities, events, and programming support through multiple media platforms." Herb Scannell, the Nickelodeon president at the time, added, "We want kids to become personally invested in living strong, healthy lives. And if we do our jobs right, kids will believe that being healthy is cool."[4] Smoothly transforming civic behavior—grassroots organizing, activism—into part of a market strategy ("if we do our jobs right"), Scannell sells the idea of "empowerment" the same way Nickelodeon sells programming and merchandise.

These two news stories, and the rhetorical strategies employed in both, demonstrate the various ways that children's media, and Nickelodeon in particular, are understood and contested within public discourse. Interestingly, while Focus on the Family laments television's role in "brainwashing" kids, and the Alliance for a Healthier Generation presumably takes a different tack, claiming to "empower" children through its multimedia platform, both strategies rely on a fairly instrumental theory of media effects and assumptions about the formation of identity through the media. Nickelodeon, a children's cable television channel, has claimed since its inception that its role is to "empower kids" and motivate children to be "agents of change." Yet these claims, and the very idea that a television network could inspire a certain civic-mindedness in children, compete with powerful ideologies, held not only by conservative groups, that children's television works to "manipulate" and "brainwash" its audiences. These two representations of children's interaction with media mirror some of the tensions surrounding how young Americans are interpellated as both citizens-in-training and consumers in contemporary culture. This book is my attempt to make sense of these contradictions, which I see more generally reflected in the social identity of a citizen in late-capitalist, "post-national" U.S. culture. Commercial media play a pivotal role in creating cultural definitions about what it means to be a citizen—indeed, our sense of ourselves as national citizens emerges *from* (not in spite of) our engagement with the popular media. Here, I am specifically interested in the role that children's media plays in both constituting and maintaining this cultural contradiction.

When examining children's media in the United States, it is impossible to ignore the significance of the children's cable television channel Nickelodeon, which is potentially the most popular and influential producer of children's programming and media in the United States—and increasingly throughout the world—today.[5] A division of Viacom International, Inc., and delivered via satellite, the twenty-four-hour Nickelodeon channel is a network of children's programs with millions of subscribers that targets broad children and adult audiences. Nickelodeon is arguably one of the most successful cable channels in history and has worked aggressively to claim and maintain its position and image as the preeminent distributor of television programs for young children, tweens, and teens in the United States.[6] The channel's success has been possible in part because its segmented programming appeals to all age groups: preschool programming in the morning (the award-winning *Blues Clues* and *Dora the Explorer*, among others), young children's programming in the afternoon (the widely popular *Rugrats*), pre-adolescent and adolescent programming in the later afternoon (*Hey Arnold!*, and *SpongeBob SquarePants*), and "tween" programming in the evening (*The Amanda Show* and MTV-style variety programs that encourage audience participation). Then, in the later evening, Nickelodeon airs *Nick at Nite*, a nostalgic programming lineup of older family shows that includes *Petticoat Junction, The Cosby Show,* and *Growing Pains,* to name only a few. Aside from the actual program lineup, Nickelodeon has also garnered critical acclaim for its original programming, featuring both animated and live-action programs that have as a selling point the idea that the channel addresses "kids as kids." In the last quarter of 2004, all of the ten highest-rated television shows watched by children under the age of twelve—on both broadcast and cable—were Nickelodeon programs.[7] But Nickelodeon's reach and influence does not stop at television programming; Nickelodeon-produced movies, such as *Harriet the Spy, The Rugrats Movie, Lemony Snicket's A Series of Unfortunate Events,* and *The SpongeBob SquarePants Movie,* are also a staple of children's media—in fact, *The Rugrats Movie* became the first non-Disney children's film to gross over $100 million.[8] And, as just a brief glance in most U.S. elementary schoolyards, malls, and athletic fields will show, many of the products purchased by or for children are licensed by Nickelodeon. *SpongeBob SquarePants* t-shirts, *Dora the Explorer* lunch boxes, *Rugrats* backpacks, and *Blue's Clues* plush animals all have a place within the consumption ethos in which American children surround themselves.

Clearly, given the broad scope of the channel, there are many stories to tell about Nickelodeon. In this book, I focus on two related narratives: the relationship between kids and commercial media citizenship, and the position of Nickelodeon as a powerful site for constructing this kind of media citizenship. I see this book as both a contribution and an important challenge to the recent (both scholarly and popular) literature on the construction of the child consumer. The first few years of the twenty-first century have witnessed an increasingly sensationalized debate about the consumption habits of young middle-class American children, and popular books lamenting new heights of kids' superficial spending have topped best-seller lists. The child consumer appears all too often in this literature as a stereotypical cultural figure, helpless against the enormous reach of media corporations and vulnerable to a bottom-line profit motive. Consider in this regard the titles of recent books on the topic: *Consuming Kids: The Hostile Takeover of Childhood; Born to Buy: The Commercialized Child and the New Consumer Culture; Freaks, Geeks and Cool Kids: American Teenagers, Schools, and the Culture of Consumption;* and *Branded: The Buying and Selling of American Teenagers* are just a few examples.[9] Much of the popular literature that laments the contemporary state of the young U.S. consumer relies upon relatively simplistic mainstream effects research on children, research which assumes a media environment of passive viewing, from which children should be protected. Although I would not deny that youth culture is commodified in contemporary U.S. culture in unprecedented ways, I also believe that acknowledging the consumer element of kids' lives and their status as consumer citizens does not indicate that children are somehow victimized and without agency. In other words, I do not nostalgically long for those days before MTV and Nickelodeon occupied every aspect of a middle-class U.S. kid's life, from clothing to food to rebellion, as a time when children were not interpellated as particular kinds of consumers. As I discuss throughout this book, there has been very interesting and important recent work within media and cultural studies on U.S. children's culture that complicates this picture in important and useful ways.[10] *Kids Rule!* intervenes in this literature by offering a rethinking of the definition and dynamics of citizenship in a niche-marketed, branded society. Unlike many traditionally progressive perspectives on the commodification of youth culture, I see the contemporary commercial environment as one that is complex and contradictory—and it is within those complexities and contradictions that youth citizenship is constituted in profound ways.[11]

This book is about a particular historical juncture in U.S. media culture, and the role that the particular communication technology of cable television plays in this juncture. *Kids Rule!* challenges some of the assumptions made in more conventional media studies about how to understand the relationship of children with the media. In many of these studies, social categories such as "innocence" and "corruptibility" are frequently measured in terms of how often and to what extent a child witnesses violence and other adult themes such as sexuality and politics in media culture. Through communication impact studies and social science surveys, the relationship of children and the media has been traditionally conceived as a kind of behavior, measurable through the presumed negative effects of violent messages and images.[12] Although not all media effects research strictly focuses on a behaviorist model that looks for causal links between stimulus and behavioral outcomes, it nonetheless remains difficult to investigate the impact of the broader social context on children and media within the confines of this research tradition. Traditional effects research and policy studies can be useful in theorizing the kinds of content in the media, as well as certain reactions of children *to* the media. However, policy decisions do not address the unprecedented ways in which children are marketed through the media, nor do they propose any change in how children are thought about as consumers. While some interventions certainly are important, effects research is limited in what it can tell us about the nature of children actively participating *with* the media.

Here, I discuss how tensions between consumer citizenship and political citizenship are maintained by the media industry within which Nickelodeon is situated: it is precisely the structure of the cable industry that allows for a more innovative and active address to a youth audience even as this industry remains structured around competitive commercial interests. Because of the flexibility of a cable network's programming—Nickelodeon airs exclusively children's programs fifteen hours a day—there are greater resources to create innovative and potentially more risky programs (especially when compared with the somewhat more constrained broadcast networks). As recent technological innovations in animation as well as a broad diversification of content in children's programs have demonstrated, the children's cable industry is clearly a valuable cultural site in which to locate recent shifts in the structure of kids' television. This media context provides youth culture with commodities, a class-based definition of "cool" culture, and an idealistic and inaccurate picture of a harmonious "multicultural" youth population. It also provides opportunities for rights, belonging, group membership, and perhaps even political action. Often these opportunities are immediately co-opted by corporate culture, but nonetheless there is potential within this media environment for a kind of meaningful consumer citizenship to be constituted.

It is within this dual cultural and marketing framework that Nickelodeon imagines its audience as a group of active consumer citizens. The fact that this imagined audience is similar for both Nickelodeon and advertisers does not automatically mean that the network is somehow disingenuous in its claims about being on the "kids' side." What it actually means, however, to be on the "kids' side," and what the consequences are for the child audience when an empowered identity is marketed as a kind of product, needs to be critically explored. The divisive strategy employed by Nickelodeon that establishes a discrete boundary between adults and children is one that functions brilliantly for the company in terms of profit. As Marsha Kinder has pointed out, the exaggerated generational conflict that Nickelodeon cultivates and markets as a kind of fun rebellion actually results in a blurring of the two identity categories. Thus, Nickelodeon presents a "convergence of generations" where adults are addressed as children on television, and children are encouraged to act like adults.[13] Within this consumer market, the two seemingly oppositional forms of address—the generational divide and the transgenerational connection—function in tandem to provide a landscape in which Nickelodeon is the entity to smooth over any kind of generationally based conflict. Both a divisive generational warfare (seen most clearly in the network's philosophy of "Us versus Them") and a transgenerational address (seen in the programming itself, as well as ads for the network that air on broadcast television during primetime) form the two sides of the Nickelodeon brand.

This book details the development of the Nickelodeon brand, from roughly 1985 to 2005. In this sense, it is a historical analysis of the channel—as with all media, the structure and organization of Nickelodeon has changed dramatically in the past twenty years, and many changes occurred even during the writing of this book. Viacom has been restructured, and has acquired new holdings and sold old ones; the structure of leadership within Nickelodeon has changed (in January 2006, Herb Scannell resigned as president of Nickelodeon and was succeeded by Cyma Zarghami); and many of the programs discussed throughout the book are no longer being produced or aired. My interest here is in charting the ways the channel developed from an upstart cable channel to a global brand, rather than giving an account of Nickelodeon's present status in the children's television landscape. Analyzing this development allows us a critical look at the strategies involved in the transformation of a small cable channel into a hugely successful network that insists that "kids rule."

CONSUMERISM AND MEDIA: CHILDREN AS CITIZENS

Needless to say, it is jarring to think about children as consumer citizens. While it is common for adults to mourn the failure of democratic politics in the United States, or to express a jaded cynicism about political process and civic behavior within the context of multinational corporations and global branding, it nonetheless remains difficult to situate children within this scenario, as similarly world-weary and disaffected. As both scholarly and popular literature demonstrates, there is an impulse to protect children from this commercial context and to prevent their victimization at the hands of profit. This book is not my attempt to ally with one side or the other of this dynamic. Rather, I want to take a look at these categories—citizenship and consumers—and not only examine the ways in which we confuse political citizenship and economic enfranchisement but also describe the logic of this slippage. Maintaining the distinction between consumerism and citizenship has performed important cultural work in terms of buttressing and understanding democracy. Without endorsing this distinction, I want to identify both a *process and logic of consumer citizenship* and bracket a reflection on whether or not this is positive or negative for the democratic process. I use the case study of Nickelodeon to describe the transformation through which this logic and process is happening, and I argue that the space that Nickelodeon *produces* is one that we presume the channel *came to occupy*. In other words, the relationship of consumers and citizens is a dynamic one, and

Nickelodeon holds this relationship that *it created* stable, so that it seems as if it has always existed. I want to argue that, in the contemporary moment, the market is understood as constitutive of citizenship through the interpellation of children, and this interpellation of children is about making subjects for that market. Nickelodeon has been significant in producing not only this dynamic but also a generation that understands consumption acts as citizenship.

In order to examine the role of Nickelodeon in creating a particular convergence of consumer behavior with citizenship, it is necessary to contrast a media-centered consumer citizenship with a more traditionally formed notion of political citizenship. Citizenship, like consumerism, has a particular history in the United States, one tied to ideological notions of exclusion and inclusion, cultural boundaries, and legal definitions. In the current consumerist environment, what gives the category of citizenship cultural substance—is it about rights? Empowerment? Access to political action? Political participation by citizens is considered a prerequisite for successful democratic societies, yet citizenship itself has been ill-defined historically—for instance, neither the Constitution of the United States nor its framers offered a clear, unambiguous definition of citizenship in the founding rhetoric of the United States. Is a citizen the same thing as a "person" in the Constitution? What is the relationship of the state—and what should it be—to a citizen, or the nation to its citizens?

The definitions of contemporary U.S. citizenship are characterized by tensions in existing dominant beliefs and ideologies. These tensions revolve around the conventional notion that citizenship is a *political* category, represented and constituted not within the world of commerce but rather in direct opposition to those kinds of material interests. Indeed, Jürgen Habermas's definition of the citizen's role in the public sphere continues to have a kind of privileged authority when it comes to defining contemporary citizenship as a category that is explicitly political.[14] Even despite the many challenges to the exclusivity of Habermas's formulation by feminists and critical race theorists, or the problematic nostalgia that shapes his version of a public sphere, the notion that citizenship is formed *via* the democratic process has both social and political currency. As a result, when it comes to defining citizenship, Habermasian themes of liberal democratic ideals such as rational discourse, rights and liberties, and political freedom have a kind of remarkable resilience.[15]

Because children are typically considered, by virtue of their youth, to be "outside" political life, they have traditionally not been addressed in public discourse as full citizens: they are not rights-bearing citizens of a nation, they cannot vote, they do not have "free choice" as choice is formally defined.[16] But when the very definition of citizenship shifts to include the commercial realm, where and how are children situated? Social theorists such as Locke and Rousseau, for instance, argued for the importance of formal education in training children to be future citizens because of their belief that a child's consciousness was a *tabula rasa* or "blank slate."[17] In the United States, particularly at the turn of the twentieth century, the role of formal education in creating children as "informed citizens" was increased. Literature, civics, and history courses, for example, were reinforced through school curricula, federal funding, and civics education and were considered important factors in fostering responsible and informed future citizens in a liberal, public democracy.[18] In the 1950s and 1960s in the United States, sociologists and political scientists became intrigued by what was called the political socialization of children, and so the ways children learned about citizenship, patriotism, and national identity—the ways children were socialized politically—were studied.[19] Questions regarding the political identities of children were seen as important, especially during the postwar context of 1950s U.S. culture, when concerns about political stability and the durability of democracies were common. Generally, it was held that the political socialization of youth occurred primarily in three places: in the family, where children and adolescents are seen to be influenced by their parents' political beliefs; at school, where citizenship and patriotism are often included in mission statements of American public schools (as well as in voluntary youth organizations, such as the Boy Scouts); and in the media, where information about official politics and political figures is disseminated.[20]

However, in contemporary culture, formal education, while maintaining a peripheral role in the training of citizens, has been superseded by the reach and influence of consumer culture and the popular media, and children are increasingly addressed as particular kinds of "citizens" in these contexts. This recent attention to children as consumers has as much to do with recognizing a particular political economic agency of children as it does to the unprecedented ways in which children are constituted as a commercial market. The tension within citizenship between consumer and political identities, for young people, is between the media address of children as increasingly important consumers in an ever-widening "youth" market, and the simultaneous desire for children to be noncommercial but active in another sense, as particular political subjects. And indeed, as Lauren Berlant has argued, despite the formal and informal exclusion of children from the realm of citizenship, the citizen consumer is often necessarily configured as a child. In the contemporary political economy, where private habits and behaviors (such as sexuality but also consumption) have come to act as the means through which public questions are negotiated and solved, national citizenry is constituted not by adults but rather by what Berlant calls "pre-citizens": "In the reactionary culture of imperiled privilege, the nation's value is figured not on behalf of an actually existing and laboring adult, but of a future American, both incipient and pre-historical."[21] This "infantile citizen" simultaneously embodies innocence and naiveté but also puts demands on the public imaginary as far as what the nation should expect from its citizens. As Berlant argues, the U.S. national public sphere is a contradictory construct that values a certain notion of intimacy—primarily associated with the logic of the family, heteronormativity, and private acts, such as sexual behavior, but also the private acts of consumption and engagement with the commercial media.

I draw on arguments about cultural and consumer citizenship like Berlant's as well as Toby Miller, Nestor García Canclini, Arlene Dávila, and others as a way to address the tensions I see forming Nickelodeon's own particular view of youth citizenship. The tensions contained in definitions of citizenship are produced through opposing cultural relations in late-capitalist U.S. society. As Miller points out, the resulting understanding of citizenship, by both the media and the citizen her/himself, is informed by two or more kinds of subjectivity. Citizens are, of course, always consumers and are in this media environment "trained" to be selfish, individualistic, and loyal to goods and services.[22] Nickelodeon clearly draws upon this element of citizenship by cultivating audience members/citizens through a kind of brand membership and loyalty. Despite the power of the consumer citizen, however, a more traditional political notion of the citizen continues to linger in media society, one that is community-minded and selfless. In this way, the community-minded individual is still created, but the community itself is part of a brand.

The last decade of the twentieth century witnessed a burgeoning body of scholarly work that theorized this shift, focusing on the facets of consumer citizenship. As Canclini has argued:

> We live in a time of fractures and heterogeneity, of segmentations within each nation, and of fluid communication with transnational orders of information, fashion, and knowledge. In the midst of this heterogeneity, we find codes that unite us, or at least permit us to understand each other. But those shared codes refer ever less to the ethnicity, class, and nation into which we are born. Those old units, insofar as they endure, seem to be reformulated as mobile *pacts for the interpretation* of commodities and messages. The definition of a nation, for example, is given less at this stage by its territorial limits or its political history. It survives, rather, as an *interpretive community of consumers,* whose traditional —alimentary, linguistic—habits induce them to relate in a peculiar way with the objects and information that circulate in international networks.[23]

In the contemporary world, the imagined national community references this community of consumers, united by "shared codes" of consumption behavior.[24] The context of globalization and transnational cultures, combined with the proliferation of cable television and the industry imaginings of niche audiences, means that the ways in which consumers are marketed to are increasingly personal and identity-based. Not only are consumers marketed to in individualized ways but the shared identity *of consumers* is increasingly one of the most meaningful *national* connections among members of a community. The rise of the youth market and the increasing sophistication of marketing trends for youth audiences indicate that consumption habits have come to be one of the most profound elements in basic definitions of youth identity. It is through this interpretive community of consumers that the definition of a nation is sustained, with young people as the "citizens" of the nation.

The contradictions seemingly inherent within consumer citizenship lie within what defines the *practices* of citizenship. Public debates about citizenship have historically been shaped by different understandings of rights and obligations of citizens and the roles and responsibilities of governments. The notion of civil and/or political citizenship, emerging from thinkers in the eighteenth century as well as through struggles in the nineteenth century, predominately referred to the rights that were understood as necessary for individual freedom, such as the rights to free speech and assembly, property rights, and general equality before the law. As is well documented, those groups (e.g., women, racial, ethnic, and sexual minorities, and the poor) who were excluded from these formal rights protested to extend the boundaries of citizenship. Indeed, the right of disenfranchised groups to protest in order to participate in the exercise of political power has historically been a hallmark of citizenship.[25]

While clearly there remain profound social, political, and economic divisions between privileged groups and the disenfranchised in the United States, traditional practices of citizenship designed to address those divisions have been redefined. "Cultural citizenship" as a term and an identity category was introduced as a way to better account for these realities. As Miller puts it, cultural citizenship "concerns the maintenance and development of cultural lineage through education, custom, language and religion and the positive acknowledgement of difference in and by the mainstream."[26] Of course, shifts in the definition of citizenship are certainly not new to the twenty-first century, and the intersections of a more traditional form of political citizenship and consumer/cultural citizenship did not originate with Nickelodeon, or with the election of the former movie star Ronald Reagan as president or, more recently, Arnold Schwarzenegger as governor, or with the increasing visibility (and importance) of celebrity activists, ranging from Bono to Angelina Jolie. Politics has long suffered a crisis of representation, especially for young people, where politicians seem continually woefully out of touch with their constituents. It makes sense, then, for politicians to capitalize on consumer culture as a way to forge a connection with youth culture so that political life does not seem alien. Entertainment and popular culture have a particular role in current practices of citizenship, but not to simply hold a place in a familiar entertainment/politics binary. This kind of simplistic binary, in which either entertainment or politics is celebrated, does not represent the various ways in which contemporary people and communities construct themselves as citizens. Yet at the same time as this binary formation is challenged, the two categories—entertainment and politics—remain discrete entities that function to inform or disrupt each other. In this book, I attempt to redefine citizenship within a media context by situating citizenship—rather than entertainment or politics—as the locus of my analysis as a way to explore new possibilities and contradictions for productive identity making.

CITIZENS AND AUDIENCES: THE MEDIA CONTEXT

One of the most important recent developments in scholarship on media and audiences has been the recognition that concepts such as consumerism, audience, and citizenship do not connect in some simple or easy-to-understand fashion but rather form a complicated dynamic.[27] For instance, Elizabeth Bird's study of media audiences theorizes these interconnections. She argues for complicating the notion of the "real" in a media world and gives evidence not only from scholarship but also from an increasingly savvy and cynical youth population that constantly questions what can be considered "real" in an age of digital simulation and easily manipulated images.[28] Yet Bird preserves a nostalgic rendering of the citizen/consumer divide, asking how audiences might "break through the grip of the media conglomerates, talking back to media as active citizens, rather than mere consumers?"[29] In formulating her question in this way, Bird misses a crucial point: consumer citizenship is not simply indicated in the way that advertisers and corporations appropriate political rhetoric in order to sell products. Rather, it is increasingly the case that people *understand* political rhetoric precisely because of their identities as consumers.

When the subject of an inquiry involving the media is youth or children, the question of audience empowerment becomes even murkier. The various ways in which children are constructed in relation to the media in the United States—the child in need of protection from the media, the child as savvy media user, the child as consumer, the child as media citizen—have come to define the American experience of childhood itself. Each construct of the child invokes different kinds and definitions of cultural or consumer empowerment. Historically, though, an important element in the cultural definition of childhood in the United States has been a *lack* of access to political empowerment and engagement (thus justifying protective legislation and media regulation).[30] According to early studies of political socialization, children were (and still are) seen as citizens-in-training, existing within a state of *becoming* political.[31] Theorizing children as *already* empowered citizen consumers thus marks not only a change in the political economy in which children participate but a redefinition of the experience of childhood.

I am interested in youth consumer citizenship within a specific political economy and body politic. Given the existing commercial context, the citizenship I'm theorizing indicates not just one's value as a consumer. I also consider the ways in which consumerism provides the terms and conditions through which people construct citizenship. I argue for a redefinition of citizenship as a category of analysis that accounts for an *interrelationship* of children as an audience, as consumers, and as members of an economically stratified community. The categories of identity both constructed and communicated by commercial media are organized by U.S. corporate culture as market demographic groups, distinguished primarily by the kinds of purchases made and a loyalty to brands. More specifically, the cultural recognition manifested in this kind of media visibility and identity formation connects to a particular vision of political and cultural enfranchisement.[32] Nickelodeon is one cultural site that not only produces this interrelationship but also makes particular claims about the cultural enfranchisement of children, contributing to sets of meanings that form a contemporary notion of citizenship—meanings that invoke a sense of membership, community, and individual agency. Brand culture, the concept of "cool," girl power, "diversity," and commercial camp and irony are all features of Nickelodeon programming that construct the child audience member as a particular consumer citizen. These characteristics of Nickelodeon programming directly relate to personal, consumer identity and are far more meaningful for a youth audience than abstract political concepts such as information about government, the workings of democracy, or the idealization of political leaders and political authority. Indeed, the tropes of irony and media savvy that characterize the current generation often explicitly mock these more traditional political concepts.[33] This move, from the world of politics to the world of media as constitutive sites for national and personal identity, is one that follows a more general consumerist trajectory in U.S. culture as marketing increasingly targets and appeals to individuals segmented by consumption habits, and citizen disaffection with "politics as usual" continues to intensify.

In order to theorize how a media outlet such as Nickelodeon is constitutive of consumer citizenship for its audience, some of the ways in which youth empowerment has been negotiated and struggled over need to be considered. As Daniel Cook puts it, "The uncertainty of children's agency renders defensible all sorts of claims and counterclaims about who children 'are' and what children 'want,' allowing most anyone to frame the child in any number of ways—for example as a competent social actor, as deserving of rights, as needing protection and guidance, and so on."[34] Consider in this regard the relationship between children and one of the traditional media vehicles of citizenship, news programming. If being a "good citizen" has meant that one is informed, politically, economically, and culturally, to encourage rational discourse, the news is crucial to the process of becoming a good citizen.[35] Nickelodeon both supports the news as an important element in constructing citizenship (through the program *Nick News*) as well as challenges the authority of the kind of information news provides as constitutive of citizenship. Interestingly, because children are seen as vulnerable to the media and in need of protection, even the process of becoming informed about the world through news is not often positively regarded. Children have been largely understood as an inappropriate audience for the news, however, because one of the assumptions of understanding children as "citizens-in-training" is that children are not full participants in constituting their political identities. Rather, they have a more passive relationship to the political world, trained and disciplined in a manner that implies acquiescence and conformity rather than active engagement.[36] As David Buckingham has argued, "With some significant exceptions, young people are defined as onlookers rather than participants in the process of political debate and political action. Despite the rhetoric of empowerment and the promise that children's voices will be heard, young people are largely constructed here in adult terms, rather than political actors in their own right."[37] Because Nickelodeon has actively formed a public image that insists on precisely this—treating children as political actors in their own right— it is not surprising that the channel's news program, *Nick News*, is one of those "significant exceptions." The program, and its host, Linda Ellerbee, challenge traditional programming by addressing children as political actors and as engaged citizens.

Nick News is the longest-running children's news program in the United States.[38] *Nick News* has aired specials on a number of important issues: the LA civil uprisings surrounding the beating of Rodney King in 1992, children with

AIDS, the Clinton/Lewinsky affair, the Israeli and Palestinian conflict, the terror-ist attacks on New York on September 11, and children with gay parents. Stylis-tically, *Nick News* does not follow a conventional news format—information is shared conversationally among a group rather than disseminated from a cen-tralized authority figure, and although clearly Ellerbee occupies a position as an authority, she sits on the floor with the children and guides the conversation rather than directs it. While the program is generally critically acclaimed, it also garners criticism for the topics on which Ellerbee focuses, precisely because the news program challenges assumptions about children as impressionable passive viewers. Yet *Nick News* is significant not simply because the show engages its young audience as active citizens but also because it challenges assumptions about the role "news" plays in constituting citizens. In other words, *Nick News* does not have the kind of immediacy of daily news—it is aired once a week, and more often than not, the program is designed as a "special edition" that focuses on a specific topic. These specific topics, however, concern precisely those issues that are significant in the identity making of children—issues of race, of fear, of popularity, of discrimination. As Buckingham comments about *Nick News*, "In different ways, these programmes push at the boundaries of what counts as news—and indeed as politics. At the same time, they adopt less conventional forms of pedagogy that address and position their audience in quite different ways from mainstream news."[39] Thus, while remaining a highly conventional commercial enterprise, *Nick News* also disrupts the assumption that only a par-ticular kind of news is the conduit to citizenship, especially in the program's special editions, which cover timely, and often difficult, topics. While clearly the commercial media gestures toward these topics through public service an-nouncements and celebrity spokespeople (in anti-drug or safe sex messages, for example), it is just as clear that the ways that commercial media primarily en-gages with difficult topics are organized around loose federal policies that hold channels to precise numbers of minutes to focus on these issues in programming. *Nick News* crafts its identity as a different sort of engagement by asking children to speak on these issues themselves.

For instance, in 2002 *Nick News* aired a special edition, "My Family Is Dif-ferent," which focused on children with gay parents and, more generally, on homophobia and antidiscrimination laws. Before the show actually aired, there was a heightened media debate over the topic: Nickelodeon received more than 100,000 letters and phone calls opposing the show, primarily from the ultra-conservative organization the Traditional Values Coalition. This edition of *Nick News* was co-hosted by Rosie O'Donnell and included conservative viewpoints from the Reverend Jerry Falwell (who was among those calling for the show to be blocked).[40] Ellerbee responded to the outcry by insisting that the show was "about tolerance . . . It is not about sex. It does not tell you what to think."[41] Although there was a significant protest to this episode by various conservative groups, Nickelodeon aired the special as planned. Because *Nick News* is more than simply a commercial product, the program (and Nickelodeon more generally) is a particularly good case study for a theoretical inquiry that examines how a particular channel "frames the child" as a consumer citizen. Yet despite the ways that *Nick News* shapes its identity as "different" from traditional news sources, in this book I look more closely at other Nickelodeon programs, those that veer even further from the traditional media spaces that are widely understood as important sources for the "informed citizen." I examine the claims that Nickelodeon makes about empowerment; indeed, the channel has been more successful than any other network (or any other media outlet) in both creating and sustaining an "empowered" child audience. Geraldine Laybourne, the former president of Nickelodeon, frequently claims that her goal when relaunching Nickelodeon in 1984 was to give children "a network of their own."[42] This goal implicitly connects empowerment with representation; ownership over a network, even if illusory, implies a kind of agency simply by recognizing children as an important group to address. Giving children "a network of their own" clearly gives the child audience a particular kind of cultural capital, pointing to the significance of media visibility in the contemporary U.S. context.

KIDS' TELEVISION

Before Nickelodeon, there was no channel on U.S. television that was exclusively dedicated to children's programming. In the United States, Nickelodeon needs to be contextualized within the two pre-cable models of children's television: the commercial broadcast model and the public broadcast model. Since the widespread adoption of television into the domestic home, the medium has been recognized as symbolically powerful as both entertainment and education, and historically the presence of advertising as well as merchandise tie-ins has distinguished the commercial "entertainment" programming from the publicly funded (and presumably invested in the "public interest") educational television.

In order to chart the history of children's television within these two spheres, it is useful to track some of the Federal Communication Commission's (FCC) policy decisions, which have had a role in both creating and sustaining a broader cultural view of the child audience. Within commercial broadcasting, at least since the 1950s, children's programming was aired during particular time blocks when children would be most likely to watch television: mornings (especially

Saturday morning) and after school—and thus where advertisers were most likely to hone in on a particular audience. As Jason Mittel argues, the "exile" of children's cartoons to Saturday morning (a shift from cinematic cartoons which were largely created for an adult audience) established a viewing programming context not only for who would be watching television at that hour but also what kind of television would be available.[43] Because children watched television on Saturday morning, and the reigning assumption at the time was that children were both an uncritical audience and enjoyed watching repeats, this time spot became a financially lucrative one for broadcasters, allowing networks to sustain fairly insignificant production costs.[44] At this relatively early moment in the history of television, cartoons were regarded as "harmless entertainment" and the narratives and creative style of cartoons were shaped to fit the (perceived) unsophisticated child audience.[45] On the other hand, as more and more advertisers began to tap into the market potential of the child audience over the course of the decades between the 1960s and the 1980s, the merchandise tie-ins with children's television increased, and the FCC was forced to pay attention to the marketing of children through television. As I discuss in more detail in the next chapter, the environment of media activism in the 1960s and 1970s (led primarily by Peggy Charren and Action for Children's Television) challenged the presence of advertising on television as well as merchandise tie-ins, and in 1969 the FCC prohibited the airing of television programs based on licensed characters, characterizing them as "program-length commercials."[46] Nonetheless, with the widespread deregulation in the 1980s of the communications industries under the Reagan administration, this FCC restriction was lifted to allow for a different kind of "public interest" broadcasting where every member of the audience, including both young children and advertisers, was considered "equal" in the free market of the media.[47] This led to a boom in the merchandising tie-in business, prompting yet another FCC intervention several years later with the 1990 Children's Television Act (CTA).[48] One of the major goals of the CTA was to increase the quantity of educational and informational broadcast television programming for children and to force broadcasters to serve the child audience as part of the obligation to the public interest. In 1997, the CTA produced the Three-Hour Rule, mandating that commercial broadcast stations air a minimum of three hours a week to fulfill the educational and informational programming directive. Commercial broadcasters needed to comply with the Three-Hour Rule in order to qualify for expedited license renewal.[49]

The federal enforcement of "educational" television as a discrete and separate genre from "entertainment" TV is obviously connected with a more general understanding of the symbolic power of the medium. Children are culturally and politically understood as "future citizens" as well as both innocent and impressionable, and FCC policies and regulatory practices contribute to the positioning of the child as such. In the 1960s, public broadcasting in the United States sought to redress some of the problems that came with broadcast television in terms of its dependence on advertising, the increasing ties with toy companies, and the general low quality of children's programming. The famous "vast wasteland" speech on May 9, 1961, by then-FCC president Newton Minow was inspired by a concern for children and the ways television was failing them in providing a model for informed citizenry.[50]

One of the programs that *was* fulfilling the "public interest" obligations of broadcasters was the Children's Television Workshop's *Sesame Street*. As is well known, the idea for *Sesame Street* grew out of 1960s altruism: it had a different agenda from commercial programming in that the show was initially designed to give underserved children a "head start" before school.[51] In essence, *Sesame Street* could either stand in for or at least supplement a preschool program, something that was primarily only available for middle- and upper-class children. *Sesame Street* has been recognized (and critiqued) for its emphasis on cognition as a crucial tool to prepare for formal education, and the program's emphasis on diversity and tolerance and representation of a variety of socioeconomic levels within its characters has certainly led to its recognition as an alternative to typical broadcast children's television.[52]

Sesame Street shares something important with Nickelodeon, however: neither *Sesame Street* nor Nickelodeon was initially subject to the same kind of economic restraints that shape network television. Because it is on "noncommercial" public broadcasting, *Sesame Street* was able to air programming that not only featured people of color but also incorporated themes that dealt with racism and diversity in U.S. culture.[53] Nickelodeon was created at the moment of television's deregulation in the 1980s and (at least initially) needs to be understood within this context, as an alternative of sorts to the *Sesame Street* model. Within this historical moment, Nickelodeon was able to create programming that responded to the low-end production of licensed character shows dominating both broadcast and cable television that were enabled by deregulation. Nickelodeon imagined programming that looked different from the typical formulaic fare on broadcast (and some cable) TV and thus, like PBS, could take "risks" that the networks claimed were impossible economically. Both channels encourage a kind of empowered sensibility on the part of their child audiences that is seen much less frequently in network television. Of course, the fact that *Sesame Street*'s original intended audience was underserved children, and Nickelodeon's audience is those children who live in households that can afford cable television, means that the "risks" each channel takes have a profoundly different target and import. Nonetheless, my point is that part of Nickelodeon's claim that it empowers kids is made possible by the commercial environment of cable (and public) television: because the economic constraints (at least in the 1980s and early 1990s) were not as stringent as those of broadcast television, risk-taking on the part of programmers was possible. During this time, Nickelodeon produced *Clarissa Explains It All,* acknowledged in the industry as a landmark show featuring a strong, intelligent girl as a lead character. Additionally, Nickelodeon explicitly refused to produce programming that was violent, at a time when violent shows aimed at young boys were enormously lucrative. Shows such as *You Can't Do That on Television,* which was often overtly critical of the ways in which television manipulated young audiences, became a hallmark for Nickelodeon's identity. In this way, through programs like these, Nickelodeon firmly established its reputation as a rebellious risk-taker in the otherwise conformist children's television landscape. But in order to even associate empowerment with a child audience, both *Sesame Street* and Nickelodeon have relied upon particular cultural understandings of children and their interaction with the media. In particular, both *Sesame Street* and Nickelodeon have rejected a commonplace view that children are innocent and should be protected from television, opting instead to advocate for *better* kid's television to more appropriately serve the active child audience.

As both Nickelodeon and *Sesame Street* demonstrate, the position of the audience member is of crucial importance to any project that involves the interaction of children with the media; not only are children the intended audience for much media but, perhaps more forcefully, children are often used as compelling metaphors for studies that theorize the power of the mass media. As David Morley points out, the "new revisionism" that emerges out of communication studies in the later part of the twentieth century works to address this infantilizing move and position the audience more like thinking adults.[54] However, while it may be the case that in studies of adult television, scholars have become more attuned to the various ways in which audiences can be active (although what exactly it means to be an "active" audience is problematic and has an uneven history), the subject of children interacting with media has stubbornly remained on either side of the debate between the passive and active audience member.[55] The use of the child as metaphor then becomes an important moment of *contention* for rethinking and reframing audience studies. While theorizing the audience as active allows for a greater understanding of adult audiences, it also maintains an essentialized relationship between adults and children as integral and fails to further our thinking about commercial media youth audiences in nuanced and complex ways.

Notwithstanding this scholarly emphasis, the figure of the "media savvy" child has emerged within *popular* discourse more and more frequently. As technology becomes more sophisticated and more difficult for adults skilled in (more) rudimentary technologies to navigate, children have emerged as a new class of experts. This is not always (or even often) met with public approval. The quick glut of products that help filter "inappropriate" material on the Internet is an interesting testimony to the anxiety many adults feel about children becoming technological experts. This anxiety stems from an assumption that the technological skills children possess outmaneuver their ability to comprehend what it is that they see on the screen. That adults have particular anxieties about the tastes, habits, and practices of the younger generation is certainly nothing new, but apprehension about the relationship of children with technology has heightened in new ways in the late twentieth/early twenty-first centuries. As Henry Jenkins argued when he testified before the U.S. Congress about "selling violence to our children," adults are afraid of children, afraid of new technologies, and most importantly, afraid of the usage by and reaction of children to digital media and new technologies.[56] Adolescence is widely understood as a confusing, liminal stage of life—indeed, as a truly alien stage of life. The recent moral panics about "friendship" networks such as myspace.com merely add to this social construction.[57] These anxieties about youth and media have functioned to reconstruct late-twentieth and early-twenty-first century childhood in the United States as a mystifying and frightening state of affairs: innocent, yet sophisticated; impressionable and in need of protection, yet world-weary and desensitized.[58]

But children are not seen as in need of protection from only new technologies. The consumer world, like technology, also has had a historically contradictory relationship with children. Despite the normalization of consumption behavior among U.S. children, there is still a powerful cultural rhetoric about the need to protect children from the commercial world. Moral panics over extravagant spending, the influence of consumer culture on antisocial behavior, and the ever-increasing fast-food industry mark some examples of this contradiction. Corporate culture has been efficient in figuring out at least one way to reconcile this contradiction, shaping contemporary understandings of *parenthood* also within a commercial framework: "good" parents are those who have the knowledge and the means to purchase what a child "needs" at every stage in development. As Daniel Cook has shown, part of what being a good mother has meant historically is the ability of a woman to broaden the domestic sphere of the home to include the department store so that purchases could be made to aid in the proper development of children.[59] The "proper" kind of consumption will ostensibly lead to "proper" children—just as "pathological" consumption habits (such as tattoos, body piercings, listening to rap music, etc.) apparently lead to pathological children. The consumer world has thus a precarious relationship with the child consumer: both in need of products and to be protected from them, the child consumer is constituted as a contradictory subject.

This contradiction is heightened in a contemporary media context, where television is simultaneously celebrated as a needed asset to parenting and lamented as a damaging hindrance to good parenting. Nickelodeon, not surprisingly, has consciously crafted its identity to provide a kind of "balance" within this contradictory dynamic: by claiming to "respect" kids, the network responds to cultural anxieties about protecting kids as it simultaneously frames this "respect" as a crucial part of the brand identity. In this way, Nickelodeon's claim to be "on the side of kids" is similar to the ways advertisers construct child audiences: sophisticated, media-friendly, and enthusiastic consumers. At the same time, the network's conscious attention to children's culture assuages parents and educators that watching Nickelodeon television will not deter "proper" development. So, for example, Nickelodeon holds a "Kids Pick the President" campaign during election years, a program that allows children to "vote" for their choice for president and to hear opinions about the presidential race from a "kid's point of view." Clearly, what it means to have agency within a media context is not as simple as "empowering" children to act in either the consumer or the political world. Indeed, part of Nickelodeon's explicit mission is to air programs that kids like to watch, not those that their parents would like them to watch; it promotes itself as a network "dedicated to empowering kids, a place where kids could take a break and get a break."[60]

THE NATION OF THE BRAND

In order to account for the kinds of possibilities and contradictions Nickelodeon presents, it is useful to take seriously brand culture as the dominant shared interpretive community that Canclini theorizes. Brand loyalty, in the case of Nickelodeon, functions as a particular kind of citizenship practice. The concept of "empowering" kids is shaped by marketing strategies, so that empowerment only makes sense in the culture of the market. One of the characteristics of niche channels like Nickelodeon is that the interstitials—the promos between programs, the ad campaigns for the channel, the product announcements—are as entertaining as the actual programming itself. The "flow" of the channel then generates a particular structure of feeling, where Nickelodeon, as one former employee puts it, becomes a "way of life."[61] The channel thus creates a provisional community through a field of shared symbols about the brand, and loyalty to the Nickelodeon brand is the ticket to membership. Importantly, Nickelodeon's branding strategies are exceptionally effective precisely because they don't look like branding strategies. The notion of empowerment espoused by the network, the address to kids as citizens, the corporation's own sense of cool and irreverence are all part of this marketing tactic. This slipperiness, this lack of discernment within different definitions of empowerment, assists in Nickelodeon's success as a brand, because brand loyalty does not seem so much about preference for commercial products as it does about everyday cultural practice.

When Nickelodeon targets a youth audience ages seven to thirteen, this particular group is construed as a *community* of consumers. These market delineations of a target audience in turn formulate the contours of social and cultural identity—as if identity (or an audience) remains within these naturalized age borders, arbitrarily placed upon kids as well as made meaningful by advertisers. Generations, of course, are more fluid than that—it is not as if a child stops watching Nickelodeon the day she turns fourteen, or that the transition from the Nickelodeon preschool block to its regular programming begins when the child ends preschool and begins kindergarten. In the structure of the cable industry, however, these fluid boundaries can be made much more predictable and stable within the dynamics of vertical integration and centralized media ownership. Viacom owns Nickelodeon, as well as Noggin, MTV, BET, VH1, Comedy Central, and Paramount Pictures, among other media outlets.[62] The interpretive community of Nickelodeon consumers can remain intact as it progresses generationally and thus demographically: after Nickelodeon, young adults tune into MTV or BET, adults over thirty-five tune into VH1, and so on. Nickelodeon exemplifies what Joseph Turow calls a "segment-making" form of media—by consciously and carefully using a generational divide as its primary form of address. By honing its Us versus Them philosophy so that it permeates every level of the network from programming to advertising, it has helped to create a discrete, powerful segment within children's programming.[63] In fact, Turow identifies Nickelodeon as a "pioneer attempt" to establish a kind of "ad-sponsored communion" within the world of cable television. Nickelodeon is a programming service designed to both create and service a particular kind of community and it does this with careful research methods, primarily using focus groups to find out "what kids want."

In her book tracing the creation of the Latino market, Arlene Dávila argues that branding is involved in the "marketing and making of a people."[64] In the

contemporary capitalist context, where commercial culture does not simply in-
fuse every aspect of our life but is constitutive of every feature of our lives, the
brand takes on added significance in terms of its importance in the formation of
identities, notions of entitlement, and feelings of belonging.[65] As Dávila points
out, marketing has always been involved in the making of public identities,
but the pervasive way that consumption habits have shaped individual and public identity is uniquely characteristic of late-twentieth and early-twenty-first-
century capitalist life.

The current context of globalization and transnationalism provides a further
dimension to the connectivity between consumerism and citizenship. As Dávila
argues, the global flow of culture (including the movement of both populations
and goods) has resulted in the constant presence of two variables: "culture,
involving the existence of particular and lingering hierarchies of race/ethnicity/
language/nationality that mediate people's position within any given society; and
consumption, insofar as—whether as exiles, citizens, permanent residents, or
immigrants—individuals are consumers first and foremost."[66] The various ways
that Latinos, African Americans, Asian Americans, and other nonwhite communities are othered in the mass media, and the ways that marketers then capitalize
on that otherness to sell products, provide a central means to situate different
ethnicities within a social, cultural, and commercial hierarchy. While children
are of course a different kind of identity group in U.S. society than nonwhite
communities (to be othered by generation requires a different mode of interpretation), they nonetheless form a particular kind of global "media community" that advertisers and marketers both create and then sustain. The commercial media, in conjunction with—and often in opposition to—other "venues of
signification" such as state apparatuses, dominant ideologies, hegemonic institutions (ranging from education to heterosexuality to legal marriage), creates a
framework of belonging around categories such as race, culture, nation, and, I
would argue, generation. Branding thus becomes a point of entry for identity—
generational identity is not simply sold through brands such as MTV, Nike, and
Nickelodeon; it is *created* and made meaningful by these brands.

Nickelodeon's branding strategies fit within a general historical trajectory of
consumer culture where advertisers attempt to connect with one's "lifestyle" as a
way to sell products. So, for instance, in the 1950s, advertisers capitalized on the
emerging American suburb and the utopic vision of the newly formed nuclear
family as a way to tap into a new consumer market. The political context of the
Cold War provided a backdrop for the advertising of home products and ap-
pliances as a way to demonstrate a national (American) superiority.[67] In the 1960s
and 1970s, as Thomas Frank demonstrates, advertisers focused on the youth

audience and commodified the concept of "cool" as a way to differentiate products and used the seeming oxymoronic theme of a nonmaterialist lifestyle (popular at the time) to sell clothing and cars to a burgeoning youth market.[68]

In the 1980s, a decade characterized by excess and the "me generation," advertisers were freed up by a deregulated communications industry, and commercial licensing and trademarks shaped the commodity landscape. During this time, marketers became increasingly adept at narrowing and specifying the target audience, and new research tools such as "psycho-graphics" and lifestyle identification—such as the Yuppie (young, upwardly mobile professional) and the Buppie (black, upwardly mobile professional)—began to tie products directly to certain lifestyles and soon characterized the advertising industry.[69] Media audiences were newly segmented into "primary media communities," as Turow argues, and the ways in which the media hailed the consumer felt more and more personal and individualized, even as individuals were increasingly understood according to their economic status. As Turow puts it, advertisers form these kinds of media communities "when viewers or readers feel that a magazine, TV channel, newspaper, radio station, or other medium reaches people like them, resonates with their personal beliefs, and helps them chart their position in the larger world."[70]

But what does it mean to "chart" one's position in the world, if you are a child television viewer? For Nickelodeon, this means adopting a stance that stands in for both parental and national authority, so that the channel becomes a sort of media family or community for its audience. This is key to successful branding, where one's loyalty to a brand should feel "natural." The fact that this "individualized" invitation is disseminated to millions of other consumers through a wide range of marketing vehicles, like kids clubs, online computer services, and magazines, is of course part of the strategy of advertising, and what Horkheimer and Adorno called in the mid-twentieth century "pseudo-individualism," where marketers would persuade consumers to buy products that were marketed to them as individuals.[71] Despite the increasingly savvy consumer, as well as the progressively more sophisticated and hip rhetoric of advertising, the strategy of marketing to millions in terms of precise individualism remains widely used in the contemporary historical moment. Nickelodeon in this context is important to consider, because of the way the channel imagines its audience as citizens precisely as a strategy to market the brand.

The way that the Nickelodeon brand is marketed also needs to be contextualized within the general history of consumer media culture and the child's role within this culture. The contemporary relationship of children with television has changed in some dramatic ways since the 1950s, when, as Lynn Spigel has documented, the damaging messages of television were seen to transform children into "juvenile delinquents."[72] But in other ways, the relationship of children to the media is as fraught as ever in the contemporary media environment, where new anxieties about children avidly participating in consumer society as fully developed consumers in their own right are often connected to commercial media use and television advertising.[73] In contemporary brand culture, consumerism is the foundation for any discussion of empowerment as it involves the media. Historically, because this kind of empowerment is found within the commercial realm, it has been dismissed as spurious, illusory, or available only to the few.[74] Indeed, legislators, academics, parents, and educators have often advocated for the protection of children from the commercial world precisely because they are assumed to be innocent and vulnerable to commercial interests. This construction of the sentimentalized child is part of a larger cultural discourse about modern notions of progress and consumerism.[75] In fact, the sociologist Viviana Zelizer argues that childhood "is actually an invention that accompanied other modern inventions that promised rational progress and innovation."[76] Part of this modernist ethos included the domestic realm, which became one of the largest targeted markets for consumer products during the early twentieth century.[77] As middle-class children and their mothers were secure in their domestic worlds, away from the harsh realities of the working world, marketers sought new ways to commercialize this space and to portray the domestic sphere as in constant need of new products.[78] Children, precisely because of their presumed innocence, were newly understood to be in need of proper guidance and motivation—a cultural construction ideal for toy and game companies, children's clothing manufacturers, and educational resources.[79] Toys and games (and later, new technologies such as radio and television) were marketed to parents as crucial to a child's development; as the industrialized world made room for and then encouraged the necessity of leisure time, parents were increasingly addressed by toy companies to buy products for children's play.[80] No longer connected to the commercial world as producers, sacralized and sentimentalized children were targeted as a new niche in the world of consumers at the beginning of the twentieth century.

Clearly, consumerism and politics have been tightly connected, despite ideological efforts to maintain these two realms as separate. As Lizabeth Cohen points out in her careful history of the relationship between citizenship and consumerism in twentieth-century America, mass consumption often provided the context for political or civic behavior. Americans emerge as two different kinds of consumers: the citizen consumer, seen as responsible for "safeguarding the general good of the nation, in particular for prodding government to protect the rights, safety, and fair treatment of individual consumers in the private market place," and the purchaser consumer, "viewed as contributing to the larger society more by exercising purchasing power than through asserting themselves politically."[81] In this way, Cohen marks a time when the definition of "consumer" became a political category, or a subject of analysis, rather than a habit, something that one does. Consumption is rather part of who one *is*.

Cohen offers a structural analysis of the politics involved in the emergence of these two kinds of consumer citizens in the United States. She focuses on labor politics and the new recognition that one's voice could be heard as a political voice through consumption—indeed, that there was something that could be called "the politics of consumption" is important to consider. According to Cohen, the marketplace can be a space for positive political activism where consumers can fight for rights as well as use the space of the marketplace itself to fight for broader political rights. There was a range of factors that allowed for a particular kind of "consumer republic" to function, and for these two categories to emerge as logical: FHA housing policies, a vibrant politically informed labor movement, the policies of the New Deal, and the "new" focus on the consumer. Cohen analyzes the ways in which concepts of political empowerment apply to the context of consumption; that is, how one becomes "political" through the consumer choices that one makes. As she points out, during the New Deal era, one's identity as a consumer was important to particular groups who historically lacked access to power: "for social groups not otherwise well represented, in particular women and African Americans, identification as consumers offered a new opportunity to make claims on those wielding public and private power in American society."[82] Children, as with other minority groups within a predominantly white, male-centered society, have historically lacked access to power.

There is a notable historical shift in this dynamic, soon after the period discussed by Cohen. The commercial media context of 1950s postwar American culture aggressively created and then cultivated the teenage market. The 1950s saw a more formal cultural definition of the teenager, and commercial popular culture quickly capitalized on this by producing goods and services specifically for this new market. As Marcel Danesi has pointed out, the rise of the television and record industries in the 1950s "courted" the teenager because of the amount of leisure time and new ways to spend and consume. Commercial media culture, ranging from the television show *American Bandstand* (first aired in 1957) to Elvis Presley to the coming-of-age film *Rebel without a Cause,* cultivated the teenage market as a special one and dedicated productions solely to this audience. Importantly, the 1950s also mark a shift in authority figures for adolescents; whereas in previous years, family, church, and neighborhood provided advice and guidance about how to construct one's identity, with the rise of the teenage market the commercial mass media came to powerfully stand in as authority figures for children.[83] This shift in authority, combined with postwar middle-class affluence, led to the predecessor of the current children's market. As Grace Palladino argues, "youth-oriented marketers, more concerned with teenage tastes than teenage futures, would now give traditional character builders a real run for their money. In the days before Pearl Harbor, adult marketers had naturally assumed that their job was to tell teenagers who they were and what they wanted to buy. Ten years later, they would be asking teenagers to speak for themselves and presenting the younger generation as bona fide consumers with a right to spend their own (and their parents') money as they pleased."[84] The teenage market began to be promoted heavily by magazines such as *Seventeen* and the television industry, and the group was soon "sold" to advertisers as it became clear that a lucrative market existed. The teenage market grew, however, once advertisers and the commercial media began to market to this group as a discrete group—not children, not their parents.[85] Like teenage media in the 1950s, Nickelodeon also arrives in a commercial media space—1980s cable television—with no precedent, at least not for an all-children channel.

In the current context of Nickelodeon, the media audience member supplants the focus on the laborer, or the individual. Children have a kind of power within the commercial world; indeed, consumer citizenship is somewhat "democratizing" in the sense that power is predicated on purchase choices rather than individual identity. Quite simply, people who are underrepresented within political and cultural realms are often recognized as lucrative markets in consumer culture, where willingness to buy products is what really "counts."[86] This is not the same as arguing, as Cohen does, that consumption becomes an issue for politics—that is, the rights of consumers, labor policies, and so on—so that purchasing goods becomes an act of patriotism.[87] While this is an important element of consumer citizenship, I see the shift at the current historical moment as one which constitutes the marketplace not simply as a platform from which to launch political goals and aims. Rather, the marketplace is constitutive of politics—political identities, rights, and ideologies are often formulated *within* the consumer marketplace, rather than in opposition to it. When Nickelodeon offers its audience a "network of their own" and pledges to create programs that deal with issues that are important to them, the channel is part of a constitutive process.

For example, consider one of Nickelodeon's most popular programs, *Rugrats*. A special episode of this show, "Rugrats Discover America," was created ostensibly in honor of Columbus Day (although neither the historical figure nor the federal holiday is mentioned in the special), and the program was aired about a month after the 9/11 World Trade Center and Pentagon attacks. The program is a widely popular animated series that features four babies who constantly get into trouble and a group of parents who are generally clueless in terms of what their children are "really" up to, a direct reference to Nickelodeon's rhetoric of generational conflict. "Rugrats Discover America" opens with the grandparents of some of the characters distributing souvenirs to the children from their recent trip across America. The souvenirs, including a Native American artifact and a toy Statue of Liberty, prompt a fantasy of the main characters involving a vacation across America in a tour bus, with stops at particular places of interest, such as the Grand Canyon, the California desert, and New York City. A side story features two older child characters taking a motorcycle trip across the same terrain, complete with *Easy Rider* outfits and a version of "Born to Be Wild" playing on the sound track (a visual and audio trope that assumes a transgenerational audience).

The *Rugrats* special offers a pointed and specific version of citizenship; focusing on popular culture and tourism, this program defines citizenship in terms of the consumer who acquires "national" knowledge at different tourist stops around the country that are then represented in souvenirs. As an American consumer spirit represented in popular film references and commercial souvenirs (a kind of cultural capital that seems to be a specific prerequisite for citizenship), this definition of citizenship is offered alongside the broader, idealist American "spirit" represented in more jingoistic displays of patriotism such as displaying the American flag. These themes combine with the 1999 marketing campaign for the network that celebrates the "Nickelodeon Nation," as well as the promises to "pledge allegiance to kids," the encouragement of its young audience to "Exercise those choice muscles," and the insistence that "You have more power than you think!" As Heather Hendershot has pointed out, Nickelodeon's emphasis on the "rights" of kids places into bold relief the connection *and* the tension between rights and modern citizenship, where rights for kids who watch Nickelodeon are most crucially the "right" to make purchases, and the "choices" that are exercised are consumer choices.[88]

RETHINKING CONSUMERISM:
THE LANGUAGE OF RIGHTS AND EMPOWERMENT

So what are the practices of youth citizenship encouraged by consumer culture? Forms of popular culture and, more specifically, commercial entertainment are not outside the realm of "official" politics; on the contrary, it is often within these realms that our understanding of and resistance and acquiescence to "official" politics are constituted.[89] For example, Maire Messenger Davies considers a more "cultural public sphere" by discussing both news and entertainment programming for young audiences on the BBC. Her ambitious study (which involved over 1,300 children, and both quantitative and qualitative data) queried about the storytelling potential of television (specifically the BBC in the U.K.) by explicitly asking how children felt about television. Her questions included wondering whether TV was suitable for children or not, whether children have "rights" in the context of the media, and so forth. Davies's study is quite useful for thinking beyond a Habermasian notion of the public sphere, since she considers the "cultural public sphere" as crucial in the construction of citizenship. As she puts it:

> In considering the role of televised storytelling in introducing children to, and allowing them to be included in, any kind of cultural public sphere, the central question is one of participation. Although it can be difficult for scholars to agree on what exactly constitutes a preschool animation, or an "entertainment" as distinct from a "factual" non-fiction programme, most childhood media scholars do agree that children should have their own needs, tastes, wants and identities acknowledged in their entertainment media, and that this is potentially a question of "rights."[90]

Davies's focus on "rights" is important given that the language of rights structures most theories of liberal citizenship. However, crucial adjustments to a formal definition of "rights" need to be made when discussing how children are consumer citizens. Rights discourse, because of the assumptions contained within it, excludes the possibility of children occupying the category of citizen—except as a future identity. In other words, a traditional model of the public sphere is built upon a number of discourses—such as rights discourse—that are profoundly at odds with the recognition of children as potential political actors. As Jessica Kulynych argues, "The theoretical vision of the public sphere and our cultural understanding of publicity invoke distinctions between public and private, insider and outsider, order and disorder that are based on the exclusion of children."[91] These binary discourses, as well as the themes that characterize a citizen within liberal thought more generally (autonomy, reason, and so forth), function to systematically exclude children from belonging in the realm of citizenry, and, in fact, *depend* on the specific and intentional exclusion of children. The dichotomies that Kulynych discusses are useful tropes for understanding how children are excluded formally from contemporary definitions of citizenship. More importantly, these dynamics are crucial for theorizing how a cable television channel like Nickelodeon challenges this traditional framework and includes children within the definition of citizen, precisely by subverting these dichotomies and appropriating them as specific means to empowerment for the child audience. The use of political language in Nickelodeon's promotional spots —the language of rights, respect, and allegiance—is an example of this kind of strategy. More obliquely, Nickelodeon programs, ranging from the animated *Rugrats* to the live drama *The Brothers Garcia,* contain themes and narratives that challenge assumptions about children as unsophisticated and unable to understand complicated metanarratives.

The language of "rights," as the authoritative discourse that helps to determine who and what constitutes a citizen, always already contains a politics of exclusion. To be "rights-bearing" one must possess a particular kind of rationality, and historically many people have been understood to be "naturally" incapable of this rationality (women, people of color, the infirm, and others). Although the exclusionary nature of the language of rights has been challenged by many scholars, from Catherine MacKinnon to Wendy Brown, the granting of rights continues to be one of the most effective and visible way to confer a kind of citizenship on individuals; one need only examine the history of human rights internationally or civil rights nationally to understand this significance.[92] Despite the lingering salience of rights discourse, the inequities in the social and cultural world (often determined and enacted based on personal identity categories, such as class, race, national origin, gender, and, in this case, age) mean that "officially" possessing political rights doesn't always correspond with citizenship.

Nickelodeon is a particularly good example to demonstrate these tensions within citizenship, as the network professes to acknowledge "kids' rights" and purposefully defines them differently from the officially recognized rights of the U.S. citizen. In fact, the channel developed the Nickelodeon "Bill of Rights," a sort of "mission statement" that appropriates the liberal language of rights, using and exposing this language as ridiculous through mocking its inherent exclusivity. The Nickelodeon "Bill of Rights" additionally overtly shifts the formation of rights as established within the context and in relation to the state to the commercial sphere. The network reframes political language for its use in establishing Nickelodeon as a particular consumer brand—a brand that is immediately recognized for its playful, ironic mode of address to its child audience. Given the symbolic sanctity of the Bill of Rights in the United States, Nickelodeon's reformulation within the context of a commercial television network is especially irreverent—and especially effective in terms of brand identity development. This is how the Nickelodeon "Declaration of Kids' Rights" is described in the employee handbook: "In the course of history, it has become pretty clear that all people are born with certain inalienable rights; among them life, liberty and the pursuit of happiness. But these rights haven't always applied to kids. And that stinks! Now, 200 years after the creation of America's Bill of Rights, this declaration proclaims to the world that you have rights too:

> You have the right to make mistakes without someone making you feel like a jerkhead.

> You have the right to be protected from harm, injustice and hatred.

> You have the right to an education that prepares you to run the world when it's your turn.

> You have the right to your opinions and feelings, even if others don't agree with them.

So there![93]

Despite the liberal rhetoric of equality ("all people are born with certain inalienable rights"), the Nickelodeon Bill of Rights does point out some important ways in which children are left out of a formal definition of citizenship. The network claims a specific entitlement: it is through *Nickelodeon*, not through the federal government, that rights will be "conferred" upon children. The government has historically excluded children, and Nickelodeon deliberately challenges this by claiming to address the concerns of children from a position of close identification: we *know* how it feels (it "stinks"), we *understand* that adults often make kids feel bad ("like a jerkhead"), and we'll *help* you challenge this patronizing position ("so there!"). The Nickelodeon Bill of Rights is one example of the idea that it is within the commercial realm where many of the questions that are distinctive of citizenship, questions of belonging, community, and representation, are both posed and answered.

CONVERGENCE: CHILDREN, CONSUMERISM, CITIZENSHIP, AND THE MEDIA

Cable television provides a unique cultural site in which to analyze different engagements of the commercial media—as a kind of pleasurable manipulation and as constitutive of identities and "notions of belonging and entitlement"— precisely because cable TV targets audiences as specific and unique identities. Cable television has also been popularly understood as the "alternative" to broadcast television—not simply in terms of an alternate choice but also in terms of its initial promise to more accurately represent a variety of audiences. In the late 1970s and early 1980s, the rapidly expanding cable industry appeared to lower barriers to entry, allowing independent entities to launch cable networks, and encouraging new media forms and programming formats to emerge and prosper. Children's channels, music video, 24-hour news, 24-hour weather, movie channels, and nostalgia channels devoted to programming long off-network were introduced. The "authentic" differences within people created by (or at least exploited by) marketers to produce demographic groups are thus vigorously engaged by cable television as part of each channel's appeal. Within the U.S. children's television landscape, Nickelodeon is the one cable television channel that has made consistent claims about its role in empowering children and has also provided a model for all other cable channels in terms of financial success. As Linda Simensky, a former employee of Nickelodeon in animation and development, has said: "Empowerment was a big part of the promises [Nickelodeon made to its audience]. The thing that was most interesting to me about Nick wanting to empower kids was telling them it was okay to be a kid. And to like kid things and that being a kid was fun."[94] Nickelodeon situates its version of empowerment beyond that of buying power and claims to "respect" children's needs and desires by encouraging "kids to be kids." Apparently, it is assumed by Nickelodeon that its audience knows what it means "to be a kid"; the vague quality of the phrase "being a kid" allows it rhetorically to fit nicely into the channel's claims about empowerment. The public service announcements on the channel, its own promotional spots, and programming narratives all revolve around the "kids only" theme.

As many media scholars remind us, the television audience is an imagined group, created for the purposes of advertisers who attempt to generalize and stabilize what is a particular and unstable practice: watching television.[95] The result of generalizing TV audiences in this way, at least with broadcast television, often occurs at the level of the content of programming (the airing of "lowest-common-denominator" programming) where for the most part broadcast television continues to be economically safe by airing tried-and-true genres, spinoffs of previously successful programs, and formulaic narratives. Yet at the same time, the contemporary U.S. media environment is increasingly sophisticated in the ways in which audiences are both imagined and addressed, and Nickelodeon has capitalized on this marketing trend, effectively positioning itself as a rebellious upstart within the larger children's television environment. Indeed, part of Nickelodeon's strategy is to challenge a notion of stable and "safe" television by addressing its audience in specific and even exclusionary terms. A character like Jimmy Neutron, from the program *Jimmy Neutron: Boy Genius,* is clearly smarter and more capable than the adults in the program (indeed, Jimmy's father seems to have only one interest in life, an obsession with ducks), and every plot revolves around Jimmy's superior intellect. In another Nickelodeon program, *The Fairly OddParents*, adults are so dispensable that the main character's parents are featured in the opening sequence as cardboard cutouts that sit on the front porch as a kind of prop. Through program narratives such as these, the network can claim to be for "kids only," celebrating a challenge to the authority of both adults and advertisers, as the network simultaneously delivers an audience of millions to its advertisers. Understanding Nickelodeon and its audience indicates a need to shift analytical focus from the text, because audience interaction is more than watching an individual program or having one specific fan base; however, it also means that the consumption of products should not be the only focus, since the "Nickelodeon kid" is engaged in more than purchasing products and constituting consumer identity. "Watching" Nickelodeon is a social and cultural practice that involves media structures and individual agency, production and consumption, text and audience.[96]

The former president of Nickelodeon, Geraldine Laybourne, argues that "Nick empowers kids by saying to them, 'You're important—important enough to have a network of your own.' "[97] In the current cultural climate, media visibility (whether on television, music, or other media outlets) equals a kind of power—especially for children. The unproblematic collapse that Laybourne makes between the realization of children as an important consumer group and perceived political power, where "you're important enough to have a network of your own," is certainly not a new phenomenon with adults, but the steadily increasing purchasing power of children ages four to eleven (American companies spend more than twenty times what they spent ten years ago on advertising for children, approximately $2 billion each year) indicates the significance of the intertwining of issues of citizenship, perceived political power, and consumer power.[98] Consumption habits mark individuals as members of particular communities and thus grant individuals a kind of power that accompanies such membership. Thus, citizenship is increasingly defined within consumer culture —as a *process* of consumption itself. Nickelodeon's self-conscious address about kids "as kids" is as much about the *purchasing* power of kids as it is about the *political* power of kids; in fact, these two discourses inform and constitute each other.

But because conventional politics and commercialism *are* in tension with each other, Nickelodeon's approach involves a more complicated arrangement than simply constituting its child audience as a new market. Although the snappy doo-wop/rap medleys that promoted Nickelodeon's campaign of "Nickelodeon Nation" may seem a bit obvious in their efforts to collapse citizenship with

1. Jimmy Neutron from *The Adventures of Jimmy Neutron: Boy Genius*, 2005.

2. Timmy Turner's cardboard cut-out parents from *The Fairly OddParents*, 2005.

consumerism, there are other ways that Nickelodeon encourages an active political participation within the bounds of its commercial structure. Thus, when Buckingham asks, "Children may indeed have acquired a new status within the private sphere of consumption, but how far has this extended to the public sphere of social institutions and of politics? Children may have become 'sovereign consumers,' but to what extent have they also been recognized as *citizens* in their own right?" one potential reply is that to be a "sovereign consumer" *is* to be a citizen.[99]

As I've discussed, an important element of Nickelodeon's self-construction is the network's insistence that kids are an active audience in their own right, separate from the world of adults. Indeed, as much of Nickelodeon's programming demonstrates, "adults just don't get it." Part of what adults "just don't get" is the consumption habits of youth, which are important markers of identity and ways of distinguishing one social group from another.[100] The boundary between the worlds of children and adults that is implied by the idea that adults "don't get" the world of children is important to the self-construction of children as particular kinds of citizens. Allison James has argued that the deliberate mystification of children's culture *by* children is crucial for one's self-conscious construction: "the true nature of the culture of childhood frequently remains hidden from adults, for the semantic cues which permit social recognition have been manipulated and disguised by children in terms of their alternative society . . . By confusing the adult order children create for themselves considerable room for movement within the limits imposed upon them by adult society."[101] A successful way of manipulating adult authority as a means to create a separate children's culture has been to select consumer goods that are distinctly outside the adult world, whether these choices be situated in popular music, fashion, or television programming. This strategy, however, does not simply establish "an alternative system of meanings which adults cannot perceive"; it also constructs children as a very important market demographic.[102] The children's media market is especially attractive because of its multidimensional appeal: children have money of their own (and more and more each year), they have influence over the purchasing power of their parents, and they are considered a market for the future.[103] The relatively newly found (or at least, newly energized) recognition of children as a lucrative market has resulted in increased visibility in the mass media—after all, part of targeting the tween market means that corporate culture needs to provide a kind of representation that is both appealing and inclusive.

These tensions are indicative of the complex relationship children have with the media. In the following chapters, I examine different dimensions of this relationship through an analysis of brand culture, the rise of "girl power" ideology, the New Economy of race, as well as other cultural dynamics. However, the questions that guide this book insist that these struggles over meanings also take place within the commercial structure of the media industry and as a result are produced by this context. I thus consider Nickelodeon not as a monolithic media empire but rather as a key player in a battle of competing discursive frames that are shaped by the contradictions embedded within the relationship between children and media more generally.

THIS BOOK'S ORGANIZATION

An examination of Nickelodeon demands a multivalent approach, one that considers contemporary media frameworks as complex, interconnected practices and ideologies. The research for this book was designed to take into account the competing frames of discourse that shape children's interaction with media, so I have aimed to examine different dynamics from a variety of vantage points. I interviewed approximately fifty U.S. children (ages eight to thirteen), from predominantly middle-class backgrounds, of different ethnic backgrounds, about the programs that they watch on Nickelodeon. The interview questions were designed as a means to determine the appeal of particular shows over others, or how children think they are "connected" to Nickelodeon, what ways are they still "left out" of media, and so forth. While I do not necessarily rely on these interviews for my central arguments in the book, I discovered a great deal through these interactions, primarily about the power and ubiquity of the Nickelodeon brand and its meaning in the lives of children who are (predominantly) avid media participants.

As a way to understand how it is that the children's television industry constructs not only its actual media product but also children's culture, I also spoke with industry professionals from a wide range of contexts. I used interviews with industry professionals to contextualize the historical development of the Nickelodeon brand, the production side of "girl power" shows, and also to understand Nickelodeon's commitment to diversity by airing minority-produced programming such as *Dora the Explorer* and *The Brothers Garcia*. This information gave me insights into the ways the tension between consumer citizenship and political citizenship is necessarily maintained by the media economy within which Nickelodeon is situated; it is precisely the structure of the cable industry that allows for a more innovative and active address to a youth audience even as this industry remains structured around competitive commercial interests.

I also examined the media representation of Nickelodeon; as one of the most successful cable channels in history, Nickelodeon is often covered in not only trade publications such as *Broadcasting and Cable*, *Advertising Age*, and *Variety* but also the dominant mass media press in the United States, including (but not limited to) the *New York Times*, the *Los Angeles Times*, the *San Diego Union Tribune*, and the *Washington Post*. I analyzed articles and press coverage about Nickelodeon as a way to determine the position the channel occupies in the mainstream American imagination as well as within the children's television industry. Finally, as a way to enrich the examination of the media discourse circulating about Nickelodeon, I conducted textual analysis on actual programming, in particular those shows that were identified (by both producers and audience members) as "girl power" programs, programs that featured diverse casts and crews, and those shows that best exemplified what one fifteen-year-old girl called "Nickelodeon humor."

In chapter 2, I offer a broad historical picture of the media industry in which

Nickelodeon emerges in the early 1980s, as a way to explain Nickelodeon's phenomenal success in the competitive children's television market. By situating Nickelodeon in the context of the media industry, I argue in this chapter that the network is not a success simply because of its philosophy or its innovative programming but also because of the economic context of the cable environment. This chapter traces the development of Nickelodeon as a network from a commercial-free "green vegetable" network (airing programs that parents wanted their kids to watch, not programs that kids themselves wanted to see) to a network that profits from ad-based revenue and is enormously successful with children. Focusing on not only the "mission statement" of the network but also on interviews with industry professionals, this chapter also examines the role that former Nickelodeon president Geraldine Laybourne had on the meteoric rise of Nickelodeon in the cable industry.

Because Nickelodeon's brand identity is so important to the overall way in which the network is received within the industry and by its audience, chapter 3 focuses on the history of this brand development, situating Nickelodeon as a specific product of a consumer society. I argue in this chapter that Nickelodeon's claims to "empower" its youth audience are successful only because the channel emerges in an already powerful cultural context of consumer citizenship. By examining advertisements on Nickelodeon, as well as offering a detailed analysis of the development of the Nickelodeon brand, I argue that within the context of the brand, it makes sense for Nickelodeon to claim that "Nick is more than just another kids' entertainment outlet; our big orange splot [the network's logo] stands for a set of ideas kids can understand and trust."[104]

The next three chapters specifically examine some of the themes on the Nickelodeon programming as crucial elements in the channel's claim to empower and respect kids. In chapter 4, I explore the contradictions between consumer citizenship and political citizenship through the lens of "girl power" ideology as it is represented on Nickelodeon. Nickelodeon has been especially outspoken in its commitment to girls; a recent industry seminar titled "Girl Power! Creating Positive Role Models for Girls" lauded Nickelodeon's specific efforts over the past twenty years to feature girls as primary leads in children's programming and its challenge of traditional gender stereotypes. In chapter 5, I turn to the network's ambivalent stance on the issue of diversity and argue that the channel gains cultural capital because of the way in which it creates diverse programming— even while Nickelodeon executives back away from owning the overt politics of these programming choices, couching them instead as "good business." And in chapter 6, I take up the often recognized intergenerational appeal of Nickelodeon and present one potential cultural space for that appeal: the politics of camp in original programming such as *SpongeBob SquarePants, Ren & Stimpy,* and *The Fairly OddParents.* In this chapter, I locate the camp style of some children's television programming as a particular kind of consumer strategy, and I argue that children's shows organized around camp, like "girl power" programs, harness a political ideology—gay identity politics, queer theory—and commodify it as an aesthetic practice. This occurs not only because of the mass media mainstreaming of camp but also because camp itself involves commodification.

Nickelodeon both produces and represents a set of tensions about children and citizenship. These tensions, between political citizenship and consumer citizenship, are not simply part of the representational politics of the network or within the aesthetic practices of the programs themselves. The construction of citizenship on Nickelodeon is also a crucial element in the production side of programming, and it functions to anchor the particular position of the network within the media industry itself. In the following pages, I hope to demonstrate that Nickelodeon provides us with a unique look at not only children's television but also at children's consumer culture, at a particular historical moment when children are conceived as a market in exceptional ways.

2 THE SUCCESS STORY: NICKELODEON AND THE CABLE INDUSTRY

To some degree, the success of Nickelodeon was lightning in a bottle, it was the environment, it was a time when there was no competition. The whole idea of there being a kids' network—it was outrageous in and of itself. Because it was basically saying, look, kids, it is okay to watch TV all day long. There's going to be something on for you all the time. So it was a radical idea.

—LINDA SIMENSKY, FORMER NICKELODEON EMPLOYEE

In the late 1970s, some thirty years after the beginning of television in the United States, television industry lore proclaimed that, despite its relatively short lifespan, the "end of broadcasting" had arrived. This apparent demise was heralded by the new television industry of cable. Beginning in the 1970s, satellite technologies and an increasingly relaxed regulatory environment provided the technological, cultural, and economic context for cable technologies to emerge as a specific and discrete industry in the United States. The optimistic early "blue sky" era of cable television was accompanied by an ever more cynical outlook on the overt commercialism of broadcast networks, leading to a simultaneous hopefulness and doubt about the symbolic power of television—especially as it concerned the empowerment of the viewer.[1] While broadcast television was still held to the public interest obligations set out in the 1934 Communications Act, by the 1970s, TV was firmly entrenched in a commercial system dependent on advertisers rather than on abstract obligations to the public's "interests."

The emergence and installation of cable technology in the American home during the 1970s was positioned and celebrated in terms of its difference from broadcast television. Cable television could offer less "lowest-common-denominator" and crassly commercialized television, less intrusive advertising, more interactivity on the part of the viewer, and generally more viewer empowerment.[2] In other words, cable TV would ostensibly "serve" the public interest in a way that broadcast television ignored. The public interest obligation of broadcast media in the United States structured radio before television and states that in exchange for using the limited electromagnetic spectrum ("owned" by the public), broadcasters are obliged to serve the public interest. More specifically, as Robert Horwitz points out, the "public interest" regulatory controls included "a requirement for public information programming, an obligation to ascertain the broadcast needs of the community, and recommendations on the maximum amount of advertising."[3] However, the definition of what exactly constitutes the "public interest" has been vague, and thus difficult to enforce and regulate. Because American media is a privately owned, for-profit industry, the relationship of radio and television to the public interest was, and continues to be, ambiguous, resulting in programming created primarily in terms of commercial rather than "public" value.

When the cable industry began to emerge in the television landscape in the late 1970s, most broadcast programs were designed to appeal to the broadest audience possible for advertisers.[4] For children in particular, despite exceptions on PBS such as *Sesame Street*, the programming choices were few and highly commercial. Indeed, children were an important subject of Newton Minow's now famous "vast wasteland" speech: "In the 1930s and 1940s, television's creators expressed their hope that the new medium would be the greatest instrument of enlightenment ever invented, a blessing to future generations. They were wrong. Broadcasters and politicians have turned it instead into an instrument of child exploitation and abuse. In the American system, children are not primarily to be educated, nurtured, or even entertained; like everyone else, they are simply chattel to be rounded up and sold to advertisers."[5] The role television ostensibly had in terms of constructing an informed citizenry through the media was, for many, sorely lacking; rather, television was doing a superb job in establishing the audience as consumers.

Because cable television does not use publicly owned airwaves, it is not subject to the same public interest obligations as broadcast television. Despite this, however, the optimistic rhetoric structuring the early cable industry implied that cable could address some of the problems broadcast television had in fulfilling the public interest obligations of the media. Indeed, the cable industry was flexible in ways that broadcast television was not because cable is not as dependent on advertising revenue. Additionally, because there was no clear recipe for success for this technology, in the early years of the industry, cable channels could afford to experiment with different formats and content.[6] Cable seemed poised to provide access to a greater variety of media forms and points of view than could be found on broadcasting sources, as increasing channel capacity, a pared-down regulatory apparatus amenable to growth of the industry, and consumer demand for new services transformed how homes received television signals. The perception of cable, within the industry and in the public alike, was that this new industry was an important alternative to the broadcast monolith.[7]

This, then, is the industrial context in which Nickelodeon emerges in 1979. This chapter examines how the various contexts shaping the television and cable industries during the 1970s and 1980s supplied a framework of ideas that informed the development of Nickelodeon about what "good" television for children should be. These factors were often inherently contradictory, so it is not surprising that the general rhetoric of Nickelodeon—the network's self-defined mission and philosophy—is also contradictory. I argue that although the structure of cable allowed for Nickelodeon's early innovations in television programming, the promise of cable—as well as the promise of Nickelodeon itself—was not fully realized. Nonetheless, the celebratory rhetoric of the early cable industry allowed for the establishment of Nickelodeon as antibroadcast, a kind of cable rebel in a conformist broadcast landscape. And indeed, the channel did in fact create programming that looked very different from broadcast. Nickelodeon, because of the ways in which it emerged within the context of cable, was both contradictory to and co-opted by media corporate culture. The channel was structured by this tension from its very beginnings.

Additionally, I argue here that the cultural context of media activism that in part encouraged the development of the cable industry was also a key factor in Nickelodeon's self-identity as a rebel. The utopian rhetoric that structured the U.S. cable industry carried over to media advocacy groups in this time period; in 1979 it was still possible for media advocacy groups to challenge the lack of good programming on television through a variety of different means.[8] Motivated by other social and cultural upheavals of the time, the media reform movements in the 1970s witnessed widespread support and participation.[9] It was also a time when the media, and specifically television, was simultaneously recognized as an important tool in terms of individual and group empowerment and was attacked for its erasure and containment of important narratives, images, and ideologies that were not supported by dominant groups. Within this framework, I examine media activism concerning children's television that shaped the politics of Nickelodeon, with a specific focus on Action for Children's Television (ACT).

THE BLUE SKY PERIOD: CABLE AS UTOPIA

Many scholars have investigated why television was initially developed as a broadcast system, with a limited number of points of transmission going to multiple receivers. As Raymond Williams has argued, television technology did not inherently demand or dictate the kind of broadcast system that TV became, such as the private, for-profit nature of U.S. television, suggesting that it is a mistake to analyze the broadcast nature of television in terms of a desire for mass communication.[10] It is significant that radio and television were primarily devised for transmission and reception, with little or no definition of the actual content that would be broadcast by these media. The technology of communication preceded ideas about the representational content of media. Because of this, Williams urges a multivalent approach to television: rather than understand it as a technology, or a means of control, or a pure system of representation, he calls for an approach that culturally engages television's phenomenology. Each communication medium builds on the history, economics, and politics of previous media, as television built upon radio and film, film built upon photography. This residual influence can be seen in more current communication technologies: the Internet upon television, film, and video, and cable television upon broadcast television.

As Williams so powerfully points out, theorizing television in terms of phenomenology provides us with a means to examine the material aspects of the media, or the specific capacities of each medium that distinguish its properties.[11] By grounding the material differences between and among media within specific historical, cultural, and political contexts, the "effect" of these properties on our experience and interpretation of the images and narratives becomes clearer. This kind of analysis also fleshes out the complexities and contradictions within the evolution of communication technologies. Williams demonstrates this dynamic by his discussion of "flow," where ads, programs, channel promos, and genre flow together as a seamless system, so that one television genre flows logically into the next, with no overt interruption. Television, then, is not simply a technology that can be easily fixed or located in space and time but rather is engaged in other cultural practices and ideologies as well. Because of its broadcast possibilities, television has potential as a kind of "public" medium, yet the private reception of television programming forces a shift in what is meant by public media.

Indeed, the adoption of the television within the domestic home in the United States forced into bold relief these contradictions of centralized transmission and privatized reception.[12] The privatized nature of the television limited the potential use of medium as a kind of public sphere, even though the public interest obligation of radio carried over to television.[13] Although television broadcasters were also expected to fulfill a public interest obligation, there was no clear definition of what "public interest" meant, and commercial broadcasters quickly adapted the rhetoric of public interest within their own interests and persuasively argued that private market interests *were* in fact interests of the "public."[14] This, of course, was a rhetorical strategy that FCC Chairman Mark Fowler later effectively used to justify deregulation of the communications industry in the 1980s. Indeed, the ambiguity implicit in the notion of the "public interest" led to an industry expectation that, as Minow points out, "in addition to public service, the financial health of the regulated private industry (and profit for its owners) was a legitimate measure of the public interest."[15]

Cable technology, like broadcast television, was the subject of both optimistic and pessimistic forecasts as to the role cable would play in audience empowerment. Cable television, or as it was initially called, Community Antenna Television (CATV), emerged as a force in the media industry in the late 1970s.[16] Although initially cable was considered by the Federal Communications Commission (FCC) as a "regulatory outcast," in the 1970s, the FCC began to protect cable as an important "element of the media system."[17] As Thomas Streeter explains, it was during this time that the FCC entered a period of "reregulation," where it altered the set of regulations governing cable television. The rapid expansion of the industry would not have been possible without this regulatory change. Within this context, where programming could be delivered by satellite, the promise was that cable could apparently address the problems that continued to haunt broadcast television. As Megan Mullen points out, early policy discussions of the possibilities of cable associated the technology with a kind of "revolution," which could eventually "remedy all the perceived ills of broadcast television, including lowest-common-denominator programming, inability to serve the needs of local audiences, and failure to recognize the needs of cultural minorities."[18] As Mullen documents, the Sloan Commission on Cable Communications in 1971 claimed that if the cable system was properly overhauled and applied, there was "a revolution now in sight." This kind of utopian language is quite similar to the language used at the emergence of other communication technologies: the telegraph, the photograph, the radio, and the television.[19] Like these technologies, cable promised to radically revise the viewers' relationship with media by encouraging a more active viewership and a newfound sense of political and cultural empowerment. And because cable was not (initially) conceived as dependent on advertisers, different channels could promise to reach a narrower audience through niche programming, thus catering more to the direct needs and tastes of the population. Through this kind of direct audience address, cable channels were seen as a possible facilitator of viewer empowerment and a potential catalyst for citizenship.[20] Importantly, this was not simply a discourse that circulated in the world of telecommunications policy. As Streeter argues, the utopian language about what cable could do in terms of the "information highway" included in the policy reports and city documents was also one that found its way into public and industry discourse.[21] Moreover, the burgeoning cable industry was not yet tied to major media conglomerates, so it seemed to exist as a communication technology that encouraged independent entities to create networks and channels that allowed for alternative kinds of programming.

As was the case with broadcast television, the technology that enabled cable was not the essential factor invoked in the public and policy revolutionary discourse. As Streeter articulates, although constantly labeled as "new," the technology of cable was not necessarily "new technology." Rather, it was the *use* of this technology that was understood as novel: the increase in channel capacity and the development of a market so that more channels were available was the potential impetus for the "revolution." Indeed, it was precisely cable's abstract "newness" that made it "possible to speak of cable, not as an embodiment of social contradictions and dilemmas, but as a *solution* to them."[22] Cable was seen as a possible remedy to all sorts of social problems, such as racism and poverty, because it could "narrowcast" and thus more accurately represent an audience. And, as Streeter argues, "Cable . . . had the potential to rehumanize a dehumanized society, to eliminate the existing bureaucratic restrictions of government regulation common to the industrial world, and to empower the currently powerless public."[23]

Scholars such as Streeter and Mullen have documented how this hyperbolic promise of cable was never quite fulfilled. In fact, the current structure of the cable industry resembles the familiar format of broadcast television in almost all ways. There was no televisually inspired "revolution," and the cable industry is now primarily governed and owned by the same transnational media corporations as the broadcast networks.[24] However, the utopian discourse that framed the early debates on cable, especially in terms of the public interest, was essential for providing a context for a network such as Nickelodeon to emerge precisely because it focused attention on television's potential to empower viewers as particular kinds of citizens. To enforce the public interest obligations would necessarily change the scope of the television industry and would certainly transform the dynamic between viewers, media owners, and advertisers. The promise that cable would transform the televisual world was an important factor in

Nickelodeon's early self-concept and mission, and the notion of viewer empowerment came to characterize the network's self-identity. Nickelodeon emerged in a cultural context where the notion of the public's interest was framed around independence from advertisers.[25]

Initially, there were two dimensions of the utopian discourse framing the cable industry in the 1970s that are important for the historical context of Nickelodeon. The first was that the enthusiasm for the burgeoning cable industry was vocalized not by radical political groups on either the right or the left of the political spectrum but by those groups who were more moderate. Specifically, as Streeter documents, contributors to the positive discourse on cable were those people who "wanted to 'work within the system' to accomplish democratic social change within the framework of the dominant power structures of society."[26] The support of progressive groups from the initial emergence of the cable industry offered these groups a chance to "work within the system" and a potential opportunity to influence policy decisions. This kind of moderate political positioning became important for Geraldine Laybourne when she became president of Nickelodeon in 1984 and relaunched (and transformed) the network as one focused on entertainment rather than education.

As important as it was to address problems within television at the level of regulation, the perception of the audience was a second important dimension of the early rhetoric on the cable industry. It was a common lament during this period (and continues to be today) that the standardization of broadcast television and its reliance on advertising support resulted in a mass of passive and presumably homogenous viewers. Cable was seen to be something that could bring back (in a nostalgic sense of community face-to-face communication) active participation through empowering viewers as citizens.[27] Nickelodeon's self-identity has been based on a commitment to an active child audience and has explicitly used the language of citizenship through a focus on rights and empowerment. The "kids only" zone that comprised the Nickelodeon audience was one that presumably had some say in what the network creates and produces. As I demonstrate throughout this book, within the world of Nickelodeon, the network's stance on encouraging an active audience is, at the very least, complicated. But the network's claim that it empowered the child audience was a crucial element in Nickelodeon's development of a very specific self-identity.

Although clearly a commercial network, Nickelodeon also embraced some of the same rhetoric as the early "blue sky" pioneers of cable, and these themes—audience empowerment, transformation, revolution, assuaging of social problems—became essential parts of the Nickelodeon brand. Nickelodeon defines these themes, of course, within the structure of the commercial world of children's television, and as such, they are as much a part of the network's industry identity as they are abstract progressive concepts. These same notions of empowerment, transformation, and rebellion were incorporated into Nickelodeon's programming, giving the network an identity that, unlike other burgeoning cable networks at the time, did not look like recycled broadcast programming. Years of struggling to pinpoint the ill-defined "public interest" obligations of television offered an opportunity for Nickelodeon to claim itself in the public interest for kids, even if cable TV was not explicitly subject to this kind of regulation the way broadcasters were. Within this context, the network tried new ideas, developed a new kind of relationship with the audience that was based on a kind of "respect," and from the beginning created its own original programming —though clearly not in the realm of "educational and informative" later specified by the Children's Television Act of 1990. In this way, Nickelodeon was a *response* to the burgeoning cable industry, not just a by-product or a recycled broadcast network. As Linda Simensky, a former employee of Nickelodeon during this particular period, argues, the success of cable depended on "the promise of cable to be narrowcasting. To me, Nick was one of the most narrow of narrowcasting channels—there was no golf channel back then, there was no specialty channel back then, everything was almost more general (networks like USA and TBS). CNN was narrowcasting, but people thought that was insane as well. To me, Nick was the first narrowcasting channel."[28]

Cable television ostensibly presented an alternative to the lowest common denominator programming on broadcast television. Within the context of broadcast television itself, however, another way to address this problem was through media advocacy. As the cable industry was burgeoning, cultural discourses circulated—within the media industry as well as general public discourse—about "good" and "bad" television for children. The apparent negative influence of advertising and consumer culture on programming content for children's media was generating a particular kind of attention by media advocacy groups, and this context of change and advocacy was another necessary condition for the emergence of Nickelodeon.

MEDIA REFORM OF THE BROADCAST NETWORKS: ACT

Early broadcast television also carried a promise of smoothing social tensions through a commercial venue; as Lynn Spigel documents about television in postwar U.S. culture, "television was depicted as a panacea for the broken homes and hearts of wartime life; not only was it shown to restore faith in family togetherness, but as the most sought-after appliance for sale in postwar America, it also renewed faith in the splendors of consumer capitalism."[29] This enthusiasm, however, was tempered by some negative attitudes toward television. As with all communication technologies, there was a general ambivalence on the part of viewers, legislators, and educators as to what television had to offer the American public. Specifically for children's television, the number of advertisements aired during a program and the regulation of children's programs to the "Saturday morning exile" inspired some groups to take action on the precise basis of the public interest clause.[30] The overt commercialism of children's programming on broadcast television, especially in comparison to the educational programs of PBS (*Sesame Street, Mister Rogers' Neighborhood,* and *Electric Company,* among others), was understood by some to run counter to the interest of the "public." In 1969, a case was filed with the FCC against the toy company Mattel, on the basis that the television cartoon produced by the company, *Hot Wheels,* was merely a "program length commercial" and thus violated the FCC's time restrictions on advertising.[31] The show was eventually pulled from the air, and this proved to advocacy groups that challenging the FCC on the basis of failing to serve public interest obligations could be an effective strategy. Encouraged by the more general context of reform that characterized 1970s culture, media advocacy groups began to challenge broadcasters on the basis of public interest obligations, in efforts to hinder license renewal with the FCC.

Television itself played a crucial role in the civil unrest and political upheavals of the 1960s, through its broadcast of some events such as the 1968 Democratic Convention and the Watts riots, as well as the Vietnam War itself. It was also during this era that the corporate consolidation of the television industry solidified and expanded. Thus, as many scholars have noted, the use of the television by activists to claim that "the Whole World is Watching" meant something quite different to advertisers: more and more consumer dollars.[32] Certainly the 1970s yielded some "good" television—in fact, some of the most critical and interesting broadcast television was produced during this period.[33] But with the shift within broadcast television to ad-based revenue in the late 1960s (as opposed to a single sponsor financing a program), the economic potential of television was clearly established—advertising, not creative production, determined the kind of programming that would be broadcast to the nation.[34]

In the world of children's television, advertisers were also starting to take notice. Although the children's market was not near its current scope (in terms of purchasing power, influence, or advertiser dollars), in the 1970s this market still represented an opportunity to target a particular audience. Not surprisingly, the embrace of the children's market by advertisers was seen as an abuse of commercial television by many activist groups.[35] Because of the assumption that television could be a catalyst for citizenship and an educator for children, and because of successful educational programs on public television, some activists saw advertising during children's programming as a particularly egregious offense. The most vocal media activist group, and the group who received the most attention from the mainstream press, was Action for Children's Television (ACT), the first prominent activist group to focus specifically on children's television. ACT was founded in 1968 by Evelyn Sarson, Peggy Charren, and others, whose primary identity was as middle-class mothers who wanted children's television to be more responsible in its programming. There were two primary objectives of the group: "increasing choice in children's programming, and stopping the 'over-commercialization' of children's media."[36]

As Heather Hendershot argues, unlike other activist groups such as feminist groups or the antiwar student protesters or the civil rights movement, the group of women who formed ACT were "safer" in terms of their politics. The familiar strategy of "working within the system" worked for ACT, as it was politically easier for government agencies such as the FCC to address ACT than other activist groups, who were seen as "extremist."[37] Unlike groups such as feminists or student groups like Students for a Democratic Society, ACT did not focus on *using* the media to articulate its political agenda but was critical of the corporate media institution itself. This would prove crucial to the self-conscious development of Nickelodeon's identity, which seemed to redefine what a corporate media institution was, at least in terms of the ways in which institutions addressed their audience.

ACT voiced its complaints with children's television not by boycotting networks (they were, in fact, staunchly against boycotting, claiming it to be a form of censorship) but by going directly to the FCC.[38] Specifically, ACT's objection was that broadcasters had failed their public interest obligations. The group asked the FCC to implement a "code of ethics" regarding children's programming, one that encouraged age-appropriate programs, prohibited the promotion or advertising of products during programs, and forced advertisers to run ads only before and after programs.[39] This, the group insisted, would force television to fulfill its basic public interest obligation by training citizens, rather than little consumers. As Hendershot points out, while the changes that occurred as a result of ACT's petitions to the FCC were in some ways negligible (the original goal was to remove children's programming from the marketplace, which clearly did not happen), the group did manage to find an appropriate way to challenge the broadcast system; the use of the discourse of public interest as a platform for challenging FCC decisions was shown to be an effective measure of protest. ACT's focus on the failure of broadcast television to fulfill its public interest obligations forced the

FCC to pay more attention to media activist groups (including those who advocated for lighter regulations for cable television), which led to an increasing number of media activist and reform groups during the 1970s.[40] As Hendershot details, "ACT was fairly successful largely because it was an incorporated organization that played by the rules not only of the FCC but also of big business. Even as it attacked certain products and business practices and called for the elimination of ads on children's shows, ACT confronted television professionally, using language and strategies comprehensible to TV and FCC executives."[41] This kind of strategy, working within the system rather than against it, is always complicated, as some principles and challenges put forth by ACT could never be realized—or even imagined—through this kind of address (such as the removal of advertising directed at children). ACT was limited by what it could and could not say to the FCC (or more accurately, what the FCC would and would not listen to) because of its refusal to challenge the "liberal reformist ideology" within which the FCC was so deeply embedded.[42]

This stance proved to be remarkably similar to the one that Geraldine Laybourne would embrace as the new president of Nickelodeon in 1984. The cultural context that made ACT such a successful media reform organization was the same one that led to the widespread adoption of cable television, and more specifically, to the creation of Nickelodeon. However, there were some key differences in goals and philosophy between ACT and Laybourne: Laybourne sought to make "good" children's television, but not in terms of the educational programming that ACT endorsed. Laybourne was not interested in noncommercial television; even though initially the channel did not accept advertising, Nickelodeon was never intended to be "public" television. As she said, "The PBS orientation to kids is different from ours. PBS begins by asking: 'How can we improve kids? There's something wrong with them.'" Laybourne's approach with Nickelodeon has been to entertain, not educate kids: "to celebrate being a kid . . . We don't try to prove kids know their alphabet."[43] Additionally, Laybourne clearly believed that "good" television was possible in a commercial environment and thus never challenged the advertising world in the way that ACT did. Finally, Nickelodeon (led by Laybourne) defined the child (and thus the child audience) differently from ACT. The child viewer was configured by Nickelodeon certainly as a citizen, but not in the way that ACT defined citizenship. Rather, the Nickelodeon definition of a child viewer was as a consumer citizen—this child was not innocent or vulnerable but rather was a savvy media consumer. The sharp division that media advocacy groups assumed between citizenship and consumers was conceptualized by Nickelodeon as a convergence. Indeed, the "Nickelodeon kid" was commodified and marketed until it became the emblem of Nickelodeon's self-identity—and ended up being the network's key to success.

NICKELODEON AND THE COMMERCIAL CHILD

Because ACT did not believe in boycotting products that advertisers promoted, the group needed to define other ways in which to advocate for better children's television.[44] Nickelodeon emerges in these cultural debates in an interesting way: although there was some alliance between ACT and Nickelodeon because Nickelodeon, like ACT, was publicly dedicated to better children's television, Nickelodeon also had a very different public stance on what constituted "better" TV. As Laybourne says about the relationship between Nickelodeon and ACT, "[Charren] always liked the people at Nickelodeon and grew to like the network because we did things like Nick News as well as doing good things for kids in general. But she was leery about Nickelodeon for a lot of reasons, and rightfully so. When we first started, we had 1.5 million subscribers, and she didn't want broadcasters to be let off the hook. They had been given this valuable license, and she didn't think they did much programming that had a higher purpose for kids—except for the occasional history minute. She was afraid of Nickelodeon in the early days because the broadcasters would say, 'Well we don't need to do that because Nickelodeon does that.'"[45] Nickelodeon's discourse challenges the cultural capital of "tasteful" and educational television directly and aggressively: TV should be about entertainment, not education. As Laybourne herself stated, Nickelodeon didn't need to prove that the network was teaching children basic skills. The role of TV as educator was clearly parental, and Nickelodeon quite carefully set out to distinguish itself from parents—the network was on the kids' side and consciously (although within limits) challenged parental authority. The child audience, for Nickelodeon, was built of savvy, sophisticated consumers.[46]

The "Nickelodeon kid" was thus aligned with a market, rather than a cultural, definition of children. As the marketing expert James McNeal has pointed out, for advertisers, children are considered three different kinds of market: children as a primary market (where they spend their own money), children as a "market of influencers" (where they influence their parents' decisions), and children as a future market (where cultivating loyalty becomes important).[47] This marketing definition of "kid-ness" is incorporated as a theme in advertising targeted to children: as McNeal argues, "To the extent a product designer can capture this kid quality and imbue any object or service with it, a high degree of satisfaction for kids on a relatively long-term basis is likely to occur . . . Further, it is suggested that the more a product can be classified as kids-only (as possessing kid-ness), the more acceptance and liking it will have among children, and the more likely it will be a marketing success."[48] More and more money is spent on children's ads in an attempt to tap into the "kid-ness" of children—often in direct opposition to "adult-ness."[49]

Part of what the world of advertising and marketing understands—and that media activist groups choose to ignore—is the implicit binary involved in the construction of the child as an innocent. As Ellen Seiter notes, "Implicit in ACT's characterization of the child consumer in need of protection is the rational adult consumer cool to advertising's persuasive whims."[50] This binary between adults and children, with the accompanying emphasis on "kid-ness," becomes the precise dynamic that Nickelodeon ends up exploiting to phenomenal success, but from a slightly different angle: children are "cool," and adults "just don't get it." In other words, the binary is not simply reversed, where children are sophisticated and adults are "innocent"; rather, there is a new emphasis that exploits the factor of "kid-ness" to a different level. Adults are boring, kids are interesting; adults are predictable, kids are spontaneous; adults are responsible, kids are wacky. This part of Nickelodeon's self-identity is absolutely dependent on a different definition from the historically powerful "innocent child." The difference between these, however, need not be an essential division according to Nickelodeon: a commercial environment and a profit motive does not affect the network's primary concern in terms of "respecting" kids and treating them as particular kinds of active agents.

THE 1980S: DEREGULATION AND CHILDREN'S TELEVISION

In the 1980s the Reagan administration's FCC, led by Mark Fowler, changed the U.S. regulatory environment and relaxed the government controls that had governed broadcast television (as well as other telecommunications) for the previous fifty years. With deregulation, commercial broadcasters were no longer constrained by these government rules, emphasizing instead the rules of the market. This "free" market mentality (which included child viewers) was assumed to naturally regulate the broadcast industry, so that instead of the FCC controlling content (even in a limited way), television viewers had the "choice" to turn off the television set if it was not providing adequate fare. Deregulation gave media owners more and more control over the industry (and allowed media owners to own more and more media outlets) because free speech rights, a protection interpreted as "freedom to advertise," protected them.[51] Additionally, the whole idea of "public interest" could no longer be used as a mechanism by which broadcasters were responsible for programming that was considered fair and balanced.

Since deregulation indicated that the public interest was best served by the privatized market, the ability to challenge broadcasters' licensing renewal (the basis on which many groups challenged broadcasters) was diminished.[52] With public interest concerns out of the way, advertising for children could be redefined and take a larger part in determining the kinds of programming that were placed on the air. In fact, Reagan vetoed the Children's Television Act, which proposed to reinstate advertising-time restrictions. Programming based on pre-existing toys would no longer be considered a violation of FCC policy or of the "public interest." As Horwitz points out, during the period of Reagan deregulation, "Only the marketplace—the middle- and upper-middle-class viewers who most appealed to advertisers—had the right to remark upon program content, and unless they were Nielsen families, their opinions could be expressed in only three ways: by changing the channel, by turning off the set, or by boycotting sponsors."[53]

This deregulatory environment and the relaxation of government rules governing the amount of time spent by broadcasters on advertising led to the characterization of the 1980s as "the decade of the child consumer." The lessening of federal oversight certainly opened the way for licensed toys and program-length commercials to dominate the airwaves in terms of programming for children.[54] But also, because children were recognized as part of the "free" market that could ostensibly regulate the TV industry, they were in turn recognized as an important consumer market. In this way, we can see a shift in cultural definitions of childhood, where children are newly understood as particular kinds of consumer citizens and garner a similar kind of "respect" as a lucrative market. The emergence of Nickelodeon within this context is clearly connected to the way in which children matter economically in this historical moment.

Thus, Nickelodeon as a *concept* as well as a network could only occur in a particular kind of environment. Because Nickelodeon was essentially attempting to create what looked rhetorically like a noncommercial environment for children—one that was about kids' rights, respect, fun, and an Us versus Them ideology—within an intensely commercial context, there were necessarily contradictory dynamics involved in both the shaping of the network's self-identity and the children's media landscape itself. As we've seen, there were contradictions within the cable industry, where the utopian and anticorporate rhetoric relied precisely on a corporate mentality for its realization. There were contradictions within the media advocacy environment, where the most successful groups, such as ACT, were successful in particular because they worked within, and not in opposition to, the media regulatory system. There were contradictions within the general conception of the power of television itself, where it was understood by the public, legislators, and educators alike as both liberatory and reactionary. Finally, there were (and continue to be) contradictions within cultural conceptions of the child and childhood, where the child is figured as both innocent yet a savvy consumer. All of these factors set the stage for the emergence of a peculiarly unique cable network. However, as with most organizations, Nickelodeon needed a particular kind of leader who would not attempt to "resolve" these contradictions but rather embody them within the very philosophy of the network.

Geraldine Laybourne, who became president of Nickelodeon in 1984, represents this kind of embodiment: her network was not pressured yet supported by advertising; she "worked within the system" to create an entity that looked entirely different from the system; she publicly supported the empowerment of children yet also sought to exploit them as a commercial market. Importantly, Laybourne was not *the* network, in that any kind of corporation always exceeds the boundaries of the individuals who create and lead it, but her vision was crucial to the success of Nickelodeon. As Simensky, who worked in development at Nickelodeon for nine years under Laybourne, commented: "Gerry really was the creator, she was the visionary who was able to articulate the vision. Everything that she did, she knew how to ask you the questions that you weren't prepared for—she just was operating at a higher plane. And it was like she could see the future, and so there was this feeling that she was like a guru, that she really was pretty magical."[55]

THE GERRY LAYBOURNE ERA

Nickelodeon technically began in 1979 as part of an interactive cable endeavor of Warner Communications. Part of the QUBE cable network, the channel was then called Pinwheel and was designed to offer children's programming that was prosocial, nonstereotypical, and commercial free. QUBE was part of an interactive cable experiment; it was a local program concept for the residents of Columbus, Ohio, and each cable subscriber received a box with buttons to push to vote on different programs, to shop, and so forth. Pinwheel was designed to be the first channel in history dedicated to children, and at the beginning the only show featured on Pinwheel was a preschool program called *Pinwheel House*.[56] This was a nonanimated show that featured educational fare (similar to *Sesame Street*), and was aired the entire day, from 7:00 a.m. to 7:00 p.m.

QUBE was a product from the "blue sky" era of cable television and in the beginning offered a wide variety of programs. As Mullen documents, the trade publications in the late 1970s were "filled with articles about the futuristic cable scenario QUBE had initiated."[57] The interactivity promised by the QUBE selector box could offer the "town meeting" ethos promised by the implementation of cable, and it was touted as one of the important ways that cable would revolutionize the television industry. However, QUBE, like most cable television, resembled broadcast television more than challenged it, and after the first five years, the interactive programming was cut back and eventually eliminated.

Pinwheel, however, was a bit more successful. In April 1979, Pinwheel changed its name to Nickelodeon, and its children's programming expanded to thirteen hours a day.[58] From its inception, Nickelodeon claimed to address an unmet need in television; although there were other channels that aired programming for children, Nickelodeon boasted original programming and program formats, mostly first-run acquired programs and in-house productions. It sought to develop a strong identity with its viewers, much like its sister station, MTV. In 1980, Warner merged with American Express, and Nickelodeon, along with MTV, became part of the programming division of the corporation, Warner-Amex Satellite Entertainment Company, eventually renamed as MTV Networks.

Pinwheel/Nickelodeon was a product of a changing commercial environment, and it focused on the educational potential of television. However, despite its lofty claims of being noncommercial, Pinwheel/Nickelodeon remained subject to ratings, and the channel was known then as "green vegetable" programming, indicating that the programs offered were liked by parents and considered "good TV" for children but disliked by the child viewers.[59] At the same historical moment, MTV was immediately a clear success. Laybourne, commenting on this history, states that what MTV did was create "a home base for teenagers. It was very hot, very sexy while Nickelodeon was 'Woe is me.' I think we had invested only $20 million in its development by the end of 1983, and we remained a last choice for kids. If there were nothing else on, kids could tune to Nickelodeon."[60] When Laybourne took over in 1983, she immediately sought to make Nickelodeon the MTV equivalent for younger children, a hip, fun home base. She switched focus from quality educational to quality entertainment programming and began accepting advertising as a way to supplement revenue.

Before it began accepting commercial advertising, corporate sponsors underwrote Nickelodeon, similar to the format of the Public Broadcasting System.[61] As a way to build loyalty among sponsors, Nickelodeon also offered unique sponsorship agreements with several advertisers. So, for example, Reebok and Converse had "exclusivity positions" in the programs *Double Dare* and *Finders Keepers*.[62] Later, Nickelodeon also had multiyear deals with advertisers, which it was able to acquire because there was virtually no competition from other children's channels. This trajectory, from noncommercial "green vegetable programming" to accepting advertising, is a crucial part of Laybourne's legacy. Laybourne accomplished a great number of goals during her tenure at Nickelodeon: she established a clear identity with viewers as a "kids-only" network; she developed an audience address that emphasized respect, not condescension; she maintained the channel's commitment to nonviolent, nonstereotypical programming; she preserved, for the most part, the channel's pledge of non-toy-based programming; and she managed to tap into an important audience niche left ignored by the children's television staples *Mister Rogers' Neighborhood* and *Sesame Street,* because she produced programming for children over (as well as under) the age of eight.

Laybourne's vision for Nickelodeon was designed to fill a children's television void left between commercial television, on the one hand, and PBS and Children's Television Workshop, on the other. Not surprisingly, given the controversies generated by children's television and advertising (largely made public by ACT), when Laybourne made the decision to accept advertising in 1983, she had to strategize over how to spin this decision to Nickelodeon's audience (especially parents). Initially, Nickelodeon prided itself on offering quality children's television not available on the broadcast networks precisely *because* it was commercial-free. Nickelodeon's self-identity had already been strongly formed around what it was *not:* commercial programming, driven by licensed toy characters, violent, stereotypical. The decision to accept advertising clearly contradicted the channel's early goals. After all, in 1983, before the channel's relaunch, the then vice-president of Nickelodeon, Cy Schneider, said about advertising, "We are not against advertising for moral or philosophical reasons . . . We don't take advertising because cable, to succeed, should be different from commercial broadcasting. It makes for a better product. When Nickelodeon was being developed four years ago, there was considerable complaint that children's programming on the networks was carrying too much advertising. Not taking advertising was a way to differentiate us. It's part of our concept."[63] The network had to be strategic about the way the decision to accept advertising was framed, given such earlier statements about the "Nickelodeon concept." This contradiction was noted in the popular press: in a *New York Times* article detailing the decision to accept advertising in 1983, the reporter asks the questions point-blank: "The quandary that all of this poses is: Will Nickelodeon have to make compromises to preserve its integrity? And if it does, will its integrity be compromised?"[64] Laybourne and the rest of the Nickelodeon staff defended the decision to take on advertising from a number of different fronts, but primarily by insisting that service to children and service to advertisers are not necessarily irreconcilable. According to this explanation, Nickelodeon attempts to provide "a nurturing, protective environment for children. While we are a business, we're responsible as kid advocates to protect them from commercial exploitation . . . That means walking a very distinct, but fine line."[65] From Laybourne's time, Nickelodeon has carefully crafted its identity as a media channel that serves consumers *as* citizens. Advertising, Laybourne claimed, would not lead to Nickelodeon airing lowest-common-denominator programs, where the audience is thought of as a monolithic audience of two to twelve years old. Rather, the channel would continue to improve its already age-specific programming, catering to children's needs, not those of advertisers. As Laybourne argued, "Age-specific programming is what Nickelodeon is all about . . . We look at the developmental needs of each age group."[66] Through rhetoric like this, Nickelodeon was able to maintain its identity as a cable upstart—even while the economic structure of the channel resembled other broadcast channels.

In addition, Nickelodeon would not air "educational television" as a way to combat the commercialism of the advertising. As Laybourne said regarding educational television shows: "They would bore kids to death . . . We look for shows with new information, shows about another culture, heroes and heroines, life styles. We look for shows that present kids as competent or interesting and have respect for them."[67] Laybourne painstakingly crafted a campaign that justified reliance on advertisers around the notion of "respect": respect for children and what they wanted to see, not respect for advertising and the commercial structure of television—as if there is a profound distinction between the two in this context. Within this kind of political economy, the idea that children deserve a kind of respect from a commercial network has everything to do with their consumer power. Nickelodeon thus produced a self-identity that explicitly positioned private interests—consumption—as a public value—citizenship and respect.

Despite the seeming hypocrisy, after Warner-Amex began accepting advertising for Nickelodeon, the channel continued to insist that they remained somehow noncommercial in a commercial environment. John Schneider, then president of Warner-Amex, claimed that Nickelodeon "will never be primarily supported by advertising because there are not an awful lot of advertisers interested in the preschool child."[68] Of course, Schneider turned out to be quite wrong; as current data shows us, advertisers are *very* interested in the preschool child—in fact, that group as well as the rest of the child audience is seen to be an especially important demographic for advertisers because of the "three-in-one" package an advertiser gets in a child. Nonetheless, in the early 1980s, when Nickelodeon began accepting advertising, the channel was sensitive to the regulatory environment and thus rhetorically framed this decision as one that was, somehow, not a commercial one—it was simply about keeping "good television" on the air. As Laybourne comments, "In those early years, the ad sales people would have been very happy if we had acquired a violent cartoon library. But we always had more revenue on the affiliate side than the advertising side and so we could always say to the advertising side of our business, 'We can't do that because of our commitments to our affiliates.' It helped us stay on the side of nonviolence."[69] And in fact, initially, there were not many ads on the channel, and the ones that aired were selected because they were in keeping with Nickelodeon's overall mission: there were only seven minutes of commercials an hour (including Kellogg, Milton Bradley, Activision video, M & M candies, and Bubblicious gum). In keeping with the channel's pledge to air only nonviolent television, advertising that promoted toy guns or other war toys was turned down.[70] Laybourne relates a story about rejecting advertising for Laser Tag, a game that involves guns and shootings: "The advertising was incredibly violent. Boy, I didn't want to do that—I didn't want to go in that direction. We were trying to keep the trust of parents, the Peggy Charrens of the world, and the cable affiliates. Imagine their response if we started taking advertising with guns. This very violent ad was going to be everywhere, and we would have been 'owned' by Laser Tag, so I objected to running it."[71] By focusing on those ads the channel *refused* because they were morally or politically oppositional to Nickelodeon's philosophy, the significance of the fact that Nickelodeon *was* supported by advertising was diminished.

After the decision to accept advertising, Nickelodeon had to convince its audience, the parents of children, the industry, and, because it helped tremendously to have the support of vocal media activist groups, groups such as ACT, that the integrity of the channel's original mission to offer quality, nonviolent, nonstereotypical programming remained intact. As Peggy Charren said about Nickelodeon's decision to accept ads: "Nickelodeon deserves every award it's gotten. It's a microcosm of what television for children should be. It has diversity. It's like a children's library that has comic books on the shelves but also has biographies of sports figures and how-to books. I hope commercials won't mean an end to that diversity. I hope we're not living through a Golden Age of Children's Television that will soon come tumbling down."[72] Laybourne and others at Nickelodeon were insistent that the channel would not develop programming just to sell products, as the broadcast networks were doing so successfully in the era of Reaganomics and deregulation. The shows on Nickelodeon, in other words, would not be about "toy-hawking" but would rather be about establishing a place in television where kids could "just be kids."

JUST BEING KIDS: NICKELODEON AS NEIGHBORHOOD

Nickelodeon wanted to be what Laybourne called "a trusted friend to kids," and it set out to forge this friendship by purposely being noneducational, not eschewing mass culture in favor of some "universal" understanding of "good" culture but rather reveling in mass culture and commercial culture in a way that excited the kid audience. In order for the network to remain a "trusted friend to kids," it needed to provide something different from the toy-based programs of Saturday morning cartoons on network television. Laybourne claimed that one of her goals, even before Nickelodeon, was to "put animated toy-related programs out of business."[73] She sought to do this by creating shows such as *Double Dare,* an early show on Nickelodeon that was phenomenally successful (quadrupled, then doubled again the ratings for the time slot). *Double Dare* exemplified some of the early goals of the channel: it was messy, irreverent, and kids were positioned as authorities. The show followed a game show format, where contestants were asked to complete physical challenges, brainteasers, and obstacle courses, among other things. If a contestant gave the wrong answer, or answered "I don't know," then he or she was "slimed"—the beginning of a Nickelodeon trademark when gallons of green slime are poured on the head of contestants. Laybourne attributes some of the success of shows like *Double Dare* to the increasingly public critique of toy-based programming: "I was trying to figure out how to break down the standard myths about kids: They only like animation, they only like fast pace, they only like action adventures, whatever. My notion was that kids only liked what they were only exposed to and that if you exposed them to other things you could elevate their tastes and move them along."[74] So although Laybourne was in opposition to ACT in terms of educational television, there remained a similarity between the two in the moral imperative to "elevate their tastes and move them along." The difference lay in how they each defined cultural capital. There was clear agreement between Nickelodeon and media activists that the typical focus of children's television on toy-based animation underestimated children's tastes, but where groups such as ACT saw children as being duped by these kinds of programs, Laybourne saw children as sophisticated media viewers. Because of the freedom of the cable industry and an environment of deregulation, Nickelodeon could exploit this sophistication, by claiming to give kids "what kids want." Nickelodeon was conceived as a crucial part of childhood; as Laybourne claimed: "there is no more important function for us than to allow kids to have a childhood. We knew that, we knew what we were doing, but we hadn't crystallized it like that."[75]

"Having a childhood" meant a variety of things at Nickelodeon. Not only did it rhetorically mean framing of the network as a place where kids can be kids; it also meant that it produced itself as a "safe" haven. Using research gathered through Nickelodeon focus groups, the channel positioned itself as a place in which to feel safe from the outside world. Taking a cue from the *Children's Television Workshop,* which pioneered the use of focus group testing to produce children's television in the 1970s, focus group research allowed Laybourne and Nickelodeon to claim a kind of authenticity that challenged the superficiality of commercial broadcast television—Nickelodeon *really* knew what kids wanted because they *asked* them.[76] Nickelodeon executive Bruce Friend, then vice-president of worldwide research at the channel, commented on the importance of research for Nickelodeon: "We want to look for the nuances and the subtleties. It's hard to get that kind of detail on the phone—especially young children. They're not very articulate. If you bring them in here, though, you can see their facial expressions to stimuli. So if, for example, we show something and the kids are squirming all the way through. Then when they say the show is 'great' afterwards, we know something's wrong. We do a tremendous amount of focus grouping."[77] Nickelodeon clearly sees itself as responsive to kids' needs regarding programming decisions. An oft-repeated story of Laybourne's is that, when researching with a focus group of children about what kids liked about being kids, the children replied that they liked being kids "because they were terrified of growing up. They had heard about drunk driving and teen-age suicide and teen pregnancy and drugs and everything that the media blitzes them with. The moderator said 'What do you like about Nickelodeon?' and they said, 'That's where we can just be kids.' And that was it."[78] Nickelodeon was that place where you did not have to grow up, where a "kid could be a kid." As Laybourne says, "We're not here to change kids or increase their reading scores . . . we think it's pretty tough being a kid today. They're growing up in households where most have a single parent or both parents work. We ought to be a place where they can just relax, where kids can just be kids."[79] The notion of allowing "kids to just be kids" has a great deal of sentimental value in a culture that values the innocence of children and where children are considered to be generally vulnerable and helpless in a world of adults.

In fact, even interrogating the idea of "letting kids just be kids" seems on the surface to be overly critical, given the currency of childhood innocence. However, as the contradictions between Peggy Charren and Geraldine Laybourne, both strong advocates for children, make apparent, it is not at all clear what letting a kid "be a kid" really means. Culture in general does not provide the answer to this: Is a kid a media-savvy audience member who has unique desires and needs? Or is a kid a media-manipulated dupe who can't help but be sucked in by the commercialism of television? One thing is for sure, what a kid *is* is impacted in a great way by television and other media: "As MTV had come to represent teen culture a few years earlier, Nickelodeon set out to define for children a new TV sensibility, distinct from any other. It would be a kind of televised kids' clubhouse, a world unto itself where children's styles, language and attitudes prevailed."[80] This TV sensibility is clearly part of a cultural definition of childhood, where creating the child audience is part of creating meanings about childhood itself. For the Nickelodeon audience, an important element in creating the child audience is that kids are fundamentally different from parents. In fact, as I discuss in the next chapter, the "big idea" of Nickelodeon is an "Us versus Them" attitude, where the television programs aired on Nickelodeon are expressly not for adults but *only* for kids. Nickelodeon, its creators insist, is a kids' network, not a family channel; the difference lies in the fact that a kids' network is created with kids in mind, whereas a family channel is created with parents in mind. As Friend commented, the difference between Nickelodeon and the Disney channel is that "Disney is more family focused. That's different from Nickelodeon, which kids see as just for them. Disney has enormous brand equity, but they are recognized differently from us."[81] The network sought to be different from any other children's channel, and part of this meant not marketing the obvious. Of course, Nickelodeon's stance on being different and cool is precisely its marketing hook.

Nickelodeon, under the guidance of Laybourne, emerged as a formidable force in the world of cable television. The network "just for kids" is a success story for not just children's television but for cable television more generally. The network tapped into an unmet need in the children's market and took a deliberate stance that was different from that of the educational channels such as PBS on the one hand and the commercial broadcast networks on the other. As the children's media executive Donna Mitroff commented, the circumstances that surrounded Nickelodeon at this time allowed for a crucial flexibility: "cable in its early stages, ratings are not the issue, the team of people who come together are allowed to try things and fail, you know, as their first thing out of the box . . . think of it—the luxury of being able to try and fail and try again without being canned. It's what made everyone want to rush over to go to Nickelodeon, because you just can't do that."[82] Media activism around children's television in the 1970s and 1980s also provided a kind of cultural screen against which Nickelodeon measured itself. While ACT and other activist groups insisted on protecting children from television, Nickelodeon proposed instead to empower them by giving them "a network of their own."

Not surprisingly, the success of Nickelodeon meant that the network became attractive to some of the bigger transnational media corporations. In 1985, a few years after Geraldine Laybourne created the strong self-identity for the channel as a kids-only zone, Viacom International took over ownership of MTV networks. At that time, Viacom already owned several cable channels, and with the addition of the three MTV network channels it quickly became one of the biggest cable operators in the country.[83] In 1987, Sumner Redstone, a substantial stockholder in Viacom and the head of National Amusements (a major theatrical exhibitor), took over Viacom. The next phase in the story of Nickelodeon concerns the shape of the network after this moment, when its identity was transformed from an upstart cable channel with MTV Networks to a major player in the transnational corporate world.

NICKELODEON AND VIACOM

The early years at Nickelodeon were characterized by a heady sense of freedom in the historically highly controlled children's television industry; as Simensky relates, "Only the people who wanted to work there [at Nickelodeon], worked there. So everyone that was there was really into it. And they knew they were building something good and they knew that the brand felt cool and it felt right and people were really proud of it. So they didn't give us a lot of money, but they gave us a lot of freedom. And it was a great place to try out things."[84] However, as scholars such as Streeter, Mullen, and Norma Odom Pecora have pointed out, cable television ended up adapting to the general structure of network television, with centralized ownership by transnational media corporations and advertising-based revenue sources, more than it disrupted this structure and offered a true alternative.[85]

The global corporate reach of Viacom, Inc. is truly astounding: in 2002, the corporation's revenues reached $24.6 billion, and it had affiliates in 166 countries worldwide. In 2002, Viacom owned, in the cable and television industries, not only Nickelodeon but also the music stations MTV and VH1, Black Entertainment Television (BET), United Paramount Network (UPN), Showtime, and the broadcast network CBS. In radio, Viacom owned Infinity Broadcasting, which operates 185 radio stations, and in publishing, Simon and Schuster. Viacom also owned the film and production studio Paramount Pictures. Viacom hardly represented an "alternative" to transnational media corporations; on the contrary, it has functioned as a model for other media corporations seeking global reach and revenue. So what happens to Nickelodeon's "alternative" mission for children's television, when cable is no longer understood as a different media option but is simply another acquisition in a broad range of media?

In some important ways, Nickelodeon held on to its original mission of offering programming for kids that is nonviolent and nonstereotypical. In other ways, however, the programming on Nickelodeon began to resemble those broadcast programs that Geraldine Laybourne was so opposed to in terms of mega-licensing agreements, toy-based programming, and dominance of animation. As Pecora states, "Although it attempts to maintain that programming philosophy, the Nickelodeon channel now carries many of the same commercial messages found on Saturday morning network programming and, in 1993, licensed more than 400 items."[86] Ten years later, in 2003, Nickelodeon had even more licensed items and a tightly interconnected domination in the world of children's media.

In 1995, Geraldine Laybourne left Nickelodeon to become vice-president for cable operation at Disney/ABC. The former vice-president of Nickelodeon, Herb Scannell, became president and continued to successfully build Nickelodeon until his departure in 2006. During his tenure as president, the children's television environment has seen remarkable growth, and his efforts to build "synergy" with other Viacom holdings chart some of this growth. One of Scannell's first moves was to build the animation department, and from the mid-1990s, Nickelodeon began to move away from the live-action game show formats of its early days, adding more animated programs to its schedules. Along with these animated programs, which lend themselves much more easily to licensed characters, came licensing agreements with Mattel and Dakin and the development of an in-house merchandising division.[87] It is clear that Nickelodeon now resembles powerhouses such as Disney much more than an alternative, rebellious cable channel. Scannell certainly increased sales at Nickelodeon since Laybourne left, and he has steered the company in the direction of animated films, increasing licensing and merchandising, and overseas expansion, among other things. While animation at Nickelodeon continues to produce "edgy," innovative programming, other children's channels such as Cartoon Network, Disney, and FoxKids have followed suit in an effort to capitalize on Nickelodeon's success. Nickelodeon thus doesn't "stand out" as different in the same way it did in its early days, precisely because of its success in this market. This growth, while clearly financially successful, has also called into question the initial goals of the channel to "empower" kids. As Pecora succinctly puts it, "Where Laybourne was the education president, Scannell has become the marketer."[88] It should be clear that Laybourne was also a "marketer"; indeed, the changes she implemented at the channel (such as advertising, increased program schedule, and so on) set the stage for Scannell to continue to increase Nickelodeon's revenue base. The political economy of cable television in the 1980s was quite different from that of the 1990s, and the two presidents during these periods reflect the vagaries of the market as much as ideologies about kids. Laybourne is recognized as the "education president" because of the way Nickelodeon changed the televisual landscape for children. According to at least one article, Nickelodeon employees have complained that Scannell's drive to increase sales has put Laybourne's mantra of "kids first" at risk.[89] Simensky, too (while agreeing that Scannell is "the right guy for the job"), says, "There have been several things that have happened over the years [such as *Rugrats* characters selling cars] that I have thought, 'I wonder what Gerry thinks of that.' Because it is hard to not think of Nickelodeon as her baby so you have to wonder about some of the decisions that have been made since she left, and what she might think."[90]

Of course, the Nickelodeon network is not the sole vision of either Laybourne or Scannell, or, for that matter, of Sumner Redstone of Viacom. Every network is built on a variety of different visions, and even if there is a dominant understanding of the network's identity, in an unpredictable and constantly changing media system there are always multiple ideas competing for dominance. Nonetheless, Laybourne seemed to have been instrumental in the shape of the network's self-identity as an irreverent, fun, "kids-only" zone. Clearly, the risks she took when president of Nickelodeon shaped the children's television landscape irrevocably. She also laid the groundwork for Nickelodeon's continued success in fusing consumerism with citizenship. In fact, Donna Mitroff attributes important shifts in the shape of kids' TV—within both cable and broadcast television—to the changes Laybourne made when president of Nickelodeon:

> It absolutely changed the landscape, no question about it. It changed what everybody does in children's programming. And the changes are not only what you do in the programming, but it also changed the—call it the geographical landscape in the sense that the growth of cable, the growth of an idea of a place for kids caused the networks to say, "We can't compete. We can't draw kids to a four-hour-block on Saturday morning" . . . it's a change in the geography, but triggered by the phenomenal success of Nickelodeon . . . All of that came out of that time period when the risks were not so great. And it has hardly ever happened in the history of organizations that they can keep that spirit going when they become formalized.[91]

When Laybourne left Nickelodeon, and as the channel became more "formalized" within corporate media culture, there were shifts in Nickelodeon's identity. Part of this involved the channel's commitment to animated programming.

ANIMATION AND CORPORATE CULTURE

Throughout most of the 1980s, Nickelodeon's programming was primarily live-action shows, often modeled after game shows and adult reality shows on network television. Aside from *Double Dare*, other popular programs were *You Can't Do That on Television*, *Kids Court* (a kid version of the *People's Court*), *Salute Your Shorts*, *Kids Rock* (a kid version of MTV), and *Hey Dude*, a dramatic series about kids on a dude ranch. While there were cartoon programs, they were few and far between—in 1984 the schedule showed only two animated series.[92] There were no merchandising tie-ins during the early years at Nickelodeon, although that changed fairly quickly with the introduction of Green Slime shampoo, a product emerging from *You Can't Do That on Television*.

As the network began to reap profits in the mid-1980s, the merchandising and toy tie-in production increased exponentially. However, Laybourne maintained her staunch position against toy-based programs, and while she conceded that some animation could be innovative, she also remained firm in her conviction that Nickelodeon would not look like the cable version of Saturday morning broadcast cartoons, where the television was often used as a baby-sitter, and advertisers capitalized on their particular "kids only" zone.[93] The cartoons in the 1980s were predominantly those "30-minute commercials" that ACT protested against: "Cartoons shifted from a mass audience theatrical label to a 'lowest common denominator' category, implying shoddy production values, formulaic stories and gags, hyper-commercialization, and limited appeals to anyone except children."[94] Laybourne sought to change this with animation on Nickelodeon; she hoped to "give kids variety, expand their imagination, give them different art styles—different animation, different shapes, sounds, exposing them to something that's not the look-alike animation they're used to."[95] Laybourne often compared Nickelodeon's animated programming against the network stations' "look-alike animation," attributing its bland and repetitive qualities to the tight connection with merchandising: "With all this toy-hawking and action-adventure—with a boy it's always action-adventure, with a girl it's cooperative villages and furry little creatures—we've lost the power of what animation can do: Animation can be funny and tell stories that can reach all of us. That's animation at its best."[96]

As I discuss in chapter 6, the presence of animation on network television enjoyed a kind of renaissance in the 1990s, helped in no small way by several animated successes with the adult audience: Warner Brothers released *Who Framed Roger Rabbit?*, Fox television introduced *The Simpsons*, and Disney's animated films such as *The Little Mermaid* and *Beauty and the Beast* were instrumental in lifting that particular corporation from a decades-long slump.[97] As Alan Larsen argues, the increase in animated programming in the 1990s was intricately connected to the vertical integration of multimedia corporations like Viacom. This increase is not because cartoons are cheaper to produce; although they are considerably cheaper than most dramatic series or sitcoms, they are usually more expensive than reality television. Nonetheless, the connection between an increase in animation and the increasing vertical integration of transnational multimedia corporations has to do with the ancillary revenue offered by animation: the merchandising, the product tie-ins, the home video market, and the potential film production.[98] Although children had been a targeted audience since the 1950s, it was really in the 1990s that kids became "big business." With this increase of a "pure" demographic, "concentration upon children's markets became a veritable bedrock of the new conglomerate era."[99]

The current shape of Nickelodeon is clearly a product of this new conglomerate era. As the channel begins to resemble commercial broadcasting more and more (or arguably, broadcast television looks more and more like Nickelodeon) and looks less like an "alternative" channel, it also increases the amount of animated programs and product tie-ins. In 1984, there were only two animated programs on Nickelodeon, in 1994, 43 percent of its programming was animated, and in 2003, 61 percent of the total programming was animated (the Nickelodeon website includes a category for "classic Nick," where all of the shows are live-action).[100] In 1997, Nickelodeon invested $350 million in original animation, which doubled its output over five years, including building a new state-of-the-art animation facility at the Nickelodeon studios in Los Angeles. The changes in the kinds of programming that Nickelodeon offers can be attributed to the network's success—as it was more and more profitable, advertisers were more willing to invest in commercial time. As Pecora argues, the success of Nickelodeon provided it with the necessary capital to invest in more original and diverse programming but also shaped the network more and more in the commercial mode.[101] The years after the network decided to take on advertising saw an increase in half-hour animated programming and product tie-ins.[102]

It is clear that the "crowded field of children's television programming" was truly motivated by the phenomenal success of Nickelodeon.[103] It wasn't simply that no one thought of programming children's television outside of the Saturday morning enclave, but that advertisers were also not interested. The success of Nickelodeon, and the way that the network captured such an enormous audience so early on in the children's television game, ignited that interest in sponsors and advertisers and led the way in exploiting the kids' market. Before the onslaught of children's television programming in the mid 1990s—channels such as Fox's Family Channel, Cartoon Network, and the Disney Channel—Nickelodeon was able to sign advertisers for multiyear deals. Inspired by Nickelodeon's success in the kids' market, other channels wanted the advertising dollars, and with the expanded field, advertisers were able to pick and choose. However, despite Nickelodeon's status as major player in the world of kids' advertising, Scannell argued that the continuing financial success of Nickelodeon would not challenge its "kids first" programming approach.[104] Inexplicably, Nickelodeon maintained a holier-than-thou attitude about advertising and licensing, although the 1998 estimate of revenue of $630 million included $300 million from the daytime kids' advertising, $140 million from *Nick at Nite,* and $190 million from license fees.[105] Despite this, Nickelodeon continued to set itself apart from other commercial networks, locating the difference in the competitors' "toys-first" rather than "kids-first" attitude. In one news report, Scannell had this to say: "With Saban and Fox, there's a whole different point of view about kids. Their philosophy about kids programming includes the aspiration of licensing. At Nickelodeon, we don't think of kids as little consumers."[106] Again, this reflects the channel's strategy to address this central contradiction (a strategy continued from Laybourne's time). Where Nickelodeon continues to grow as a business and increasingly makes decisions (whether about programming, licensing, or advertising) based on this growth, it nonetheless continues to insist that the child audience it caters to is not seen as a market demographic.[107] This rhetoric is evident in an interview with a Nickelodeon program developer, when the discussion turned to decisions that are made regarding character licensing in the studios: "Licensing plays no role for our studio. It plays a tremendous role to the networks. They want to have programs with characters that are prettier so that they will sell well. There comes a point when the owners of the studios and the networks have to dig their heels in and state what they won't do."[108]

While Nickelodeon clearly led the pack in television, one of Viacom's goals for the network was to expand its reach into other markets, following the lead of Disney in this area. Disney, through its prolific production in the 1990s in film, television, merchandising, licensing agreements, and home video, aggressively cultivated the children's market and provided the motivation for conglomerates such as Viacom to follow in their footsteps with Nickelodeon. Nickelodeon in the 1990s and early twenty-first century strikingly resembles Disney: the vertical integration of Viacom has Paramount Pictures producing Nickelodeon movies; the video-sell-through (where a consumer buys the video rather than rents it) is a huge revenue; and in 2004 Viacom acquired the broadcast television network CBS, which aired Nickelodeon cartoons on its channel on Saturday morning.[109] Both Disney's cable channel and Nickelodeon were considered alternatives to the broadcast system, but as Pecora points out, in the context of increased media centralization, "these 'alternatives' function within the context of a profit-driven system and, increasingly, they have adapted to that model. Although cable and public broadcasting were set up in opposition to commercial broadcasting, commercial has come to be the defining factor . . . PBS, Nickelodeon, and the Disney Channel become the brand names that readily identify a place for children's entertainment."[110]

Donna Mitroff comments that the "Nickelodeon difference" in the early days of cable was an issue of pragmatism as much as anything else: "It's not a group of wonderful creative people at Nickelodeon sitting around and saying, 'We need to do the right thing.' They had the luxury of being early, not being trapped by ratings, because the expectations were so different for cable. And so you had the opportunity to experiment, and to look around and say, 'What are the other people not doing?' instead of 'What's everybody else doing that's getting ratings that we have to find some clone of that.' So you know, its timing too, as much as anything."[111] However, this alternative feel was reframed in the 1990s and early years of this century by a slicker, more corporate lingo that stresses partnership with corporate entities, licensing agreements, and distribution alliances—even though the central "mission" of Nickelodeon has not rhetorically changed. As Nickelodeon began to be integrated with the other Viacom holdings, such as Paramount Pictures, the press coverage of the network focused on its revenue as much as its child audience. In 1996, for example, when Nickelodeon and Paramount Home Video allied in a multiyear distribution arrangement for Nickelodeon titles, the president of Worldwide Video for Paramount Pictures, Eric Doctorow, said: "The Nickelodeon brand is an extraordinary asset to the Viacom family, and with this new alliance, all of Nickelodeon's Video's current and upcoming titles will be consolidated under the Paramount banner." Catherine Mullally, vice-president of Nickelodeon Video, went on to say about the partnership, "This mix of 'toons, pre-school and movies provides a consumer-driven, well-focused presence at retail. Paramount offers powerful marketing and operational strength to our line of video products, and Nickelodeon is delighted to be working with them."[112] Since the mid-1980s, but particularly in the mid-1990s, Viacom has been particularly aggressive in forming "strategic alliances" with other corporate entities as a way to extend Nickelodeon's already impressive corporate reach. In 1997, for example, Nickelodeon partnered up with the fast-food chain Burger King, where the restaurant supported Nickelodeon with exclusive promotions focusing on the *Rugrats Movie* and television series. The Viacom press release read: "Nickelodeon is fortifying its relationship with kids and securing its position as a leading kids' marketer by creating a strategic alliance with Burger King Corporation, one of the largest quick-service restaurant chains in the world." The release also quotes Tom Harbeck, senior vice-president of Nickelodeon marketing: "This strategic alliance with Burger King offers Nickelodeon the chance to leverage our brand as a top kids' entertainment company and market to kids even more effectively with another potent brand and marketing partner."[113] This kind of rhetoric is quite different from the earlier rhetoric of Nickelodeon, which stressed "respecting" and "listening" to kids, not effectively marketing to them. It also underscores the fact that although Scannell, like Laybourne, claimed that Nickelodeon doesn't think of kids as "little consumers," the key to the channel's success has been the fusion of citizenship with consumption. Other corporate alliances followed. In 1998, Nickelodeon partnered with Paramount Home Video (also from Viacom) to launch the successful preschool series *Blue's Clues* on home video. Also in 1998, in a joint venture with Children's Television Workshop, Nickelodeon launched the first-ever educational television network for kids, Noggin. In 1999, Nickelodeon joined with Kraft Foods in a "Smell-O-Vision campaign" incorporating Nickelodeon's logo on scratch-n-sniff game cards and 3-D glasses in 100 million packages of Kraft brands. Toysrus.com and Nickelodeon online formed an e-commerce alliance in 2000 to create a new Nickelodeon boutique channel on Toysrus.com, where a Nickelodeon link on the toy site offered Nickelodeon licensed products and cross-promotions.[114] Aside from the Toysrus.com alliance, in 2000 the network signed a multiyear worldwide licensing agreement with Mattel establishing the toy company as the "master toy licensee" of all Nickelodeon entertainment properties across a broad spectrum of toy categories including action figures, dolls, plush toys, games, handheld games, puzzles, and infant and preschool products. Finally, also in 2000, Nickelodeon joined forces with CBS, and Nick Jr. (the channel's preschool programming element) became the program supplier for CBS's Saturday morning schedule, in addition to cross-promotion and program development between the two companies.

The vast reach of the network looks quite different from the 1980s and early 1990s, when Nickelodeon was known more simply as a "kids-only" zone. The continuing corporate shaping of the children's channel consistently brands Nickelodeon as just for kids, but in the intensely competitive kids' market and multinational corporate context this concept that is so identified with the network increasingly means a particular market demographic for advertisers, sponsors, and corporate partnerships more than the idea that the network empowers kids. This is not to say that Nickelodeon, while under the watch of Laybourne, was noncommercial but that the channel's self-identity was different, as was its corporate reach. As Mitroff comments about Laybourne during the earlier years, "When Gerry first launched Nickelodeon, it was as she says, it was going to be broccoli television. And she quickly found out that that wasn't going to work. But it was an experiment that they were free to try, and when it didn't work, she didn't get thrown out on her ear. Which is what happens when the stakes are so high.

But you know, the stakes are very high now. You know, the real question is 'can they still experiment?' Not, 'could they experiment back then?' "[115] In 1988, Laybourne claimed that a kids' television network needed to address very particular needs of contemporary children, who were perceived as victimized by things like single or working parents.[116] Nickelodeon was conceived as that place where kids can "just relax." In 2001, thirteen years later, a Viacom press release put it this way: "Nickelodeon, now in its 22nd year, is the number-one entertainment brand for kids. It has built a diverse, global business by putting kids first in everything it does."[117] Obviously, both statements are rhetoric—both intended for the mass-market press, and both invested in perpetuating the Nickelodeon brand. However, the means by which each crafts its rhetoric are quite different. Laybourne's more informal, relaxed lingo allows parents to feel as if Nickelodeon is like one of them; part of the network's explicit agenda is to award children the status of citizen. In the Viacom rhetoric, on the other hand, the network is framed much more formally and within the discourse of commerce. While the press release does say that Nickelodeon "puts kids first," it has built a "diverse, global *business*" by doing so.

Laybourne was certainly not anticorporate—as I've argued, she worked within the media system by accepting advertising and some licensing agreements, and she successfully managed to create Nickelodeon as a particular corporate product. However, while president of Nickelodeon, she maintained an ethos of "noncommercial commercialism" which centered on a belief that a "free-press" society means that advertising doesn't always influence television content and decisions. Yet these goals were formulated within a different media context—in the current environment, Laybourne could not take the risks she was able to take in the 1980s. Viacom's Nickelodeon is well established as a corporate product, and there seems to be as much research devoted to expanding its corporate reach as there is on finding out "what kids want." In the next chapter, I detail the ways in which the Nickelodeon brand attempted to capture exactly "what kids want" through elaborate campaigns. Through the framework of the Nickelodeon brand, I argue, consumer citizenship represents part of a larger dynamic of citizenship that constantly moves between agency and conformity in media culture. Indeed, I argue that Nickelodeon would not be nearly as successful as a network that claims to "empower" kids if there wasn't *already* a powerful cultural context of consumer citizenship.

THE NICKELODEON BRAND:

BUYING AND SELLING THE AUDIENCE

I think one thing [Nickelodeon is] doing right is offering
programming that empowers children or involves them. It
has children appearing on camera, voting on who should
be president, calling in. To some extent, it is allowing kids
to take ownership of a station. Of course, it's an illusory
ownership, but it shows respect for kids.
—RONALD SLABY

We, the People of Nickelodeon,
in order to form
a more perfect world for kids,
promise to:
provide the best in kids' entertainment
protect kids' rights, and
promote the cause of kids everywhere!
—NICKELODEON'S DECLARATION OF KIDS' RIGHTS

On June 7, 1990, on the opening day of Nickelodeon Studios at Universal Studios in Florida, the children's cable channel announced
the "Nickelodeon's Declaration of Kids' Rights." According to the
employee handbook, this declaration "transforms a traditional adult
form into something potent and meaningful for kids. It uses language
that doesn't patronize kids, but empowers them."[1] The role of Nickelodeon as transformative media for children constitutes the crux of the
channel's stated mission, a mission that purports to challenge dominant ways of understanding kids as impressionable, passive television
viewers and instead recognizes this audience as empowered, active
citizens. This goal was formulated at a moment in the United States, in
the late 1980s and early 1990s, where the idea of empowering the child

viewer had a particular kind of cultural—and economic—currency. Within this media setting, Nickelodeon tapped into something compelling with the stated goal of specifically empowering children. However, what it means, exactly, to "empower" children within the context of a liberal, capitalist, and media-driven culture is ideologically complex. Indeed, connecting power with children —recognizing that children are empowered—raises the cultural stakes considerably, as this kind of recognition poses a threat to a long-standing ideology about both children and adults. One of the most powerful symbols of the current media age has been the use of children as both metaphors and literal figures to signify a variety of moral agendas involving the future, the past, hopes, fears, anxieties, and national identity. Within this ideological framework, children are often situated as innocents in need of protection—often (indeed, especially) from the media.

At the same time as the use of children in the media has functioned powerfully to shore up dominant ideologies, children in the contemporary era have also *used* the media more than ever before.[2] As new media use ranging from the Internet to digital technologies to file sharing becomes normalized within youth culture, children as "experts" of the media occupy a position of agency that challenges the historical (and federally legislated) stance of protecting children from the media. Children increasingly use the media as producers themselves, in a culture where DIY (Do It Yourself) cultural production (such as blogs and 'zines) is more accessible and common.[3] This is not to suggest that children have historically only had access to a passive relationship with the media, but it does indicate that the early twenty-first century offers a different kind of moment to theorize the dynamic between children and the media. New technologies, a changing youth demographic, and increasing youth technological expertise create a different potential for political agency and consumer citizenship, and because of its wide reach and massive youth audience, Nickelodeon is an especially important channel to examine within this context.

The relationship between multinational media conglomerates and U.S. youth culture was explored on a 2001 PBS *Frontline* special, "The Merchants of Cool."[4] Specifically, the documentary explains, five multimedia conglomerates—Viacom, Disney, News Corporation, Vivendi Universal, and AOL Time Warner—exert unprecedented power in marketing messages and products to young people, capitalizing on the lifestyle culture of "cool" and incorporating what historically have been subversive and anti-establishment ideologies as the very center of their marketing strategies. This marketing trend has been a major impetus for the development of brand culture, where the brand matters more than the product, and corporations sell an experience or a lifestyle more than a thing. As the cultural theorist Naomi Klein points out, "What these companies produced primarily were not things, they said, but *images* of their brands. Their real work lay not in manufacturing, but in marketing."[5] The relationship between commercial culture and youth has become one based on brand bonding, where differences between "authentic" youth experiences and the experiences sold to youth through corporate branding are no longer (if they ever were) distinct. In fact, in the "Merchants of Cool," Todd Cunningham, senior vice-president for strategy and planning for MTV, commented about his company's efforts to target teens, "The more often that we are in touch with them and in contact with them; then translating what they've told us and what kinds of issues they're dealing with; the more often that we hit a home run—the more often that we actually succeed in terms of developing a relationship and a bond with them, a great brand relationship. So the next time that we come out with a program, the next time we come out with a message, anything that we are building in terms of our brand, they're more open to it, because there's an understanding: 'This is my brand.' They, in fact, talk about MTV as being 'their brand' and seeing it as something that is an extension of themselves."[6] The language of the brand is maintained by personal narratives—lifestyle, identity, empowerment—more than a more historical language of advertising, which relied heavily on a product's efficiency in a competitive market.

Brand culture thus provides the context for the cultural and economic developments that have shaped Nickelodeon's distinct identity in the television landscape. These developments include the emergence of the cable industry, the subsequent development of niche networks, and the progressively more formidable presence of the children's market in the media economy. In this chapter, I focus on the latter, specifically on the increasingly dominant strategy of branding as a way to advertise a product or a group of products as well as to inculcate a loyal youth audience. Within this context, I also examine the ways that contemporary strategies of branding work to commodify a particular definition of *experience*—not just a product—for their audience. For Nickelodeon, this experience is about kids' empowerment and a specific kind of citizenship, where the network claims to "respect" kids by creating a network just for them. Within the Nickelodeon context, though, empowerment is not a discrete political function or privilege, or action taken by the child, but rather a product itself, a crucial element in the brand identity of the channel. The network addresses its child audience as empowered citizens who are able to make decisions about politics, culture, and relevant social issues, by virtue of membership in the brand community. Brand loyalty thus becomes far less an inclination to buy a particular product than a kind of cultural affiliation, where being a "Nick kid" means experiencing a shared community and common values about current youth culture. As a fifteen-year-old girl commented when I asked her about what it meant to be a "Nick kid": "I think [Nickelodeon] understands kids, because they have kids—like, they have little kids, they have older kids with little sisters, all types of people, so anyone can relate to at least one of the shows on the network."[7] This young audience member saw the efficient brand development of Nickelodeon in terms of a kind of kinship network, so that the channel becomes personalized, constituting itself as a family, to which any kid willing to affiliate may belong. The historical development of the Nickelodeon brand is thus an ambitious market strategy that appropriates political (and personal) rhetoric about empowerment and agency as a way to promote the network. As the Nickelodeon employee handbook states, "Nick is more than just another kids' entertainment outlet; our big orange splot [the network's logo] stands for a set of ideas kids can understand and trust."[8]

The early loyalty of a child audience is important for television networks. According to the marketing expert James McNeal, the kids market has been growing tremendously each year since the mid-1980s. In 2001, four- to twelve-year-olds had their own annual income of approximately $40 billion, and children as an influence market are responsible for over $300 billion.[9] Within this kind of economic environment, accompanied by hyperbolic rhetoric, where kids are thought to represent "more market potential than any other demographic group," competition for the attention and loyalty of children within media companies has become even more intense. Combined with the continued reach of the cable industry into more and more niche channels, including children's channels, the brand identity of channels (and specifically the marketing of brands as particular experiences) has achieved a new economic significance. Effective branding strategies that result in attracting both narrowly specific audience and advertisers concerned with reaching those same specific audiences have become the norm for transnational media conglomerates such as Viacom.[10] Nickelodeon is often touted as a particularly successful brand for kids and has clearly provided an economic model (in terms of both brand success and advertising revenue) in the media landscape for channels such as Cartoon Network and Fox Kids. In order for a network's brand campaign to make sense to a child audience, however, the child needs to be cultivated as a consumer and, in the present media context, as a consumer citizen, a member of the brand community, as well.

Consumer citizenship in this regard represents part of a larger dynamic of citizenship that constantly moves between agency and conformity in media culture. That is, consumer citizenship indicates a certain willingness to participate in consumer culture through the purchase of goods as well as a more general affirmation of consumption habits, but it also points to something broader, where the distinctions between cultural and social practice and consumption are not so finely drawn. This ambiguity allows Nickelodeon to claim, not disingenuously, to "empower" kids within the cultural context of consumer citizenship. However, empowerment means not only the power to make consumer choices. The branding strategies of Nickelodeon also frame the language of empowerment and kids' rebellion in a way so that the channel—an enormously successful one—ironically adopts a kind of counterhegemonic, "underdog" identity. This identity is then marketed to children as a means of empowerment, specifically in relationship to adults.

COMMERCIAL MEDIA AND CHILDHOOD

As I discuss in chapter 1, despite recent hype and media attention, the child consumer is not a newcomer to the American landscape. The child consumer is an identity blurred with other social categories such as love, parental obligation, and education and is a commonplace way of understanding children in global capitalist societies. Unlike the early part of the twentieth century, where arguably the U.S. public was "training" to be a nation of consumers, in the contemporary context consumption is as much a part of life for U.S. children (albeit in different ways for different socioeconomic groups) as formal education.[11] In fact, cultural definitions of who—and what—a child is interconnected with consumer behavior. As Stephen Kline, Daniel Cook, and others note, the actual physical and intellectual development of children—the definition of childhood—is charted, mapped, and in some ways defined by how the market characterizes this development.[12] In the current brand environment, the early cultivation of children as loyal consumers is particularly important to corporate culture.[13] However, this strategic, aggressive cultivation intervenes in the dominant discourse about children as inherently innocent and in need of protection. On the contrary, it is precisely the *sophistication* of children in terms of their real and potential income, their influence with parents, and their potential as a future market that advertisers rely upon.

Consequently, while advertisers are certainly influential in terms of constructing cultural definitions of childhood, the ideological notion that children are innocent lingers and continues to structure political and social agendas, definitions of morality, as well as hope for an imagined future. This is yet another contradiction that structures the construction of the child-citizen: despite the normalization of consumption behavior, there remains a powerful cultural rhetoric about the need to protect children from the world of consumption. It is within this cultural economy that Nickelodeon imagines its audience as a group of active, consumer citizens. The fact that this imagined audience is similar for both Nickelodeon and advertisers does not automatically mean that the network is merely giving lip-service to its claim to be on the "kids' side." What it actually means, however, to be on the "kids' side," and what the consequences are for the child audience when an empowered identity is marketed as a kind of product, need to be critically explored. The divisive strategy employed by Nickelodeon that establishes a discrete boundary between adults and children is one that functions brilliantly for the company in terms of profit, formulating the crux of the channel's brand identity. Within this consumer market, the two seemingly oppositional forms of address—the generational divide and the transgenerational connection—function in tandem to provide a landscape in which Nickelodeon is the entity to smooth over any kind of conflict motivated by generation. Both a divisive generational warfare (seen most clearly in the network's philosophy of "Us versus Them"), and a transgenerational address (seen in the programming itself, as well as ads for the network that air on broadcast television during primetime) form the two sides of the Nickelodeon brand.

CHILDREN AND ADVERTISING

Nickelodeon airs two primary types of advertising: corporate advertising for products and services, which provides a source of revenue for the channel, and the network's own brand advertisements, which celebrate Nickelodeon and encourage kids (and their parents) to be loyal to the network. When I refer to advertising on Nickelodeon, I am referencing the actual ads that are sold to the network and are situated between programming. Since, as I discussed in the last chapter, there is a specific history concerning the decision to use advertising as a central revenue source for the network (as opposed to commercial-free programming such as the Public Broadcasting System, or, on cable, a pay channel such as Disney that is ostensibly commercial-free), it makes sense to separate an analysis of the ads on Nickelodeon from an analysis of the network's own conscious self-promotion and branding campaigns.

Children and their responses to television advertising have received a great deal of scholarly attention since the advent of the medium as a household item in the late 1940s and early 1950s. Social science research in this area has largely focused on the relationship between children's cognitive development and the interpretation of advertising. More specifically, children have often been positioned in this relationship as incapable of distinguishing between programming and advertising.[14] This ostensible lack of critical ability makes the child more vulnerable to the commercial address of the advertisement, and more susceptible to manipulation. As many scholars have pointed out, however, the research on the effects of advertising on children has focused on the various ways in which children do not understand commercials compared with adults. As Ellen Seiter argues, "The assumption has been that children's immaturity accounts for their interest in commercials, along with the implicit—and dubious—notion that children will lose interest as soon as they achieve a normal, adult state of rationality."[15] Presumably, once one becomes a mature adult, the appeal of commercials will wane because adults *know* this particular form of media to be manipulative, to be about selling something, as they are more sophisticated interpreters of persuasive messages (which of course runs counter to other outmoded theories of the mass media that assume *all* audiences, adult and children, to be passive and easily manipulated).

However, assuming that the problem with advertising to children is their inability to distinguish between commercials and television also implies that the rest of television, namely, the programming, is somehow *not* commercial—or that there is, in fact, a noncommercial address to be found on television. Although, as Dale Kunkel points out, it is clear that the advertising landscape has become more "cluttered" than ever, with corporate sponsorship, paid advertising, and product placement as dominant contemporary media practices that blur the boundaries between commercial and noncommercial content, the exposure of children to ads has still been largely conceived of as an issue of protection, where children need to be sheltered from the overt commercial message of the ads.[16] This research has typically led to findings about the effects of advertising on children, both intended (such as children's recall of television commercials as well as brand preferences) and unintended (ranging from materialistic attitudes among children to junk food habits and, more recently, an epidemic in childhood obesity).[17]

This kind of research is congruent with the historical construction of childhood and children as innocent and in need of protection. However, the economic configuration of childhood—that is, the way in which children are constructed as consumers—is more complicated than assuming that kids are either innocent or not. Children represent an enormously powerful demographic in the world of advertising and marketing and thus are afforded a kind of economic power—power as both a primary and as a future market—that they do not receive in other cultural realms. In fact, in the current historical moment, where purchasing power is an important element in constructing identity and gaining visibility, ads address kids in a particularly "empowering" way. In the specific case of

Nickelodeon, even though empowerment in this context is primarily about purchasing power, it is rhetorically framed and marketed by Nickelodeon as a more traditional form of political or social power that every kid has a "right" to possess. In this way, empowerment becomes not only a kind of product that Nickelodeon markets for its audience but the meaning of the concept is also redefined within an economic framework, so that an "empowered kid" is not necessarily an active agent capable of political action but rather signifies a savvy consumer.

As Kunkel and others have pointed out, most kids' advertisements are primarily for food and toys, and the ads on Nickelodeon are no exception. While Nickelodeon typically carries less advertising than a broadcasting network (Kunkel and Gantz found in 1992 that network television had an average of 10:05 minutes of advertising per one hour of children's shows, and Nickelodeon had 6:28 minutes per hour),[18] a characteristic afternoon programming block on the cable network will carry an ad for juice or a fruit snack, a "girl" toy such as a Barbie, Care Bear, or another type of doll/stuffed animal, a "boy" toy such as Legos, and a breakfast cereal. One of the problems that Kunkel and Gantz found with advertising that targets children involves the content of the ads, where instead of offering detailed information about the product, ads often associate the product with abstract ideological concepts such as fun or irreverence. Again, since children ostensibly cannot make proper determinations about the product itself, ads for children are often considered as more dangerous, though clearly ads targeted to adult audiences also sell ideology as much if not more than actual products.[19] This argument continues to have cultural currency, as ads for junk food and candy have been a central target in the moral panic about obesity and American children.

Ellen Seiter argues that children "are a special audience," but not because they are more susceptible and impressionable in the context of children's advertising. Rather, one of the reasons that children's ads are interpreted with such disdain among adults is not necessarily because they are so effective at training children to be little consumers but because the ads themselves imply a kind of exclusivity—these ads are created for a world in which adults are not the authoritative ones in power. I found this notion to resonate with many of the children I interviewed; when I asked them about ads on Nickelodeon, it was clear that they noticed that ads were geared toward children. As one girl said, "I noticed that there's not really like adult commercials. They do a lot of advertising for their own products, like Nickelodeon magazine."[20] This comment sparked a nostalgic exchange among a group of three teenage girls about the Nickelodeon ads that they remembered:

A: The magazine commercial always annoyed me.

J: It's for Nickelodeon magazine, and like they have all these different ways to get your parents to call. They wake up and there's a sign attached to their arm, buy a Nickelodeon subscription.

A: And with the "groooowwwwing mind."

Me: What's the "grooowwing mind?"

C: It's the same commercial: "full of interesting facts for grrroooowwing minds." Then the big stack of magazines falls over. And the slime cake.

[laughter]

Clearly, this exchange, based on a memory of an advertisement on Nickelodeon, contained a rhetoric of exclusivity—the ad encouraged children to "get their parents" to buy a magazine subscription, and there was clearly a particular kid-centered code to the ad. Moreover, the ad itself is remembered as a part of Nickelodeon, in the way that a particular episode of a program might be discussed. Indeed, many of the children I interviewed discussed ads and programming in similar terms—but not because they couldn't tell the difference between the two. Rather, ads and programming on Nickelodeon are both crucial building blocks in the channel's brand identity.

The generational divide between adults and children that gives rise to the philosophy of the Nickelodeon enterprise is built into the message of the ads themselves, and it is to this that adults might object: "Commercials seek to establish children's snacks and toys as belonging to a public children's culture, by either removing them from the adult-dominated domestic sphere or presenting these products as at odds with that world."[21] In kids' commercials, Seiter argues, "kids rule," and the world presented in ads is utopian for children—there are no central authority figures, often no visible "rules," and the aesthetics of the ads (colors, music, design, etc.) are tailored for the taste and desire of children, not adults.[22] Children's ads conflict with the middle-class idea of what "good" TV should look like, and Seiter argues that it is *this* clash, not the central idea of selling to kids, that is the object of distaste for educators, legislators, and parents.

The rhetoric of ads for children is thus plainly constructed similarly to kids' entertainment television. Whereas educational television tends to have a patronizing tone (as in "this show is good for children"), much entertainment programming figures the child centrally—often at the exclusion of adults. For Nickelodeon, this emphasis on generation is framed in terms of "respect," where the network positions itself as a rebellious entity that respects children and is capable of liberating them from the stifling world of adults. This strategy functions effectively for the network, whose primary branding philosophy is that kids are oppressed by the adult world. By then "respecting" kids more than adults, the channel authorizes children as kinds of citizens within the context of the network brand. This "respect," in other words, is *already* a kind of product for Nickelodeon, so that the network's signature brand of "kids rule!" is not only about recognizing that kids influence consumer habits and behaviors in the household; it also offers the very notion of the empowered, respected kid as a kind of product.

The "kids rule!" rhetoric of contemporary children's ads follows a historical patterning in advertising which presents a utopian world for its audience, often by referencing and highlighting social and cultural divisions in a kind of anti-establishment manner. Thomas Frank, for instance, discusses how ads in the 1960s (Volkswagen ads in particular) often challenged consumer culture itself as a way to sell products, "The advertising style of the 1950s had been profoundly contemptuous of the consumer's intelligence, and consumers knew it: in the wake of *The Hucksters, The Hidden Persuaders,* the quiz show scandals, and the various FTC lawsuits against fraudulent advertisers, consumer skepticism toward advertising was at an all-time high. The genius of the Volkswagen campaign . . . is that they took this skepticism into account and made it part of their ads' discursive apparatus. They spoke to consumers as canny beings capable of seeing through the great heaps of puffery cranked out by Madison Avenue."[23] This method of advertising—commodifying the irony and skepticism engendered by advertising itself—emerged with significant force in the 1990s as an effective way to sell products, to youth audiences in particular.

Current advertising uses irony and a kind of self-reflexivity to both critique and ultimately sell products. Malcolm Gladwell, Naomi Klein, and Alyssa Quart, among others, have analyzed the strategies employed by corporations to conduct "cool hunts" in order to find out what is hip, cool, and not overly advertised.[24] As media and product companies such as Sprite and MTV discovered, the quickest way to destroy a product's value was to overly advertise its merits to an increasingly cynical youth audience. Thus, the trick is not to figure out the most effective way to "train" a child as a consumer within a media-saturated context but rather how to best cultivate that same child as a loyal brand user by appealing to that very same cynicism and skepticism. As Gladwell puts it, "The paradox, of course, is that the better coolhunters become at bringing the mainstream close to the cutting edge, the more elusive the cutting edge becomes. This is the first rule of the cool: The quicker the chase, the quicker the flight."[25] Figuring out this game, as well as managing the balance between the "chase and flight" dynamic in advertising, is often the tipping point in having a product stick in a consumer's mind. "Selling cool" with an ironic tone resonates with a contemporary youth audience; as Klein says about major corporations such as Nike and Microsoft, "If they were going to turn their lackluster products into transcendent meaning machines—as the dictates of branding demanded—they would need to remake themselves in the image of nineties cool: its music, styles and politics."[26] No more obvious plugs for products—rather, the "wink wink nudge nudge" style of popular culture became the dominant mode of advertising in the 1990s.

Nickelodeon is a clear example of this kind of branding. The tag words used in the network's self-promotion—respect, power, cool, oppression—are the same words that are used in the language of rebellion and counterhegemonic activities. Nickelodeon, like its corporate sibling MTV, smoothly incorporates this language so that the commercial interests of the network are marketed as ironically outside the world of (adult) consumerism. The ads on Nickelodeon that stress generational divide do so within the more general flow of the network, so that they become a seamless extension of the brand itself.[27] As a sixteen-year-old Nickelodeon fan commented about the "flow" of Nickelodeon, "I think with other networks, they have their specific timeslots and everything. Where with Nickelodeon, I don't think of timeslots. It's not like 'Oh, the new *Hey Arnold!* comes on every Thursday at five' . . . It's just kind of like you just watch Nickelodeon and the theory is there's going to be a show on that you like. You don't watch it for certain shows, you just watch it because you like the network."[28] Another girl, fifteen years old, agreed: "Because it's like one kind of genre altogether, where NBC there's so many different kinds of shows where it's not—you're gonna view them on an individual basis. Nickelodeon's more like at it all day."[29] Another young ten-year-old boy commented that Nickelodeon "was on TV like 24/7 . . . It's like the most popular kids' channel."[30] Even if one chooses not to watch Nickelodeon, or cannot afford cable television, the channel has an immediate recognizability among young children; as one ten-year-old said to me, "Some people don't have cable, so they can't see it . . . but . . . but they still know about it. They know it but they don't watch it."[31]

This transformation of a product—Nickelodeon programs—into a brand, where one doesn't even have to tune in to "know" Nickelodeon, is evidence of the channel's corporate reach. This transformation is facilitated by the channel's efforts to conduct research on children. The network regularly employs the research firm of Yankelovich Clancy Shulman to see if Nickelodeon viewers think that the network "understands kids," and in 1992, 93 percent said yes.[32] The research Nickelodeon conducts on "what kids want" gives the channel cultural capital in the children's television industry—it is yet another way that Nickelodeon consciously constructs itself as different from other children's channels. As Bruce Friend (then vice-president of worldwide research and planning at Nickelodeon) commented, "Everything we do here is informed by kids. That's our philosophy. And while some of us may have kids, most of us don't live with kids. So we do research to update us on kids' lives. It starts here. The research gives us what we like to call 'kid instinct.' "[33] Indeed, young fans of Nickelodeon seem to understand the channel's efforts to cultivate a "kid instinct"; as one sixteen-year-old audience member commented about the various claims Nickelodeon makes about "respecting" kids: "I think also that if they're gonna like, make such a big deal about being the only network for kids, the first network for kids or whatever, they're obviously doing some kind of research into this stuff and it's obviously working because people—like little kids aren't as affected, like 'oh, the first network for kids, I have to watch it.' They're gonna watch what they like and they obviously like it."[34] This comment demonstrates a kind of savvy on the part of the young audience member, as she points out that often young children don't understand how and when the channel is engaged in brand development. On the other hand, it is also clear that for at least this audience member, Nickelodeon's brand development is about more than selling products—the channel is "obviously" doing research into what kids like.

While Nickelodeon positions audience research as a kind of evidence to its audience that the network really does care about kids, the idea that Nickelodeon "understands kids" is equally as important to advertisers. Indeed, advertisers on the channel rely upon audience research data and try to use the same Nickelodeon rhetoric and feel in their ads, so that there is a flow between programming and some ads. In other words, the language of empowerment and respect is often successful rhetoric for advertisements; as the reporter Joseph Winski puts it, advertisers like how Nickelodeon "speaks the kids' language" and "really hits hot buttons."[35] The director of kids/entertainment marketing at Pizza Hut discusses the partnership between Nickelodeon and Pizza Hut: "Pizza Hut is so taken with the network's ability to connect with its audience it has adopted the Nickelodeon attitude, if you will, in our efforts to reach kids."[36] This "Nickelodeon attitude" is a crucial element in the network's claim to consider kids as empowered citizens, even as it is the key to Nickelodeon's "strategic alliances" with other companies. The economic imperative and the political message of the network are thus indistinguishable, through the careful construction of Nickelodeon brand as a discrete place, where "Nick kids" are created and marketed by the network as empowered citizens.

COMMUNITY, BELONGING, AND THE BRAND:
NICKELODEON'S IDENTITY

Naomi Klein argues in her book *No Logo* that branding, in the 1990s, became the key symbolic frame of reference for contemporary identity. As she says, "'Brands, not products!' became the rallying cry for a marketing renaissance led by a new breed of companies that saw themselves as 'meaning brokers' instead of product producers."[37] Corporations transcend their own products; Nickelodeon's "slime" is a product that is an extension of the Nickelodeon philosophy of kids first, or Us versus Them. As Klein argues, "companies such as these integrated the idea of branding into the very fabric of their companies. Their corporate cultures were so tight and cloistered that to outsiders they appeared to be a cross between fraternity house, religious cult and sanitarium. Everything was an ad for the brand: bizarre lexicons for describing employees (partners, baristas, team players, crew members), company chants, superstar CEOs, fanatical attention to design consistency, a propensity for monument-building, and New Age mission statements."[38]

Nickelodeon, as a company, fits quite clearly within Klein's scenario: as one former employee told me, the offices of the corporation are designed to be anticorporate and were not organized in an obviously hierarchical way. The presence of toys and games and the use of bright colors transform Nickelodeon's corporate offices so that they look more like a kid's clubhouse than a media powerhouse.[39] Industry executive Donna Mitroff confirms this notion that Nickelodeon focuses less on individual shows and more on the brand itself. She states, "What Nick did was so systematic about this whole branding thing that they were doing, so the programming and the thing were all woven together. And you didn't just pick shows in isolation because someone liked them. It all had to merge to create that concept which was Nickelodeon. And they spent a lot of time with kids, trying to figure out what that would be. I mean, that's how the big orange blob came to be, the splat . . . That was all by spending time not just with your branding people, but with kids."[40]

The corporate employee handbook, *How to Nickelodeon*, discusses the imperative for Nickelodeon employees to "find the kid" in oneself in order to really fit in at the company. As I discuss below, Nickelodeon employees are certainly fanatical about the design consistency of the logo, and there is a clear mission statement and the "Bill of Rights" for kids displayed in the offices and within the handbook. The brand loyalty of Nickelodeon is not simply about the Nickelodeon products that are consumed by the public but also about what one former employee calls "the Nick way of life" or "the Nick voice."[41] This notion, that Nickelodeon is a "way of life," or has a distinct voice, or can function as a kind of verb, for that matter, something that one *does*, or that one *is*, rather than a product that one consumes or uses, is part of a relatively new culture of branding. This shapes the practice of watching Nickelodeon programs as a kind of cultural practice, akin to other citizenship practices, such as national affiliation and loyalty.

Nickelodeon not only emerges but flourishes within this culture of the brand. The channel's audience is imagined as empowered citizens, situated within the culture of "cool," part of a landscape rife with symbols of kids' apparent oppression. In an article aptly titled "The Nickelodeon Experience," the then-president of the network, Geraldine Laybourne, details the way in which the concept for the channel developed: "Nickelodeon decided to do what nobody else was doing—raise a banner for kids and give them a place on television that they could call their own. In doing this, we reevaluated everything from the program lineup to the logo. We replaced Nick's original inflexible silver ball logo with a bold, brash and ever-changing orange loop that can take as many shapes as kids can imagine. This became the symbol of Nickelodeon's new identity and mission, and in January 1985, we relaunched as a network dedicated to empowering kids, a place where kids could take a break and get a break."[42]

From the time that Laybourne envisioned a new image for the network that erased the trait of "green vegetable television" from the audience mind, the channel was conceived as a place, not a product, a set of ideas, not as merchandise. Nickelodeon subsequently became many different things to its audience. Martin Davidson argues about brands: "If successful, that image will become a brand property forming the basis for future theme advertising, a theme that the product will slowly reabsorb back into itself as its unique brand value. A brand is a product that has a personality that we relate to as though in dialogue with it."[43] Nickelodeon is a partner in this dialogue—indeed, as Laybourne puts it, the channel is not simply something a child turns on and off at whim but is rather a kind of "understanding friend" who "is always there, from breakfast to bedtime, everyday, whenever kids want to watch. Nick is their home base, a place kids can count on and trust."[44] But is this kind of media dialogue a means to empowerment? And what are the consequences of considering a television channel one's most trusted friend? The costs involved when children adopt the Nickelodeon idea that they are victims in an adult world and can become empowered by watching a television station are, needless to say, rarely examined by the network. The ubiquity of the channel (at least for families who can afford cable), where Nickelodeon is shown twenty-four hours a day, airing programs that are either designed for children or, in the case of Nick at Nite, appropriate for children,

3. An example of the
new logo concept, 1991.

means that the channel *is always on*—and hence can position itself as something
(or someone) that children can trust—even more than their own parents.[45]

Laybourne, and the parent company of Nickelodeon, Viacom, certainly capitalized on the newly emerging brand context in the relaunching of Nickelodeon
as a discrete brand rather than a television product. It was not only the increasing
presence of the logo as part of a marketing landscape that made the Nickelodeon
brand so successful, however. As I argue in chapter 2, the historical parallel of
recognizing the youth market as a powerful "three-in-one" market, the increasing technological acuity on the part of children, and the general (although often
reluctant) acknowledgment of the media savoir-faire of children provided the
context for Nickelodeon to become "Nick."[46] The Nickelodeon viewer is the
savvy consumer, one who knows brands, has strong name recognition, and can
easily move between the television set, the computer, and the mall. As children
themselves become more confident in their use of the media, the advertising and
branding campaigns that attempt to cultivate them as loyal customers also become more sophisticated and hipper so that the distinctions between popular
culture and consumer culture are increasingly difficult to discern. Even more
significant, the cultural definition of what it means to be a savvy, empowered kid
is *created* by networks like Nickelodeon, so that the network's claim to empower
kids becomes a kind of self-fulfilling prophecy: Nickelodeon crafts the definition
of a contemporary empowered kid, so that what it means to be empowered is to
be a "Nickelodeon kid."

This kind of brand development marked a definite shift in children's television. As Donna Mitroff points out, in the 1980s, "branding wasn't as big an
issue. Standout programming was. When it changed was as the competition
increased, and the only way to set yourself apart . . . was by programming, always,

but you also had to set yourself apart in that chaotic world with your brand. So that you could tell kids, you had a way of short-handing, and saying, 'If you are this kind of kid, we are the place for you.' "[47] The cool status of Nickelodeon is reinforced through the various themes that compose the narrative of the brand. In the following sections, I discuss two interrelated themes that are crucial to Nickelodeon's brand identity: the Us versus Them philosophy, where kids are "oppressed" in an adult world; and the Nickelodeon Nation, in which the network can be a "home" or neighborhood.

US VERSUS THEM: KIDS RULE!

Nickelodeon has built its brand identity around a primary core idea: Us versus Them. This idea developed in part as a response to the cultural debates over educational and entertainment programming for children that were coming to a head in the mid-1980s. Advocates of educational programming, such as educators, legislators, and media watchdog groups like Action for Children's Television (ACT), recognized the symbolic power of television and saw the potential of television to be a kind of educator. Obviously, *Sesame Street* and the Children's Television Workshop capitalized on this notion and enjoyed great success.[48] As I argue in chapter 2, Nickelodeon very purposefully constructed its brand identity in opposition to the educational potential of television.[49] Framing this kind of television as patronizing for kids, Nickelodeon shaped the network's identity around the ideology of Us versus Them. As the employee handbook states about the network's identity: "It's an adult world out there where kids get talked down to and everybody older has authority over them. For kids, it's 'Us vs. Them' in the grown-up world: you're either for kids or against them . . . we were on the kids' side, and we wanted them to know it."[50] In a cultural context of media advocacy, where Peggy Charren of ACT was frequently cited in the popular press as *the* advocate for children, Nickelodeon claimed a different sort of cultural territory and legitimacy.

In an ironic twist, Nickelodeon insisted that children needed to be protected from precisely those who claimed to want to protect them. Nickelodeon would not be the authoritative adult world but would rather be "one of them," deep in the trenches of a media war: " 'Us vs. Them' became, and remains today, the Nickelodeon battle cry. We stand up for kids, expose their injustices and celebrate their triumphs. 'Us vs. Them' is the 'big idea,' the informing principle behind everything we do at Nick."[51] As the former Nickelodeon employee Linda Simensky says about this philosophy, "[Those at Nick] were very sincere in this need to say to kids that they didn't have to grow up quickly and that it was okay to be a kid as long as you wanted to be a kid and it was okay to have fun. The whole adults versus kids, Us versus Them thing really did pervade everything, every aspect of the network. In the course of development, one of the things I would look for was, did the show have a certain Us versus Them quality to it—there was branding in the shows, it wasn't just in between the shows."[52]

The difference between the tones of address utilized by the network can be quite clearly seen before and after the mid-1980 "relaunch" of Nickelodeon led by Laybourne. For example, part of the early Nickelodeon advertising campaign that first launched the network in the fall of 1982 included an ad, featured in *People* magazine, directed to parents. The main text of the ad read, in large block letters, "THE FIRST CHANNEL FOR KIDS." While this is not incommensurate with the later rhetoric of Nickelodeon as a "kids-only zone," the rest of the text is much more conventional: the ad features images from four Nickelodeon programs (*Pinwheel, Reggie Jackson's World of Sports, The Adventures of Black Beauty,* and *You Can't Do That on Television*), and underneath the images, the small text reads, "Like most parents, you're probably not all that crazy about what your kids see on TV. That's not surprising. Because game shows, soap operas, and police shoot-em ups aren't really designed with kids in mind. But now there's an entire channel that is. It's Nickelodeon and we produce quality entertainment for kids. All day. Everyday. Available only on cable, Nickelodeon is the only channel ever endorsed by the National Educational Association."[53] The ad also includes the fact that Nickelodeon shows are "receiving a lot of acclaim from critics. They're getting rave reviews from kids, too." This kind of patronizing rhetoric is precisely the kind that the more current Nickelodeon employee handbook warns against in a section of the text listing ad campaigns that "don't work." The company rejects rhetoric that "talks down to kids, and tells them what adults want." The above ad, of course, does not address children at all but rather their parents. In fact, this ad reads much like pledge campaigns on public television (PBS), where the channel appeals to the parents' sense of what is "good" TV for kids: educational, diverse, noncommercial. In this Nickelodeon ad, children are a kind of afterthought: "They're getting rave reviews from kids, too," a statement obviously implying that the reviews that count the most are those from the critics. In fact, despite the heavy emphasis on "kids" as the core of Nickelodeon, the network recommends that writers, when writing ads, use words other than "kid," as this word, like "fun," apparently condescends to children and reveals an adult agenda. The handbook borrows from advertising rhetoric and suggests instead that the writers use the word "You" in order to produce a particular kind of subject position: "Talking to You is powerful and empowering—it makes your message more personal and will draw your audience in."[54]

For Nickelodeon, empowerment means, in part, a particular tone when "speaking" to a child through the network—a tone that apparently references a media-defined notion of respect. As Simensky comments about this rhetorical strategy, "I always thought it was interesting—and right on—that you could never say something was 'fun' or 'cool.' You couldn't tell kids that it *was* something— you just had to present it. And kids could decide if it was fun or cool, but you just had to present it in a fun or cool way, then you didn't have to say it, you didn't have to qualify it. I think that is really smart. You watch other networks—you watch the Disney channel and they say 'watch our show—it's cool, you'll have fun!' That feels wrong to me."[55] Simensky is referencing a tension between speaking for kids, or on behalf of kids, and allowing kids to speak for themselves or make an independent judgment or decision about what they like and what they do not like. The idea that kids are capable of rational decisions is reframed by Nickelodeon as a crucial factor in its brand identity, where kids are situated as active citizens. The tension Simensky references is often invoked in power struggles, and in this case, Nickelodeon promotes and sells generational divide as the most important power struggle in a child's life. While it is clear that Nickelodeon *is* in fact speaking for kids—it is the network, after all, that defines what empowerment means for its child audience—it does so in a way that capitalizes on contemporary notions of "cool": cool means anti-establishment, the underdog, the oppressed. Most significantly, liberation from this kind of oppression comes not from traditional political action but rather from choosing the right television network. This is one way in which Nickelodeon maintains a constant tension between a residual notion of political citizenship and marketing.

Nickelodeon smoothly adapts political rhetoric in a way that indicates that it is through watching television that children can become empowered. What kids "need," according to the network, is simply better TV. Even outside of the protectionist rhetoric this is a difficult balance to maintain, because the general dominant ideology about childhood (an ideology produced by parents, medical professionals, legislators, and educators, among others) is that children should watch less television. Interestingly, during my interview with Simensky, I asked her what she thought of the commercial nature of television. She rightly pointed out that it isn't as if there is a noncommercial nature of television—television *is* commercial culture. As she said, it is a conscious choice to work in the television industry, "so you kind of get over how commercial it is, we accept that." She continued by saying, "The bigger issue is: you're going to be working in television, and you have important decisions to make. You can make crap or not. You can make toy-based shows, or not. You can make things that are up-lifting for kids, or you can do dark stuff. You can do funny, or good versus evil, and there are a lot of things you can do. So everyone there was influenced not by the fact that they were working in television, but again, about doing the right thing— they were making the right shows, making better shows than the ones that were out there. You would look at Saturday morning TV and say, this stuff is better. This stuff is better for kids. Kids are going to watch TV. Gerry [Laybourne] was the first one to say, kids should not watch TV, but if you're going to watch TV, watch this stuff."[56]

This idea of "better TV" for kids was a crucial element of the relaunch of the network in 1984, which involved a continuous set of promotional spots on the air called "promise spots," commercials that highlighted the new claims and "promises" of the network to its child audience. Through the kids-only rhetoric of the Nickelodeon promises, these promos seamlessly incorporated the Us versus Them philosophy as part of the network's core ideology, rather than as an efficient marketing tactic. In an apparently unselfconscious manner, these conformist promises "define Nickelodeon and ensure that everyone talks and thinks about Nick in the same way. They serve as tools for thinking about the network and describing our differences from the competition."[57] Above all else, the "promise spots" "turn Nickelodeon, the TV network, into Nick—a place where kids know they can relax and be themselves." Some of these promises include "Nickelodeon Is the Only Network for You," "Nick Is Kids," and "Nickelodeon Is Every Day."[58] As Simensky comments, "[These thirty-second promos were] just drilled into kids in those early years, these promises of what they were going to get. It was just branding in every possible way—it was smart to do that because kids would hear that and they would believe it . . . and it was true."[59] And indeed, because each of the network's promises had to do with Nickelodeon being the only network for kids, and because in this branding environment it was necessary for Nickelodeon to actively define a contemporary empowered media citizen, the promises *were* true.

For example, one "promise spot" offered on Nickelodeon is "Nickelodeon Is the Only Network for You." In part the promise means this: "Nick talks directly to kids and appeals to their sense of humor. Nick is the place where kids come to take a break and get a break. Nick empowers kids by saying to them, 'You're important—important enough to have a network of your own.' "[60] In a commercial context of media visibility, having a "network of your own" offers an interesting twist on the meaning that Virginia Woolf's "room of one's own" had in the early twentieth century: it inspires independence, freedom of thought, and ownership over one's body and thoughts, but in the specific milieu of a commercial media network. In fact, in the Nickelodeon universe, the concepts of independence, freedom of thought, and ownership over one's body *have meaning*

only within this context—these definitions of identity and subjectivity are pre-
packaged products that the channel encourages the audience to buy. Consequently, empowerment from having "a network of your own" only has meaning within the landscape of commercial television—outside this environment,
ownership over a network, even if illusory, has no power and indeed no significant meaning. Not only does this imply that "real" power is consumer power; it
also renders cultural realms outside the commercial media as invisible or at the
least unimportant for citizenship.

Nickelodeon taps into another aspect of consumer empowerment by emphasizing the idea that, within the world of consumption, kids are oppressed by
adults. The channel strategically uses the concept of oppression as part of its self-
identity; specifically, Nickelodeon claims to alleviate the oppression kids apparently feel simply by living in today's culture. Kids are different from adults,
Nickelodeon insists: they have different needs, different desires, and require
different kinds of entertainment. This binary between adults and children, like
many other binaries that Nickelodeon exploits as part of its brand identity, is
difficult to maintain. In the early years of the network, Nickelodeon's insistence
on kids' oppression by adults backfired; one of the early station promos "warns
children not to let their parents watch Nick because adults are untrustworthy;
they wear deodorant and ties, they shave under their arms, they watch the news
and do other disgusting things frequently depicted in television commercials."[61]
An early report on the network characterized it in this way: "But the line between
empowering children and pandering to them is fuzzy, and some critics argue that
Nickelodeon's effort to make kids reign supreme goes too far, becoming anti-
grownup at times and teaching children that talking back is cool."[62] These kinds
of network promotions generated complaints to the network that the ads were
disrespectful of adults, and the network had to find a new, and less divisive, way
to instrumentalize Us versus Them. The network needed to take some of the edge
out of its branding strategy and create a kind of "kids only" zone that functioned
as a place to "revolt" and feel good about doing so without actually rebelling
against media culture.[63]

The network did this by finding an effective logo and mascot.[64] When Nickelodeon was relaunched in the mid-1980s, the channel wanted to symbolize its new
irreverent, playful attitude through its logo. The constantly changing orange logo
ostensibly functions as a symbolic metaphor for what Nick offers kids: kids
against the adult world. Ironically, in order to achieve the apparent flexibility of
the "orange splat," Nickelodeon designers must follow explicit, precise rules and
regulations concerning its design and display. The color must never vary (so
much for the "irreverence" of the color orange), and the word "Nickelodeon"

must always be easily decipherable. The shape itself changes depending on the context, so that form follows function: a turkey shape for a Thanksgiving promo, a flag shape for a Fourth of July promo, and so on.

The paradox between the network's claim of flexibility with its ideas and its insistence on conformity is evident, as Simensky comments, in the way Nickelodeon employees were talked about in the industry as "bleeding orange . . . People joke now that it was a cult . . . you know, do you drink the Kool-Aid. You believe Nickelodeon's the only way to be but there was just something about it that was right and part of it was that there was never any sense of exploiting kids—that was never part of it. If anything, there was this sort of idealizing kids— it was about respecting them, almost 'over-respecting' them—people really felt like they were working in service to kids."[65] The idea of "over-respecting" kids in such a commercial environment is, needless to say, a bit ironic—if the network was indeed created for serving children, then *doing that* would hardly constitute "over-respecting" them. More to the point, what does it mean, in this context, to be "working in service to kids"? This is not to say that Simensky's claim that there was "never any sense of exploiting kids" is insincere, but the idea of creating a commercial network that is intended to serve kids begs the question of *how* they are being served. In other words, the logo, like the network itself, capitalizes on the political valence of irreverence and flexibility and transforms the logic of these concepts to better fit the commercial environment.

Alongside the logo, during this time Nickelodeon was represented by a material artifact: green slime. Green slime is part of Nickelodeon promos, programming, and magazine articles, as well as a product in and of itself. The presence of slime (or "gak," which is a similarly gooey, messy substance) on Nickelodeon apparently clearly translates as a symbol of kids' oppression—it is anti-adult, anti-authority, and kid-centered. As the corporate handbook puts it: "Mess, slime and gak are more than a gag or theme, they are Nickelodeon's mascots. Pretty much by accident, on shows like *You Can't Do That on Television* and *Double Dare*, we discovered that green slime and mess excite kids emotionally, symbolize their rebellion and totally gross out adults."[66] Slime is clearly much more than simply a licensed product for the network (although not insignificantly, Green Slime Shampoo was the first licensed product ever to emerge from Nickelodeon); it is an important symbolic object that, in its messiness, its refusal to stay within conventional spatial borders, its sheer disgustingness and audacity, characterizes not only the mission of the network but also the personal identities of its audience.

Slime was first used on *You Can't Do That on Television*, where every time an adult or a child on the show used the words "I don't know" he or she was

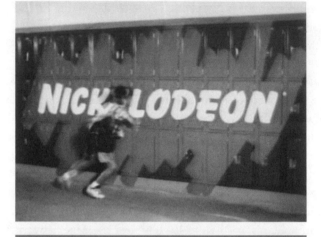

4. The Nickelodeon logo painted on school lockers, 1991.

5. Nick Jr., the channel's preschool lineup, has its own unique logo, always figuring a parent/child configuration, 2004.

6. The Nickelodeon logo in its new flexible form, 1991.

"slimed"—a huge amount of green slime was poured on his or her head. Slime is used as a visual in some of the promos (where green slime will run down the screen), but it is also an enormous element in the network's first true mega-hit, the game show *Double Dare*.[67] Slime, because it is understood to be fundamentally anti-adult, is construed by the network as a part of its commitment to respect children rather than condescend to them. The copyright-protected toy product, for the Nickelodeon universe, becomes a particular kind of unifying symbol, one which signifies a specific meaning that makes sense in a contemporary context where market forces and cultural politics have encouraged a generational divide. Slime is precisely what "adults don't get" on Nickelodeon—and the network works to keep it that way. As the handbook continues: "Kids watching at home identify with the poor kid on TV who gets slimed. They say to themselves: 'He's like me, he's just trying to get through his show and he's getting dumped on. I'm just trying to do my best to get through life and I get dumped on.' Green slime becomes a symbol for kid oppression and solidarity. It's like a great common denominator. A slimed kid says to all kids: 'You're not stupid and you're not alone! We all get dumped on!' "[68] To be "dumped on" obviously has at least two meanings in this context: the literal dumping of slime on the child in the game show, but also the metaphorical meaning of being "dumped on"—kids are victims here, oppressed by adults, by network television fare, by life in general.

Indeed, in this context, childhood itself is a state of victimization and can be thus considered part of contemporary liberalism, where liberalism (and by extension, citizenship) is understood primarily in terms of identity positions or identity politics. Within this version of liberal citizenship, Nickelodeon is the savior, by not only creating a material artifact that is a symbol "for kid oppression and solidarity" but also "standing up" for kids in this kind of oppressive environment. This, of course, has been an effective strategy within liberal politics: create the problem, thus creating an opportunity to resolve it. Nickelodeon generates an imagined space of oppression through its relentless focus on the cultural divides between adults and children. Because the channel is dedicated to "kids only," it—rather than parents—can then liberate the child from that oppression through the use of an anti-adult artifact. This "liberation" is quite clearly contained and commodified, where the members of the audience are then encouraged to feel solidarity with each other. Kids watching at home "identify" with the kids on TV, and the basis for this media "community" is shared appreciation for and use of a commercial product—just as the basis for this kind of media empowerment is commitment to a particular television network. Consumer citizenship is built around this kind of identification, where shared consumption of products provides for a kind of safe liberal practice. The representation of oppression symbolized within consumer artifacts such as slime thus suggests an underlying dynamic: liberation is also gained by consumption. In this sense, Nickelodeon's branding establishes a particular kind of social identity, where loyalty to the channel offers a kind of temporary or provisional liberation from adults. The network then can claim to be for "kids' rights" that are constituted in opposition to those of adults, or to the way in which adults treat them.

This use of slime as a symbol for oppression recalls Allison James's work on the relationship between children, penny candy ("kets"), and the adult world. The super-sugary, brightly colored, cheap "kets" popular among the British children represent not simply a good bargain in James's studies but also a conscious distance from the world of adults: " 'Kets' . . . are, by their very nature, removed from the adult domestic sphere and belong to the public, social world of children. In name, taste and consumptive experience, 'kets' belong to the disorderly and inverted world of children, for in this alternative world a new order exists which makes the 'ket' an eminently desirable product."[69] Like "kets," slime and mess on Nickelodeon represent a "new order" for children, one in keeping with the overt philosophy of the network. It is not so much—or even especially— that children understand the significance of slime in Nickelodeon programming, but that *adults don't*—that is the crucial importance of the symbol. James discusses how the ritual of eating "kets" inspires adult abhorrence—they are messy, kids share them in an unsanitary way, they are the opposite of refined foods. " 'Kets,' therefore, are the antithesis of the adult conception of 'real' food while, for adults, sweets are metonymic meals. 'Kets' involve a rejection of the series of rituals and symbols surrounding the concept of the meal and are regarded as rubbish by adults. Because they are despised by the adult world, they are prized by the child's and become the metaphoric meals of childhood."[70] Slime too represents a rejection of the rituals of the adult world, and the adult world is manipulated so that what is of value to adults is seen as ridiculous, and "what adults despise is invested with prestige." Because of the extreme difference in how adults and children define slime, slime becomes *the* symbol for Us versus Them— it embodies the playful, flexible logo of Nickelodeon itself. And importantly, slime is not just an anti-adult statement but it is also an affirmation of kidhood. Thus, slime is not about humiliating the kid but rather is framed as a "triumphant event" that symbolizes kids' rebellion. Constructed specifically to alienate adults, slime is a symbol of the cultural definition of "play" that Nickelodeon maintains.

The careful construction of slime as Nickelodeon's mascot paid off for the network, which became known for its signature program of *Double Dare*. Slime has entered the everyday lexicon of children as another word for Nickelodeon and symbolizes the antiviolence stance of the network. As one reporter put it: "Nickelodeon adopted a new strategy: Let's not give the kids what we think they want. Let's give them what they want, build self-esteem and feel good about being kids. An important role for us is to be a fun playground where their sense of humor is appreciated . . . Enter slime. They would slime the kids. Gross, but not violent."[71] In light of these kinds of branding strategies, David Buckingham argues that Nickelodeon's approach to children contributes to shaping a broader change in the status of children as a distinct social group.[72] Since an important part of Nickelodeon's brand identity is to insist that kids are sophisticated media users, the network challenges the conventional notion that the media manipulates children. Rather, it is the media that aids in their liberation from adult manipulation—the media, rather than adults, provides the safe haven, the secure neighborhood. Nickelodeon is specifically set up as a "place" where kids can confront other parts of their lives and identities: rules, adult authority, schoolwork. Nickelodeon is the neighborhood for hanging out, the cool place to be.

CITIZENS OF THE NICKELODEON NATION

Establishing the network's brand identity as specific place—the transformation of Nickelodeon into "Nick"—was a crucial precedent for the network's 1999–2000 brand campaign, "Nickelodeon Nation." This campaign follows an even more contemporary brand design than the "promise spots," although the Nickelodeon Nation campaign also followed the mission of Nickelodeon carefully. The appropriation of nationalist rhetoric by a children's cable channel seemed seamless at that historical moment. The design of the network's brand identity as a "nation" is multidimensional and taps into several different cultural conversations circulating at the time: consumer patriotism, branding loyalty, the transformation of products into generalized brand ideas, such as nationalism, all the while maintaining the Us versus Them ideology.[73] As one reporter described the campaign: "Nickelodeon wants world domination. Or at the very least, its own nation."[74] The network launched the Nickelodeon Nation campaign in October 1999, on network television, during what is widely considered a favorite American national event, the World Series. Ruth Sarlin, the senior vice-president of brand and franchise marketing for Nickelodeon, says that the campaign was developed as something that was relevant to kids but also could appeal to adults without alienating kids. According to Sarlin, the Nickelodeon Nation theme represents "ubiquity in kids' lives."[75] As Phillips Business Information put it: "The launch leveraged a media buying strategy designed to position Nick as an ever-present force in the kids' world, a trusted brand for adults and a multimedia guru in the entertainment industry."[76] Veering from its "kids only" rhetoric at least for this campaign, the network courted a more transgenerational audience with Nickelodeon Nation: the campaign was aired in primetime and late night programming and during the early morning news shows *Today* and *Good Morning America*. Print ads to advertisers were run in trade magazines such as *Advertising Age* and *Adweek* and ads aimed at gaining (and keeping) subscribers were directed to audience members in magazines such as *TV Guide*.

The theme of a network for the "nation" was a particularly effective one in the context of intense competition for brand recognition within the television landscape. What better way to establish loyalty and trust than to rely upon a traditional rhetoric of patriotism and loyalty to country? Nickelodeon Nation represents an imagined community of the early twenty-first century; the "deep, horizontal comradeship" that Benedict Anderson saw facilitated by print capitalism in the eighteenth and nineteenth centuries is, in this context, a comradeship that is held together by the everyday lexicon of the brand and the normalization of consumer loyalty. Nickelodeon Nation, like other successful brands, has become synonymous with the name of the company, but more than that, the hyperbolic claims of the campaign—the network *as* nation—captures both the way in which Nickelodeon dominates the children's television landscape and the rhetorical insistence that the network is more than just TV—it is a place, a nation, a feeling of belonging. Thus, the Nickelodeon Nation is not just about programming, although programming is an important element; it is about the experience of the brand. As Mitroff points out, during a department heads meeting at a kids' network, this is what occurs: "the branding people are sitting there with the programming people and the programming people are concerned about making standout programs. But the branding people are saying, 'If it's a standout program but it doesn't fit our brand, we're throwing it away.' So they have to mesh."[77]

The ads that formed the heart of the Nickelodeon Nation campaign always featured several children, both boys and girls, of a variety of ethnic and racial backgrounds, dancing with each other in the street, in playgrounds, and in neighborhoods. These ads became immediately recognizable because of their snappy doo-wop sound: a medley of hip-hop and nostalgic pop music. The "Nickelodeon Anthem" was a revision of The Dixie Cups' 1965 hit tune "Iko Iko":[78]

2, 4, 6, 8—SPLAT!!
Me and my generation
Don't you like kids who look like that
Nickelodeon Nation
Talk about Hey Now (hey now), Hey Now (hey now)

Going to Celebration
I believe in Nick 'cause Nick believes in me
Nickelodeon Nation!

The color print ads usually featured only one child, caught in a candid moment of laughing or playing, and included large orange print that said "Nickelodeon Nation," or "We Pledge Allegiance to Kids." The rhetoric of these ads, placed in TV Guide, People magazine, and other mainstream magazines, clearly resonated with the television ads that more directly targeted the child audience (assuming that adults are more likely to read TV Guide and People magazine) in terms of the construction of the network as a specific place of empowerment and belonging.

Nickelodeon Nation advertisements were also placed within advertising trade magazines, so that the campaign was not only seen by both the adult and child audience, but also was directed to advertisers themselves. These versions of the Nickelodeon Nation campaign stressed the importance of kids as consumers, as Cindy White and Elizabeth Preston point out, with text that labels kids as "amazingly powerful consumers" and the idea that "They may be small. But if you're a marketer, kids can be positively superheroic."[79] As White and Preston argue, with these kinds of ads, "Nickelodeon tries to capitalize on its undisputed brand identification as a service singularly devoted to attracting child consumers and uniting them with appropriate advertisers."[80] More than simply attracting the child consumer, however, the use of national rhetoric in these appeals allows the network to *create* its audience as a particular kind of consumer citizen. White and Preston point out that "the young inhabitants of this community, this nation— Nick-branded kids—are not simply citizens: they are powerful consumers of the products that litter its landscape."[81] In fact, these "Nick-branded kids" are citizens in this context precisely *because* they are powerful consumers—it is their consumer behavior that authorizes them as citizens of the Nickelodeon Nation. The Nickelodeon Nation promotional strategies signal the various ways in which Nickelodeon understands both itself and its audience as an empowered force in the consumer market. This kind of empowerment, created by Nickelodeon as a particular kind of product, is not one to dismiss lightly, and it is the central feature of the present-day child consumer citizen.

It is not simply the network's ubiquity that makes it the Nickelodeon Nation. The children's market that Nickelodeon has both created and captured forms its national borders, where the other "nations" are other channels and other market shares. The consequences of framing a television station as a nation are important: this construction is more than simply a fan relationship but indeed encourages children to identify and personally invest in Nickelodeon as citizens of a nation. Based on consumer participation and commercial belonging, this kind of child citizen is encouraged to actively participate in the way Nickelodeon defines political participation: "voting" on the *Kids' Choice Awards,* where kids determine favorite pop stars, music, actors, and so forth, or choosing a candidate on *Kids Pick the President,* where during an election year children "vote" for president. As one fifteen-year-old girl recalled about her participation in *Kids Pick the President,* "[The channel] also like, at 1:52, they interrupt the show or right before the show starts back up from the commercial, they talk for about a minute about a recent event that's just happened that's important that we should know . . . only about a minute long because kids'll wanna know what they're talking about. I remember watching the election . . . when I was in fourth grade, they had like the whole thing on the election. They went through who the candidates were and stuff. And because everyone was talking about the election, I wanted to know stuff. So they had a little special."[82] This kind of consumer-driven political action, where election coverage is used as a kind of interstitial between programming, in short sound bites for easy understanding, helps the notion of media nationhood have resonance with audiences. In this scenario, divisions between a kind of "real" national identity (ostensibly built upon political action and civic agency), and a consumer national identity, one that connects empowerment with the purchase of products, are illusory at best.

The patriotic rhetoric of Nickelodeon's campaign was particularly effective because it tapped into many of the "essential" ingredients for a successful brand.[83] For instance, the organic shaping of nationalism as an idea, or an "imagined community," takes a particular form that is understood as constantly under threat: nationalism is competitive, and patriotism is often the act of insisting upon national superiority. But acts of patriotism also rely on what Michael Billig calls "banal nationalism," where in established nations there is a "continual 'flagging' or reminding, of nationhood . . . this reminding is so familiar, so continual, that it is not consciously registered as reminding. The metonymic image of banal nationalism is not a flag which is being consciously waved with fervent passion; it is the flag hanging unnoticed on the public building."[84] The brand strategies embedded within Nickelodeon Nation work as this kind of constant reminder to the network's audience. In so doing, they clearly establish Nickelodeon's superiority in the landscape of children's television, and they confirm the network as the key competitor in terms of programming content, style, and promotional campaigns.

This strategy is evident in the history of Nickelodeon with other cable networks. While initially Nickelodeon enjoyed success in part because it had no other competitors, in 1999 there were four full-time children's cable networks competing: Nickelodeon, Disney, the Cartoon Network, and Fox Family Channel. The Nickelodeon Nation campaign needs to be interpreted within this context: the campaign can be read as a familiar, continuous reminding that Nickelodeon was (and is) the standard against which these other channels could be measured. Given the intensely competitive commercial environment of cable television, all niche networks attempt to define themselves in ways different from—and superior to—their competition, and Nickelodeon was certainly no exception. As the branding "expert" Alina Wheeler characterizes this sort of relationship: "Competition for recognition is as ancient as the heraldic banners on a medieval battlefield. No longer limited by physical terrain, managing perception now extends to cyberspace and beyond. As feudal domains became economic enterprises, what was once heraldry is now branding. The battle for physical territory has evolved into the competition for share of mind."[85]

The competition between Nickelodeon and other children's networks is often noted in the media, in part because Nickelodeon had so thoroughly captured the market that when Disney entered into the fray the competition itself provided a kind of media event. As the reporter Josh Young describes this struggle for territory, it was "the battle of enchantment versus empowerment: . . . in this schoolyard showdown, the Big Orange Bully (the industry nickname for Nick's citrus-colored logo) has already thrown the first punch."[86] In its branding strategy and self-definition, Nickelodeon implicitly mocked Disney as the goody-two-shoes of children's television, again capitalizing on the commercial potential of being the cool channel. Disney is construed as the patronizing (and infantilizing) parent, and Nickelodeon as the hip best friend, adding to the channel's brand tactic of having a renegade and indeed, counterhegemonic, identity. The standoff between enchantment and empowerment between children's television channels gains a kind of attention that resonates in the environment of the child citizen and works clearly in Nickelodeon's favor. Even Cartoon Network, which clearly has a more irreverent style than the Disney channel, seems often a thin imitation of Nickelodeon. As Simensky commented about the competition between Nickelodeon and Cartoon: "If you look at [Cartoon's] Friday night packaging, they might as well run a line that says 'we'd like to be Nick—how can we do it? E-mail your suggestions to us.' Because they are trying but they're not pulling it off. They have a bad case of Nick envy. Disney also has Nick envy."[87] Nickelodeon's dominance in the kids' television market allows the channel to take the moral high ground; as Cyma Zarghami, then senior vice-president for programming, commented when asked about Nickelodeon's competition: "There's the Superman quote that with great success comes a great responsibility. We will remain responsible, but there's a lot of irresponsible ways that will be used to get ratings. That's what alerted the government to begin with. Kids' programming is like food. If you give them candy, they'll eat it. We try to make our programs more nourishing. We won't do anything gratuitously in a show."[88]

Yet, despite Nickelodeon's self-conscious claim to be the "alternative" choice in the television landscape, by the mid-1990s the rhetoric of the network had even less of an upstart feel and more that of a major global corporate player. In fact, the former president of Nickelodeon, Herb Scannell, used the exact words as Wheeler when speaking about Nickelodeon's attempts at capturing new audiences with different media venues: "The battleground for tomorrow is not just for share of TV audience, but for share of mind . . . With Nickelodeon now in magazines, online and in movies, we have three more opportunities to reinforce the Nickelodeon brand."[89] The multimedia reach of Nickelodeon is of an enormous scope; in addition to publishing Nickelodeon magazine, the channel is a corporate sibling of Paramount Pictures, which released *The Rugrats Movie* in 1999, the first non-Disney animated film to gross more than $100 million. Paramount is an important part of the empire building at Nickelodeon as well as an effective way to edge out competition such as Disney or the Cartoon Network. The reporter Marc Gunther claims: "The game they're playing at Nickelodeon these days isn't *Guts* or *Double Dare*. It's Extend That Brand. Name a category that touches kids, from toys to macaroni and cheese, and there's a product out there with Nick's name on it. The cute little children's channel that once ran no ads at all now looms over the kids' market for just about anything."[90]

Yet the network's identity remains that of a rebel, a place where kids can be "liberated" from the "real world." As Laybourne and others repeatedly put it, kids are "terrified" of growing up, in part because of what they witness in and on the media: drugs, crime, homelessness, pain, anger. As part of its commercial identity, Nickelodeon seeks to redress this by offering something different: here, the network becomes a refuge, a significant part of a safe neighborhood, an imagined national community. Just as the media (specifically Nickelodeon) can "save" children from adults, it can also "save" them from an adult-defined, hostile world. The self-conscious construction of the network as a specific place is obviously in part about audience share; as Karen Lury writes, "How do the channels secure their audience if there is so much choice and if the child can catch the same programmes at different times on different channels, or even on the same channel? The strategy of the channels is to define their identity as a brand, and through this, effectively to establish them as a place. Branding makes the space of transmission, the channel, into a place you can go to."[91]

When Nickelodeon began to emerge as a distinct identity in children's cable television in the 1980s, a particular set of historical conditions provided the context for the nascent channel. A general cultural fear circulated about the lost innocence of children (especially girls)—certainly not a new fear, but one with some new referents: AIDS, drugs, "latch-key" kid worries, crime, delinquency. There was also a growing body of research about the effects of television on children with a specific focus on commercialism and violence. These studies emerged in part because the environment of deregulation that characterized the 1980s allowed for the production of a different kind of television, where the "free" market rather than the FCC dictated the kind of television people watched.[92]

Within this increasingly cluttered landscape, there is a need for networks to create both particular and universal appeals to maintain audience share, and to establish television viewing as a "safe" alternative to real life fears concerning children. In this regard, a network's identity cannot be too specific because of the potential to alienate viewers; rather, "universal" themes such as family and neighborhood are used for appeal. As White and Preston argue, "corporations are attempting to promote brand identification with their own programming by constructing their on-air and on-line properties as authentic places where kids may play, make friends, participate in games, and interact with characters and one another."[93] Historically, with children's programs, the idea of the television as neighborhood has connected with the audience, as we witness with the success of such programs as *Mister Rogers' Neighborhood* and *Captain Kangaroo,* and of course, *Sesame Street,* a show which created itself as a destination for kids long before Nickelodeon. Building on the television as neighborhood motif, *Sesame Street* even opened (and continues to open) with a theme song in which kids ask how to get to Sesame Street, played over visuals of children and Big Bird walking to Sesame Street.[94] White and Preston discuss the importance of children's networks as "places" to visit in the minds of their young viewers and examine various strategies of the more recent networks Fox Kids and Disney as efforts to encourage an attachment of the viewer to an "authentic" place of the network. They suggest that the strategy of Fox Kids is to rely on geography, or physical location, as a way to appeal to viewers. Disney, on the other hand, cashes in on a historical framework of family, morality, or the "right" kind of values, to articulate the idea of place for its network: "while Fox Kids uses geography to organize social relations, Disney uses social relations to organize geography."[95]

I argue that Nickelodeon does both. In other words, Nickelodeon, like Fox Kids, constructs itself as an authentic destination—the Nickelodeon neighborhood, or in Laybourne's words, a "safe haven." But the framework that is used by Nickelodeon to establish this particular neighborhood is based on a clear historical economic relationship the network has with its viewers as a place for kids only, characterized by a manufactured spirit of irreverence and rebellion (quite

7. The urban landscape in *Hey Arnold!*, 2004.

different from Disney). The "place" of Nickelodeon resembles one of its own original animated series, *Hey Arnold!*, a program about a young white boy living in the inner city surrounded by kids of different races and ethnic backgrounds. The neighborhood in *Hey Arnold!* is diverse, edgy, a little bit gritty, plagued by easily containable urban problems, and run by kids with the exception of a few rather enigmatic adults.

Nickelodeon capitalized on the fear and anxiety generated by this cultural environment by creating something that is coded real and authentic, or at the very least, "cool." The fact that this "real and authentic" place existed only virtually through the media is rarely acknowledged as a paradox—in fact, this feeling of authenticity is crucial to the development of the brand. Thus, the authenticity of the place is only genuine in the sense that the connection is between a consumer and a product, even though the rhetoric implies real geographic boundaries that ostensibly hold some "citizens" in and keep others out. It is also a kind of social territory, where it encourages affiliation within the imagined community of the network. For the "neighborhood" of Fox Kids, that meant referencing a kind of "friend" that is accepted in the network/neighborhood: "The neighborhood then is a place of acceptance as well as fun. There are no entry requirements or any other of the pressures that inhibit acceptance and haunt kid's relationships."[96]

For the Nickelodeon Nation, there is a similar ease of entry into the nation—as long as one is a fan/customer of Nickelodeon, that is enough for a shared cultural identity and shared set of values: "me and my generation . . . don't you like kids who look like that, Nickelodeon Nation." The differences between kids that can be divisive—race, gender, class, sexuality, and other so-called labels—are erased in the branded Nickelodeon Nation, where the only important element of identity is affiliation with the brand. The fact that one has to subscribe to cable, so that the citizens of this nation are primarily affluent child consumers, is rendered invisible in this construction of the media nation. Like the "people" referenced in the U.S. Constitution, the media network creates an ideal citizen against which all others are measured. With Nickelodeon, the ideal citizen is the "kid"; the network often claims that its programming does not cater to any one kind of child (i.e., girls, or kids of color) but rather is about the "average, everyday kid." This all-encompassing claim positions generation as the only dividing marker of identity, which is crucial to the maintenance of the Nickelodeon brand. That socioeconomic status is also key to membership in the Nickelodeon Nation—is just as important as "just being a kid"—is obscured. Citizenship in the Nickelodeon Nation is accessible to (certain) kids only.

BRANDING IDENTITY: CONSUMER CITIZENS?

The rhetoric that structures Nickelodeon's branding strategies references a politics that is fundamentally about empowerment: rights, respect, security, and liberty. This kind of political rhetoric has made a different kind of sense—indeed, has a different kind of logic—depending on its historical context, and what it is structuring and supporting. When the language of rights and empowerment is appropriated as the language of a commercial brand, it becomes quite clear that the boundaries between these two realms of social life are not necessarily distinct and oppositional. Rather, as Buckingham argues, economic and social dynamics function in tandem with each other, as allies, not enemies:

> There is a fundamental blurring or confusion between the notions of children as potential or actual citizens and the notion of children as consumers. In the discourse of Nickelodeon, for example, the "rights" that are being talked about are essentially the rights of the consumer. Children have a right to consume things that adults provide for them; and if children have their own culture, it is a culture which adults have almost entirely created for them—and indeed sold to them.[97]

For example, the notion that children are "media savvy" in the twenty-first century does not necessarily mean that they are political actors—it could very well mean "simply that they are very quick to change channels when they see something they don't like."[98] But it also means that it is through the media that children (as well as adults) are forming their political self-identities *as* their consumer identities.

The brand strategies of Nickelodeon tap into these ideologies about consum-

erism and citizenship and present to the audience a network—and an identity—
that seems ironically noncommercial. Cultural anxieties about advertising to
children and training them to be "little consumers" were, and continue to be,
based on an exploding kids market, more and more segmented age-specific
programming and advertising, and the increasing purchasing power of children,
especially tweens. Nickelodeon responded to these anxieties in a way commensurate with the contemporary branding environment: by positioning itself as the
renegade, the cool network, the outsider. The "respect" Nickelodeon has for its
child audience is not necessarily insincere, but it is based on commodifying and
packaging trends and values important to particular age groups and then profit-
ing off the revenue. Importantly, this *becomes* empowerment for a child media
audience—empowerment exists for this generation within the bounds of consumer culture. This is not to assume a distinct binary between "real" culture and
marketing culture, but it is to argue that Nickelodeon's claim that the network
empowers kids makes sense only within the culture of the market. The strategies
of this kind of empowerment are built into each element of the structure of the
network; as Mitroff points out:

> When we're talking about adolescent angst and they're trying to capture it,
> you know, a lot of people in the industry talk about Nickelodeon as a place
> for—has been, traditionally—for school-aged kids, and then we get Nick Jr.
> And what happens as kids get a little bit older is that there's no place for them
> to go, so if you finish Nickelodeon, kids are scared to jump to MTV, but that's
> what's next. There's nothing in between . . . Now, look at what Nickelodeon's
> trying to do . . . you take that school-aged block and you throw in a few things
> that appeal to the adolescents and once you get them, then you say, "Now
> we're creating something for *you*." And that's going to be "N" [a new offshoot
> of Nickelodeon geared toward a tween audience]. So once you've attracted
> them to your network and you build that audience, and you tell them there's a
> place for them, then you take that programming and you put it over there and
> you say, "Now we want all of you."[99]

In the Nickelodeon universe, having a network of one's own is constructed as a
cultural right. However, as is evident from the desire of the network to be
omnipotent—"now we want all of you"—the attainment of these cultural "rights"
translates into market share and audience purchasing power.

In the following chapters, I examine the various ways in which the network
articulates a discourse of cultural rights through its original programming. Although it is quite clear that media power is in large part dependent on consumer
power, it is also important not to dismiss certain political accomplishments of

Nickelodeon—such as leading the way in the industry with strong, interesting girl characters, or with industry practices that include not only media representations of nonwhite groups but also a commitment to hiring marginalized people to produce these representations—as simply part of the discourse of consumption habits. One thing is evident: through its creative use of traditional branding techniques, and appeals to both spatial delineations and a transgenerational address, the Nickelodeon brand has been successful in both political and consumer discourse.

GIRLS RULE! GENDER, FEMINISM, AND NICKELODEON

I think that shows like *As Told by Ginger* [challenge stereotypes]. She isn't like part of the popular group and she has those issues with getting into the popular group, but she's like her own person still. I don't know, she still has fun. That show makes it okay to not be a popular person and you still have friends and have fun.
—K., A FIFTEEN-YEAR-OLD NICKELODEON FAN

In June 2000, the Museum of Television and Radio in both New York and Los Angeles presented a three-month retrospective that honored Nickelodeon. The retrospective, "A Kid's Got to Do What a Kid's Got to Do: Celebrating Twenty years of Nickelodeon," featured screenings of past and current programming, hands-on workshops, an interactive gallery exhibit, and seminars for families. One of the seminars, titled "Girl Power! Creating Positive Role Models for Girls," lauded Nickelodeon's efforts over the past twenty years to challenge traditional gender stereotypes on children's television by featuring girls as primary lead characters. A "girl power" seminar had a particular cultural resonance in 2000: the connection between these two concepts—"girl" and "power"—once thought to be completely absent from the world of children's popular culture had become normalized within the discourses of consumer culture. In the contemporary cultural climate, the empowerment of girls is now something that is more or less taken for granted by both children and parents and has certainly been incorporated into commodity culture. In fact, an important part of Nickelodeon's claim to "empower" its audience has been specifically connected to the production of shows that featured strong female lead characters, garnering the channel an industry and public reputation as a vanguard in challenging television stereotypes about girls (ironically achieved by Nickelodeon's insistence on "gender-neutral" programming).

The cultural context in which Nickelodeon emerged was crucial to the network's ability to position itself as "gender neutral." Indeed, the rhetoric of "girl power" has found currency in not just television but almost every realm of contemporary children's popular culture. In the mid 1990s, the Spice Girls, a manufactured, pop-music girlgroup, adopted "Girl Power!" as their motto. And, at the same time, the alternative Internet community the Riot Grrrls incorporated girl power ideology in their efforts to construct a new kind of feminist politics.[1] T-shirts emblazoned with "Girls Kick Ass!" and "Girls Rule!" became new hot items for both high school and elementary school girls, and Nike's "Play Like a Girl" advertising campaign skillfully used the concept of "commodity feminism" to sell athletic gear.[2] In the sporting world, the success of the 1999 Women's Soccer World Cup tournament, the public focus on the tennis superstars Venus and Serena Williams, and the creation of the Women's National Basketball Association brought new attention and prestige to powerful female athletes. In the world of popular psychology and everyday culture, books such as Mary Pipher's *Reviving Ophelia: Saving the Selves of Adolescent Girls* (1995) and Rosalind Wiseman's *Queen Bees and Wannabes: Helping Your Daughter Survive Cliques, Gossip, Boyfriends, and Other Realities of Adolescence* (2002) recognized problems unique to young girls growing up in the 1990s and immediately became bestsellers.[3]

And, in the world of children's television, programs about self-confident, assertive, and intelligent girls such as Nickelodeon's 1991 hit *Clarissa Explains It All*, and the network's more recent animated programs such as *As Told by Ginger*, *Rocket Power*, and *The Wild Thornberries*, initiated a new trend in programming that actively rejected the conventional industry wisdom that children's shows with girl leads could not be successful.[4] Aside from these kinds of entertainment programs, Nickelodeon also addresses gender issues on the network's nonfiction news program, *Nick News*, with episodes devoted to body image, bullying, and girls' sports, among others. In this chapter, I focus on the cultural context that produces girl power practices and commodities, and I specifically situate Nickelodeon as a key producer of girl power culture. Part of my inquiry here regards how young people use and make sense of the media in the context of their lived social experiences. I focus explicitly on gender and discuss the complicated nature of gender representation on children's television, and Nickelodeon's position on such representation. Girl power is an important aspect of contemporary consumer citizenship, and thus it is necessary to closely examine the dimensions of this cultural, economic, and material "phenomenon" as constitutive of Nick elodeon's consumer citizenship. Is contemporary media—and Nickelodeon in particular—simply capitalizing on a current trend, or does girl power ideology signify a new direction for feminist politics? I argue here that girl power is not just a fad, although it is that; it is not just about empowerment, although it is that too. Girl power powerfully demonstrates the contradictions or tensions that structure postfeminist politics, especially for young girls.

It is not my aim to "resolve" these tensions or to expose postfeminism or girl power as a commercial hoax. It is my goal, rather, to theorize how the often contradictory media representations of girl power on Nickelodeon function as a kind of feminist politics and, as such, work to constitute audiences as particular kinds of cultural citizens. Indeed, as I will discuss in this chapter, I see the dynamics and disconnects between post- and Second Wave feminisms to have a corollary in the dynamics and disconnects within the category of consumer citizenship. The same problems and distinctions that plague feminism also plague consumer citizenship: nostalgia, imagined golden past, superficiality, rhetoric of choice reframed in terms of consumer choice, and so on. Like consumer citizenship, girl power (represented in postfeminism) is profoundly, indeed necessarily ambivalent. One of the means through which Nickelodeon "empowers" its audience is by addressing girls as powerful players in brand-dominated consumer culture. And since Nickelodeon is such a media powerhouse, the channel does not simply exploit the commercial market of girl power but is also a significant *producer* of girl power culture—especially since Nickelodeon attracts a large audience of pre-adolescent and adolescent girls.

It is this tension between Nickelodeon's embrace of the girl power consumer market and the network's role as a producer of girl power ideology—and the ambivalent feminism resulting from this tension—that I explore in this chapter. But what does it mean to say that a huge corporate entity such as Nickelodeon enables girls to be *producers* of their own culture? Certainly, it can be argued, as Mary Celeste Kearney does, that alternative cultural productions along the margins of mainstream popular culture—'zines, for example, or Riot Grrrl websites —illustrate how girls can produce girl power culture in ways that challenge some of the mainstream girl power products.[5] But Nickelodeon programs are hardly "alternative" and are clearly a part of mainstream, commercial culture. To get at how part of Nickelodeon's more general claim to empower its audience is dependent on the channel's ambivalent feminist politics, in this chapter I analyze three of the network's programs: *Clarissa Explains It All,* which first aired in 1991; *As Told by Ginger (ATBG),* a contemporary popular animated series; and *Nick News,* the weekly news program for children that is hosted and produced by Linda Ellerbee. I examine *Clarissa* because the program is widely noted as a "breakthrough" show in girl power programming—it was among the first children's series to feature a strong, independent girl lead character, and through this program, Nickelodeon became well-known in the industry as a champion for girls. I then look at *ATBG* as a way to account for the trajectory of girl power ideology in the decade since *Clarissa* first aired, taking specific note of the program's use of irony and self-reflexivity as a more current rhetorical strategy of girl power. Finally, I examine *Nick News* for its representation of girl power themes, as well as its role as a producer of girl power culture through both the themes of the episodes and the figure of the host, Ellerbee, herself. Although *Nick News* differs from the other programs in that it is nonfiction, the themes on the news program—body image, popularity, parental authority—are similar to the themes in the entertainment programs, and thus it makes sense to look at all three as rich examples of mass-mediated girl power. The content of these particular Nickelodeon programs illustrates some of the contradictions within the relationship between media visibility, commercialism, and the production of girl culture—the same kinds of contradictions that, as I discuss later in this chapter, also structure postfeminism.

REPRESENTATIONS OF GENDER IN CHILDREN'S TELEVISION

The way in which women and men are represented on television has been the subject of scholarly inquiry since television emerged in U.S. society. As the symbolic and representational power of television was increasingly evident, the influence the medium had on establishing and consolidating dominant understandings of gender became clear. Depending on where one was situated regarding scholarly research, television was theorized as an active agent of socialization regarding gender roles, a constitutive element in dominant norms of gender, an important element in the symbolic recognition of dominant gender roles, and as a "feminized" medium in and of itself.[6] The television industry was keenly aware of gendered divisions in the audience, and programming was often designed to appeal to one gender or another.[7] However, gender is more complicated than the language of "target audience" allows for, and while many TV shows have demonstrated a commitment to normative definitions of masculinity and femininity, it is also the case that gender representations on television have not always been read as privileging masculinity. The many different variations of definitions of masculinity and femininity necessarily refute an essential idea that there is one single, unified truth about what gender is, or what it should be. Other factors such as race or sexuality shape the way we experience gender, so that even the language of "stereotypes," as Stuart Hall argues, is problematic because it assumes an essentialist position on gender, where "underneath" the stereotype there is an apparently "real" or authentic gender representation.[8] Indeed, as many scholars have pointed out, even television programs that are male-identified contain narratives and mythologies that appeal to feminine pleasure, desire, and empowerment.[9]

Although scholarship on primetime television and gender representation has continued to become more complex (and television itself has become more "open" to a variety of representations), children's television and the issue of gender representation has not received as much attention (in either a scholarly or more mainstream context). The most common critique or analysis about the gender politics of kids TV is that male characters and male themes dominate, and that female characters are primarily depicted as hyperfeminine and sexual. Indeed, concerns about representations of female sexuality in children's television programs have been a constant since the emergence of U.S. television (a legacy of anxiety that follows all mass media developments in the United States). Precisely because of the presumed innocence of the child viewer, media images and narratives of sexuality—especially female sexuality—have been intensely contested issues for media creators as well as media advocates and parents. The power associated with female sexuality (however contained and controlled it may be) contradicts the powerlessness that has constantly defined girl characters. The easiest and safest way to depict female sexuality (and power) in children's media has been to associate it negatively with corrupt female villains. Ranging from early debates over how best to animate the female form in Disney's *Snow White*, to protests over the overtly sexual *Betty Boop*, to feminist challenges to the hyperfeminine animated characters in children's TV shows such as *Josie and the Pussycats, Scooby-Doo, The Jetsons,* and others, the issue of how to represent the sexualized female form on children's television has been complex and contradictory.

These early concerns mirror some of the anxieties that television network executives had about racial representations in cartoons in the 1950s, where programs that were produced (or recycled) remained safely white; because there was no consensus on the appropriate way to represent nonwhite characters, characters of color were left out of early television cartoons altogether.[10] Similarly, because the female body is always already sexualized, representations of gender within children's media were often constructed within the context of protectionism. This resulted in a predictable dichotomy of feminine representation: power, when connected with female characters, was almost always corrupting, evil, and lethal. On the other side of the binary, innocent and pure (both sexually and in terms of power) princesses seemed always on the verge of abuse by power-hungry queens and stepmothers. Susan Douglas, for instance, argues that powerful female characters in Disney films "had way too much power for their own good, embodying the age-old truism that any power at all completely corrupted women and turned them into monsters. In their hands, power was lethal: it was used only to bolster their own overweening vanity, and to destroy what was pure and good in the world."[11] This dichotomous gender representation left girl audiences with only two choices: "the powerless but beloved masochist or the powerful but detested narcissist."[12]

For children's media culture, then, gender representations have by and large continued to be, like the imagined child audience, simplistically rendered. Since children television viewers are assumed to be innocent and naïve, children's programming has historically categorized identities (such as nonwhite characters, or girls, or violent criminals) as stereotypically "positive" or "negative" with little apparent nuanced complication in between. What determines the "positive" or "negative" nature of an image depends on the cultural and economic context in which it is produced. Heather Hendershot calls this "light-switch logic," where "many reformers conceive of television as endangering its potentially dangerous viewers: innocent children will imitate whatever sexism, racism, and violence they see on 'bad' shows, or they will copy the good behavior broadcast on 'good' shows."[13] The simplistic ideology that constitutes the cultural trope of the innocent child lends itself to an equally unsophisticated rendering of the television world as comprising "good" and "bad" images. In turn, this construction of children assumes that, at worst, children don't participate in the media except as brainwashed victims or, at best, are not productive members of media culture—instead, children are merely subjected to it.[14]

Not surprisingly, from the position of the television industry, gender representation has rarely been framed in terms of whether images are "good" or "bad" in terms of gender identity, but rather whether particular images sell better than others. The industry's primary goal is to get the most children watching at any given time. Gender representations, then, need to satisfy an economic imperative for advertisers, and historically this has meant the division of programs into easily understood (and thus easily divisible into markets) "girl" and "boy" shows. There are at least two primary reasons for this: one, quite simply, is that children's television resembles primetime television (and most other media forms, for that matter) in that it is male-identified. Clearly, U.S. society and culture continues to be structured by institutionalized politics of gender asymmetry and continuing male dominance, and this is symbolically recorded and consolidated in the media. That there are programs that could be called "prime time feminist" programs, or that there is certainly a widening spectrum of roles for women on television, is important, but it remains the case that women are typically cast in the less socially valuable (and/or simply less visible) roles in comedy and drama programs.[15] This trend is replicated in children's programs, but in an even more distinct way: there are clearly "girl" shows and "boy" shows in children's television, and far fewer "crossover" programs that would appeal to both girls and boys than on primetime television. Thus, the most efficient way to appeal to a broad audience is by neatly segmenting children's programming according to borders that are easily navigated—those that reinforce dominant mythologies and practices of gender in an uncomplicated way.

The second reason that male-identified programs continue to dominate in children's television is related to the first but is more clearly an economic reason: conventional industry wisdom claims that boy shows—those that feature action heroes, violent or aggressive (or "action") themes, and male lead roles—are more financially successful than shows that feature a more feminized narrative or girls as lead roles.[16] In the U.S. television industry, with such high costs of production, few networks feel that they can "afford" to take risks by creating programming that features girls.[17] Perhaps most important of all, especially from a marketing point of view, boys and girls are considered fundamentally and essentially *different* and thus desire different products and respond to different advertising appeals. Barrie Thorne has argued that this "different cultures" model regarding children has worked to create gender arrangements that are necessarily distinct: this model situates boys and girls according to a set of what Thorne calls "static and exaggerated" dualisms that are built from stereotypes and conventions of gender.[18]

Even in the 1980s, when, as Ellen Seiter has pointed out, there were more characters for girls to choose from owing to the licensed character boom, these characters were hardly empowered. Nonetheless, although the heroines of such 1980s programs as *My Little Pony* and *Strawberry Shortcake* were not necessarily powerful, intelligent characters, they were, Seiter argues, at least female, which challenged the earlier invisibility of girls on children's television.[19] Economically, in the context of deregulation that characterized 1980s broadcast television, shows that targeted a specifically female audience were perceived as probable market failures, and thus it was more financially viable to create programs that featured exaggerated, hyperstylized representations of both masculinity and femininity. Indeed, one of the more memorable moments of this television era was when the ABC executive Jenny Trias (impulsively) said, when asked why there were so few girl programs, "Girls won't watch what boys watch. We don't even think about girls."[20] While she was resoundingly criticized for this remark, she was merely revealing the ways in which gender representation on television is dependent on the market. Because Nickelodeon was a cable program in the early days of channel proliferation, it didn't have to produce the kind of safe, cautious TV constrained by the economics of broadcast television. As Donna Mitroff, an industry executive, says about the relative freedom of Nickelodeon to take programming risks during the early 1990s, "You know, they were a small group of people who worked very closely with each other. They sparked off each other, they didn't have all the rules that they have now. You know, they've become an institution. Then, you know, it's in the history of organizations. It's not as easy. So let's go back to the common wisdom, which said, 'boys won't watch what girls watch.' So along comes Nickelodeon and says, 'Hey, you know, we can take chances.' "[21]

In 1991, when Nickelodeon's *Clarissa Explains It All* debuted and became a hit with both boys and girls, the conventional wisdom about boys not watching girl programs was clearly challenged. However, *Clarissa* did not emerge as a media product in a cultural vacuum; on the contrary, it was precisely the context of a consumer-oriented "girl power movement" that provided the cultural and economic conditions in which the creation of a show like *Clarissa* was possible. Girl power was not only a popular politics, however. Nor was it simply a marketing fad that yielded financial results. Indeed, as I discuss below, within the television industry more women were taking positions of presidents of networks, heads of programming divisions, as well as writers and producers of television shows. Institutionally girl power also had a presence, and it is clear that girl power is multidimensional, expressing itself at the cultural, economic, and material levels.

THE POWER OF GIRL POWER

Over the course of the last decade, then, a media-defined movement of girl power, often connected to postfeminism, has emerged in U.S. adolescent culture, and Nickelodeon programming and the network's overall insistence that children are empowered "citizens" have contributed to this girl power movement. As such, Nickelodeon, like postfeminism, and like girl power politics, offers its youth audience a contradictory or, at best, an ambivalent message about social and cultural empowerment, and about citizenship itself. This media context of girl power, combined with the increasing cultural recognition of adolescent girls as both powerful citizens and consumers, offers what at times looks like a radical gesture in terms of disrupting dominant gender relations. However, this consumer feminism is often individualized and constructed as personal choice or individual equality, and thus figured quite differently from Second Wave feminism's emphasis on social change and liberation. Because of postfeminism's focus on the individual, we can read the mainstream embrace of girl power as a restabilization of particular categories of gender, so that this "radical" challenge can also move toward the entrenchment of conventional gender relations.

Nonetheless, if the Spice Girls and the WNBA are any indication, gender politics is no longer popularly understood as the preserve of angry Second Wave feminists stuck in the 1960s and 1970s, a group historically demonized by the media and public alike.[22] Rather, the decade of the 1990s brought a novel kind of attention to gender politics, and female "empowerment" became the buzz word—not in marginalized political communities, but squarely within mainstream commercial culture. While this kind of empowerment clearly references economic power and the recognition of adolescent (and pre-adolescent) girls as an important market segment, it also seems to address a politico-social power represented in terms of feminist subjectivity. As I've argued throughout this book, Nickelodeon has built its entire self-image around this concept of empowerment. Within the context of girl power, the channel's claim to empower its audience has particular resonance, since television's history as a medium that favors boy characters and boy-based programs means that the relationship between "empowerment" and children's television is especially fraught. Thus, while part of an emphasis on the empowerment of youth clearly signals a larger cultural shift in definitions of childhood itself, it is also reflective of shifting feminist politics, where access to female empowerment is increasingly found within commercial culture, rather than "outside" the hegemonic mainstream.[23]

Clearly, to invoke the term "power" in direct connection with girls is an ideologically complex move and has several different facets. Of course, the most economically significant way in which power connects to girls is the increasing recognition of young girls and adolescents as an important consumer group—a group that has more and more money to spend each year on "girl power" products.[24] Another important way in which power is connected with girls in the media context of Nickelodeon is through the particular gender representations on the network's original programming. In 1991, Nickelodeon launched its hit "tween" program, *Clarissa Explains It All*, featuring a young girl as its lead character. Much of Nickelodeon's claim to empower children rests in the way in which the network stands out as "different" in an increasingly competitive children's media market. In the early 1990s, focusing on girls in children's television programs was certainly different. The curator of the Nickelodeon retrospective, David Bushman, commented: "I think Nickelodeon has empowered kids in a lot of ways . . . but I think they've specifically empowered young girls, and that's a really important thing that Nickelodeon deserves a lot of credit for. This whole idea that you could not make girl-centric shows because boys wouldn't watch them, they disproved that theory."[25] Some industry professionals mark the debut of *Clarissa Explains It All* as a crucial turning point for Nickelodeon, the moment in which the network established itself as an organization dedicated to taking risks to more accurately represent and appeal to a child audience—the moment when Nickelodeon's "difference" clearly made a difference in how the channel was perceived by the industry. The success of *Clarissa* was undoubtedly a motivation not only for Nickelodeon to continue to produce shows about girls (it followed *Clarissa* with other successful programs: *The Secret World of Alex Mack* (1994), *The Mystery Files of Shelby Woo* (1996), *The Wild Thornberries* (1998), *The Amanda Show* (1999), and *As Told by Ginger* (2000), among others) but also for other networks to create programming that challenges "the boys-won't-watch-girls" myth. In this sense, Nickelodeon is an important *producer* of girl power politics, as it explicitly connects commercial representation, the sheer visibility of girls on television, with a larger recognition of girls as important empowered subjects in the social world. And this role of Nickelodeon was noticed by not only the larger children's television industry but also by at least some of the channel's audience. As one fifteen-year-old girl I interviewed discussed, many of the everyday life issues she encountered—things like popularity and fitting in socially—were mirrored on broadcast television: "We had a club and we got in trouble . . . because we weren't letting everybody in the little club and stuff. And I think all that came from like, you know, the whole like television stereotype. And I don't think we were really thinking for ourselves. Like, we just wanted, 'Oh, let's be the popular group, just like on TV.' "[26] Nickelodeon offered something different to this girl and her friends—a different set of gender dynamics than those in which, in her words, "Moms are dumb and ditzy, cheerleaders are mean, jocks are stupid." These girls saw Nickelodeon programs as important in terms of how they challenged particular stereotypes (especially those that related personally to the interviewees; several of them were high school cheerleaders). For them, in any case, Nickelodeon programs offered something "different," perhaps something even empowering.

Of course, the claim that representation and greater visibility of girls in the media results in a particular kind of empowerment assumes several things. First, as I've argued in this book, to assume that media visibility leads to empowerment is to consider adolescent television audiences as active agents who position themselves in a variety of relationships with the ideological structures and messages of the media. While this may be true, it is also certainly true that these very same ideological structures and messages of the media privilege a commercial context that connects social power with consumption activity. The children I interviewed were Nickelodeon fans, and within this identity construction, they often felt that the network was paying attention to them.

8. Clarissa Darling and her best friend Sam in the opening sequence of *Clarissa Explains It All*, 1991.

This leads me to the second, and related, point about media empowerment: the acknowledgment that adolescent girls compose an active, "empowered" audience does not necessarily "free" them from the commercial power of the mass media. To the contrary, as we witness with the increasing visibility of gay and lesbian representations on television, this kind of recognition insists on the ever-more important *connection* with the commercial power of the mass media.[27] The cultural dynamics that produced "girl power" within the constant flux of media representations of gender in the 1990s not only produced a hip new slogan but was also part of a more general shift toward "mainstreaming" feminism into popular and dominant culture.[28] Undoubtedly, this kind of media visibility carries with it a *kind* of power, in a cultural context where visibility is so often conflated with power and influence. Indeed, many of the girls I interviewed noticed that girls were often the main characters in Nickelodeon programming, but this did not seem odd or unusual to them—precisely because their generation watches television in which girl characters are more normative, a feature of contemporary television that is clearly indebted to historical efforts to make girls more visible.

Another aspect of empowerment behind the girl power movement is a more institutional one and involves not only the accounting of girls as producers of their own culture (rather than simply consumers). It also entails the transformation of the media industry itself, where more and more executives and producers are female. While, as Joy Van Fuqua argues, the relationship between women in positions of power at networks and the proliferation of strong female characters is certainly not guaranteed, it is also worth noting that, for example, the former president of Nickelodeon, Geraldine Laybourne, led the way in the children's television market in terms of creating programming with powerful girl lead characters.²⁹ As I argued in chapter 2, Laybourne was skilled at working *within* the media system as a way to change the television landscape. As Linda Simensky told me,

> Sometimes you can be more effective by working within the establishment and changing things, than you can be from sitting on the outside and complaining. So I think that a lot of people who were [at Nickelodeon] were sort of not in total agreement with the way that kids' TV was, but they found this environment where they could do things differently and feel proud. And that was Gerry [Laybourne]. That was Gerry saying, we don't have to make toy-driven shows, we don't have to work with the Hanna Barberas of the world, we can find these creators and we can make things that are better than what is out there and we can make things that are absolutely for kids, with kids in mind. Not just what adults want kids to watch, but what kids really do want to watch.³⁰

Clearly, Laybourne was invested in brand development, and highlighting girls was a sure way to construct Nickelodeon as a "different" network, thus adding to the channel's successful development as a brand. Yet it remains the case that despite the market motive and the ways in which Laybourne's commitment to "girl programming" was part of a smart brand campaign, the channel *did* produce more shows for girls. Another important female executive at Nickelodeon, Linda Ellerbee, adds to the feminist ethos at the channel, where Ellerbee's production company, Lucky Duck Productions, produces the widely acclaimed *Nick News*. The news program is also hosted by Ellerbee, who often injects a relatively progressive political ideology into her perspective on relevant news, from racial hate crimes to problems with bullying girls at school. This institutional side of girl power production coexists with a proliferation of less mainstream forms of girl power culture, such as 'zines like *Bust* and *Hues* and "Do It Yourself" (DIY) forms of cultural production.³¹

These elements of empowerment—as a consumer group, as media visibility, and as cultural producers—are, as I've argued, all crucial elements in the constitution of media audiences as consumer citizens, as well as necessary for the articulation of girl power–oriented identity. The dynamics between these variations within the theme of empowerment are complicated and represent significant tensions and even ambivalence within feminisms. Media visibility is an important component of empowerment, but it is far from unproblematic, as scholars such as Stuart Hall, Herman Gray, Larry Gross, and Bonnie Dow have pointed out.³² As Gross, writing about the increasing media visibility of gays and lesbians, succinctly put it: "as we're learning, visibility, like truth, is rarely pure and never simple."[33] One of the key tensions regarding girl power exists not between the mainstream media and feminism but rather within feminism itself, and the assumed generational differences between Second Wave and postfeminists. In order to better situate Nickelodeon's commitment to girl power, we need to first situate girl power within the politics of feminism itself.

GENERATIONAL DIFFERENCES: FEMINISM FOR WHOM?

In her discussion of contemporary forms of popular culture, Angela McRobbie identifies the 1990s and early twenty-first century as a "postfeminist cultural space." This space, she argues, is a context in which "we have a field of transformation in which feminist values come to be engaged with, and to some extent incorporated across, civil society in institutional practices, in education, in the work environment, and in the media."[34] However, this engagement most often results in a denial of those very same feminist values so that "postfeminist" popular culture is more accurately antifeminist in its trajectory. Postfeminism, understood in this manner, is thus a different political dynamic from Third Wave feminism, which is positioned more overtly as a kind of feminist politics, one that extends the historical trajectory of First and Second Wave feminism to better accommodate contemporary political culture and the logic of consumer citizens. Postfeminism, on the other hand, is, as McRobbie puts it, "feminism taken into account," a process in which feminist values and ideologies are acknowledged only to be found dated and passé and thus negated.

Importantly, McRobbie sees this process of repudiation taking place in the popular media, where, "a field of new gender norms emerges (e.g., *Sex and the City, Ally McBeal*) in which female freedom and ambition appear to be taken for granted, unreliant on any past struggle (an antiquated word), and certainly not requiring any new, fresh political understanding, but instead merely a state into which young women appear to have been thrown, or in which they find themselves, giving rise to ambivalence and misgiving."[35] Part of young female identity in this contemporary context means to engage this media narrative about new gender norms—not in a traditional politically engaged way but rather in what McRobbie calls a "ritualistic denunciation." This denunciation occurs when feminism is acknowledged, but in a trivialized fashion, shelved as something that may have been useful in the past but is clearly out of date in today's world.

This denunciation of feminism thus informs the ways in which postfeminism situates issues of gender within commercial and popular culture. This commercial embrace of postfeminism is often invoked as the crucial difference between it and other feminisms because postfeminism is understood as more representative for a new generation of women. This struggle over the "ownership" of the politics of feminism seems to be the primary lens through which contemporary feminisms are understood; indeed, one of the most impassioned discourses involving feminism lately has not been generated by differing particular political platforms, or a specific egregious act of discrimination against women, but from the arguments, contradictions, and general disavowals between different manifestations of feminisms. Within the contemporary context there are different feminisms (just as there were many different feminisms that made up the broad "Second Wave Feminist Movement" in the United States). Postfeminism thus has a vastly different political focus from Third Wave feminism, where the former eschews gender politics as rather old fashioned and dreary, and the latter refigures gender politics in a commercially bounded culture. There is clearly a lack of generational cohesion here between the various feminisms, making it difficult to figure out one's position within feminism. And yet, as Lisa Hogeland points out, generation is not a significant explanation for differences. The alternative, recognizing problems within feminism, means confronting the "unevenness" of the movement itself and "fundamental differences in our visions of feminism's tasks and accomplishments."[36] One of these differences concerns media visibility. In part because of the proliferation of media images of strong, independent female characters, many contemporary feminists seem to regard consumer culture as a place of empowerment and as a means of differentiating themselves from Second Wave feminists (although empowerment itself is read differently by postfeminists and Third Wave feminists), which have tended on the whole to be critical of the misogyny of popular consumer culture.

The embrace of consumer culture is the site for tension around the concept of the individual within feminisms as well. One of the key differences between the "cultural space of postfeminism" and Second Wave feminist politics in the United States and the United Kingdom is the focus on female individualism and individual empowerment. As McRobbie points out, postfeminism shifts feminism into something in the past—not just the ideas and values of feminism but the emancipatory politics and community activism of feminism as well.[37] Key to this shift is that in postfeminism there is what McRobbie calls a "double failure": "In its over-emphasis on agency and the apparent capacity to choose in a more individualized society, it has no way of showing how subject formation occurs by means of notions of choice *and* assumed gender equality coming together to actually ensure adherence to new unfolding norms of femininity."[38]

This move toward focusing on individual empowerment rather than coalition politics or structural change forces consideration of the following questions:

once feminism is represented as a commodity in precisely the mainstream it has traditionally challenged, can we still talk about it as political? Can the social elements of feminism be represented and enacted within the context of popular culture's relentless celebration of the individual, or is popular culture by design misogynist, as many feminists have argued? Are we simply living in, as Naomi Klein claims in her book *No Logo,* a "Representation Nation," where visibility in the media takes precedence over "real" politics?[39] Again, for those who consider themselves to be Third Wave feminists, such as Jennifer Baumgardner and Amy Richards, authors of the Third Wave feminist tract *Manifesta: Young Women, Feminism, and the Future,* the argument is made that this kind of media visibility is absolutely crucial to politics.[40] For those who position themselves as postfeminists, media visibility is precisely the evidence needed to "prove" that feminist politics is history. And yet, as Bonnie Dow argues, while the liberal feminist politics of equal opportunity and equal pay for equal work have been somewhat normalized (although the material reality of these politics is not always or even often achieved), it is also the case that the process of "mainstreaming" an oppositional politics often functions as a hegemonic strategy to diffuse those very politics. In other words, the normalization of feminism has prevented it from existing as a discrete politics; it rather emerges as a kind of slogan or a generalized "brand."[41]

However, for Third Wave feminism, this normalization of feminism within the media and popular culture has encouraged an embrace of feminism as political; as Baumgardner and Richards argue, young women who make up the Third Wave are "born with feminism simply in the water," a kind of "political fluoride" that protects against the "decay" of earlier sexism and gender discrimination.[42] The struggle for "positive" representations in the media is certainly not over, but we also do not experience the same media that we did even ten years ago, when, as Susan Douglas contends, the most pervasive media story remained "structured around boys taking action, girls waiting for the boys, and girls rescued by the boys."[43] There has been a clear historical trajectory of incorporating feminist ideologies into mainstream popular culture, ranging, as Dow points out, from the 1970s television show *One Day at a Time* to shows in the 1980s and 1990s such as *Murphy Brown* and *Designing Women.*

As a contemporary social and political movement, then, feminism itself has been rescripted (but not necessarily disavowed) so as to allow its smooth incorporation into the world of commerce and corporate culture—what Robert Goldman calls "commodity feminism."[44] This commodity feminism has resulted in a complex dynamic that is directly concerned not only with general gender issues but also with issues of cultural territory: as part of a general self-identification,

Second Wave feminism is at times overly romanticized in terms of its commit-ment to social protest politics, and there seems to be a kind of reluctance on the part of Second Wave feminists to rethink and redefine politics according to the stated needs and desires of contemporary feminism (Susan Brownmiller, in a now infamous *Time* magazine interview about Third Wave and postfeminists, claimed, "they're just not movement people").[45] Part of this reluctance to rethink contemporary feminism concerns the ways in which gender identity is also always about racial identity; perhaps because of the commercial "urban" context of many contemporary feminists, the intersectionality of race and gender has been acknowledged in ways that challenge the exclusionary history of Second Wave feminism. For many Third Wave feminists, the territorialism that sur-rounds some of the current politics of feminism seems to be about salvaging the name of *feminism* (and, presumably, the politics that ground and historicize the name). Baumgardner and Richards, Barbara Findlen, and Naomi Wolf, for ex-ample, participate in this kind of salvation project, the project of not necessarily appropriating a historical concept of feminism but widening its borders to in-clude more contemporary manifestations of the politics.[46] While in theory this makes sense, and certainly these authors at times do justice to the legacies of feminisms, Baumgardner and Richards also insist that "underneath all of these names and agendas is the same old feminism."[47] However, it is precisely *not* the same old feminism that structures the politics of postfeminism. The insistence that it is stems from a range of sentiments, from nostalgic yearnings for "real" social protest movements to respectful acknowledgments of political practices that open up economic and social opportunities to a sheer base desire to "be-long" to something. Without discounting these sentiments, it is also the case that the lingering in this generational territory battle between Second Wave and postfeminism has paralyzed the debate and prevented the further development and refinement of a feminist praxis and material feminist politics. In turn, this paralysis has allowed for a more conservative postfeminism to become dominant in media representation, so that feminist politics—be it Second Wave, post-feminist, or some other version—is rendered obsolete in the contemporary his-torical moment of hip empowerment.

Part of the complexities of the current feminist landscape means that the idea that "we" all share a feminist politics, that we all "want the same thing," is highly problematic, as it clearly connects to history: not only does this commit the same mistake made by many Second Wave feminists who insisted on a universal femi-nist standpoint but it also functions as a kind of refusal to identify what the "thing" is that we all apparently want.[48] In other words, if "we" all want the same thing in feminism, what is it? A liberal version of equality? Or a more radically

configured understanding of liberation from patriarchy? Or simply a more frequent, more "positive" media appearance? And if this is true, does contemporary
feminism address other factors of identity, such as race and sexuality, in ways that
challenge the exclusive nature of Second Wave feminism? This struggle over
territory has encouraged feminisms to exist primarily as a turf war. The politics
of feminism is quite obviously different for different generations, and Third
Wave feminists and postfeminists are produced in a very different cultural and
political context from that of feminists of the twentieth century. It then becomes
impossible to cohere contemporary manifestations of feminisms as a singular
"movement"; rather, feminisms exist in the present context as a politics of contradiction and ambivalence. Rather than dismiss these politics as an elaborate
corporate masquerade, one that intends to encourage an ever more vigorous
consumer body politic at the expense of social change, it makes more sense
to theorize how power functions in contradictory ways within the context of
consumerism.

One way to do this is to situate postfeminism as an ironic configuration of
power, a configuration that, as McRobbie points out, skillfully uses the language
of feminist cultural studies "against itself."[49] The ironic use of oppositional language and counterhegemonic practices within contemporary mainstream commodity culture has been widely theorized; for instance, Naomi Klein understands
today's brand culture to be using the language of identity politics as an effective
means through which brand loyalty can be assured; Malcolm Gladwell has theorized the economic importance of "cool" in the contemporary political economy; and Joseph Heath and Andrew Potter have argued that countercultural
values have always been, ironically, "intensely entrepreneurial." In fact, as they
point out, the commodification of rebellion reflects "the most authentic spirit of
capitalism."[50] McRobbie theorizes a similar kind of dynamic within postfeminist
consumer culture, where much of contemporary advertising and popular culture
uses a particular kind of irony when representing women, as if to suggest that the
"problem" of objectification of women's bodies is one of history; women "get it"
about objectification, and *because* of this understanding, it is acceptable—indeed,
even ironically empowering—to objectify women's bodies in the most blatantly
demeaning ways. Thus, popular media functions as a kind of critique of mainstream culture through the strategies of irony, camp, and a kind of postmodern
cynicism—but within a conventional narrative framework. Current advertising
uses this kind of self-reflexivity to both critique and ultimately sell products.[51]
Indeed, decades of economic seesawing, progressively more sophisticated marketing strategies, and gradually more blurry boundaries between consumption
habits and political and cultural beliefs have produced, among other things, a

generation that is savvy, "smart," and generally perceived to be disaffected or cynical about culture. This general ideology makes it difficult to sustain "old-fashioned" feminist politics that involve understanding women as victims of patriarchy, or the theorizing of structural impediments in terms of employment and child-care, or even more general assumptions about the various ways in the contemporary climate in which women are oppressed because *they are* women. In other words, the cynicism of the current generation is directed not only toward consumer culture but also to historical political formations, such as feminism.

Part of this has to do with the fact that irony as politics is a much more personal kind of politics than a more activist, public politics. As Jeffrey Sconce says about "smart films" of the 1990s, "American smart cinema has displaced the more activist emphasis on the 'social politics' of power, institutions, representation and subjectivity so central to 1960s and 1970s art cinema (especially in its 'political' wing), and replaced it by concentrating, often with ironic disdain, on the 'personal politics' of power, communication, emotional dysfunction and identity in white middle-class culture."[52] The consumer culture that Klein characterizes as "ironic consumption" seems to evacuate politics from the landscape in one sense because of the intense focus on personal identity. And it is this focus on personal identity and the rhetoric of choice that characterizes not only post-feminist culture but, as I discuss in the next chapter, also the "new economy" of race, where representations of personal success and media visibility seem to provide enough evidence that historical struggles over the enfranchisement of minorities and minority communities were crucial interventions but no longer necessary in the current media economy.

NICKELODEON AND GIRL POWER PROGRAMMING

Catherine Driscoll, in her recent study of adolescent girl culture, points out that "the opposition between pleasure in consumption figured as conformity and pleasure against the grain of such conformity does not provide a useful model for considering girl culture, where resistance is often just another form of conformity and conformity may be compatible with other resistances."[53] The ideological themes of girl power that are represented in Nickelodeon programs such as *Clarissa Explains It All* and *As Told by Ginger,* where the girls are strong, independent, and often unruly, are situated in relation to normative definitions of girls as obedient and docile—even as these "resistant" themes are marketed as a particular kind of product. So, for example, during the commercial break for an episode of *As Told by Ginger,* an animated program that features a group of intelligent and often ironic middle-school girls, one could easily see an ad for a "girl power" doll: girls playing with Barbie, or something similar, dressed up in sporty clothes carrying a skateboard or a radio. In ads on Nickelodeon, the presence of "girl power" does not rule out that of "girly," as one might also see an ad for something such as Care Bears or My Little Pony toys, which are hyperbolically feminine and encourage traditionally gendered play involving care and nurturing. Nickelodeon will not accept explicitly violent advertising but apparently has no problem accepting sexist ads that run counter to the kinds of values the network promotes in "girl power" shows. Indeed, this kind of juxtaposition so often shown on the media, between a kind of political agency and a commitment to consumerism, is one of the reasons that it is so difficult to theorize what exactly girl power is, as well as whether or not it is a "feminist" discourse and practice. That is to say, the typical categories that are used to talk about agency do not really apply to this contemporary context, since, like contemporary consumer citizenship, girl culture is ambiguous from the ground up.[54]

Discussing the exaggerated negative reaction to the Spice Girls and the subsequent dismissal of the group by critics as "inauthentic" and manufactured, Driscoll asks, "Can feminism be a mass-produced, globally distributed product, and can merchandised relations to girls be authentic?"[55] Driscoll understands girl culture to be primarily characterized by "unresolvable tensions" between agency and conformity. She argues, "To actually embrace the community alternative girl culture imagines requires a degree of complicity with systems with which they claim to be incompatible, and they produce legitimated models of agency within the systems they say exclude them."[56] This complicity with the system is precisely where Nickelodeon steps in; the discourse of girl power created a new niche in television programming and led to the creation of girl-centered and girl-powered shows. Nickelodeon programs can be seen as potentially innovative efforts to address gender representation in children's television. Not only does the channel create more programming that features girls; it also actively works against reinforcing gender stereotypes about feminine appearance. Several executives mentioned this element of Nickelodeon's commitment to kids; as John Hardman, an executive developer, said when asked if Nickelodeon made programs just for little girls: "We try to reach as many bases as possible. It's quite a challenge because the marketers say that girls don't buy certain toys. Marketers say we have to make the girl attractive to be a good selling product. Take the *Wild Thornberries* for instance. Our philosophy with the little girl in that program is that she's not as beautiful but she's smart, capable and industrious. That's important to us."[57]

However, the presentation and rescripting of gender identity for girls on Nickelodeon is not as seamless as the network's subtext of girl power would lead one to believe. Nickelodeon demonstrates Driscoll's point about the "unresolvable tensions" between agency and conformity: the network overtly situates gender identity (or "positive gender portrayal") as an important element of programming, but at the same time, the network's definition of empowerment is part of a larger system of consumer citizenship, where the recognition of an audience as a potentially lucrative one confers power on that same audience. As such, the network shies away from being "too political" when it comes to gender politics, framing programming decisions in a liberal rhetoric of personhood—or, in this case, "kidhood." This allows Nickelodeon to occupy a position of general inclusion rather than appear to be specifically invested in a particular group. In this way, the channel constructs girl power as ambiguous—gender asymmetry within television needs to be addressed, but through the framework of "gender neutrality" so that Nickelodeon's stance never becomes overtly invested in gender politics. As Nickelodeon executive Cyma Zarghami, when asked about why there are so many girl protagonists on Nickelodeon programs, said: "There aren't any more than boy protagonists. It just feels like a lot because we have some. We care less about gender in our programs and more about kids. Our demographic research shows that boys will watch programs with girl protagonists, so we've shattered that myth."[58] Without diminishing the importance of myth shattering, it is the development (and subsequent affirmation) of Nickelodeon as a *brand* that takes risks on behalf of kids that constitutes the politics at the channel— not necessarily a feminist commitment to alleviating gender inequality. As one fifteen-year-old girl I interviewed commented on Nickelodeon's "gender neutrality," "I think another thing is, Nickelodeon, with the exception of ones like *Alex Mack* where it's a good versus evil one, where it's just like a kind of a regular life thing, the antagonists aren't like completely bad. They always show like their good side. So even if the cheerleaders are stuck up, there's always one or two episodes where they come out of their shell and they're nice."[59] Another Nickelodeon executive, Bruce Friend, commented when asked if girls are explicitly targeted for focus group research, "It's not something that we go out of our way for. We have a gender-neutral philosophy. Some shows test better with girls but often, we're surprised by what girls like. Take the movie *Good Burger.* People thought it would be a movie for boys, but in our research, girls tested very well too. We have a very open mind about what they will like."[60] Having an "open mind" allows the network to accumulate cultural capital in the industry and with frustrated parents looking for programs that feature positive images of girls. At the same time, Nickelodeon's "open mind" avoids alienating boys (and antifeminist or unconcerned parents) while enjoying the status of being a "different" network. Indeed, as Donna Mitroff points out, the politicizing of Nickelodeon as being the "channel for girls" has a great deal to do with fortuitous timing.[61] Nickelodeon parlayed this good sense of timing into incredible success—and, along the way, changed the landscape of children's television, especially in terms of girl-themed characters and programs. This reflects a central contradiction within consumer citizenship, where the *consequence* of a market-driven strategy may be more positive gender representations, but this consequence is framed in nonpolitical terms. This dynamic is commensurate with postfeminist politics in general, which generally disavows power as a constitutive factor in gender construction; as such, a postfeminist critique often neglects a careful consideration of power relations in contemporary performances of gender. Indeed, as McRobbie argues, when mainstream feminism became a kind of commodity in the early 1990s young feminists embraced this move rightly as important and significant. However, a superficial focus on the postfeminist slogan "girl power" allowed for a deflection away from some of the ways in which mainstream feminism became connected with dominant forms of power and subjugation. Calling specifically for a reengagement with theories of power, McRobbie makes a crucial point: "Without serious engagement with Freud, or with the work of Foucault, or indeed Deleuze, the dynamics of pain within pleasure, the uncertainty and ambivalence of pleasure, the whole pink and frilly world of affect and emotion within which the girl herself is permitted to 'become,' the intensity of focus on body and its surfaces, and of course the heteronormative assumptions underpinning these endless rituals of sexual differentiation, which are conditions of youthful female subjecthood, have been quite absent from much of this recent dialogue."[62] This is the case with Nickelodeon, in its deliberate move away from politics and critiques of power by consciously adopting a "gender-neutral" position.

CLARISSA EXPLAINS IT ALL

With the debut of *Clarissa*, Nickelodeon became known for risk-taking in programming and was specifically recognized as a champion for girls in television. According to the Nickelodeon press release about the show, the main character, Clarissa Darling (played by Melissa Joan Hart), "is an imaginative and very contemporary teenager who makes no bones about detailing her likes, dislikes, and fantasies. Breaking many conventions of the sitcom and using special video effects to highlight Clarissa's thoughts and plans, the series examines life through her eyes."[63] The idea of portraying "life" through the eyes of a young girl is innovative in and of itself, especially given the historical context of 1991. Nickelodeon very purposefully marketed *Clarissa* as a break-out kind of show, and the success of the program illustrated the effective marketing: boys seemed to watch

9. Clarissa Darling, 1991.

the program along with girls, and the show clearly seemed to tap into the burgeoning cultural climate of girl power. The early 1990s were already emerging as a new era for pre-adolescent and adolescent boys and girls in terms of their spending power and consumption habits, and the character of Clarissa seemed to fit perfectly in this context. Indeed, Clarissa is not the stereotypical feminine heroine who relies on a man (or a boy, in this case) to save her from the various scrapes of contemporary teenage life. Although boys are featured regularly on the show—Clarissa has a younger brother, Ferguson, who often provides the annoying foil for Clarissa's thought processes, and her best friend, Sam, is a boy her own age with whom she has a platonic relationship—the program really does revolve around the antics of Clarissa.

As the lead character, Clarissa is portrayed as an unusually mature teenager who narrates her life to the audience as one that is full of surprises, haphazard coincidences, and typical teen dilemmas. Her parents, Janet and Marshall Darling, are caricatured as "ex-hippies," and their (media-defined) sense of social responsibility shapes each episode (for example, Janet is a health nut, and Marshall is an environmentally aware architect). Each episode opens with a monologue by Clarissa, where she voices some clever remarks about the theme of that day's show. Often these opening remarks are sarcastic and self-reflexive; for example, in the episode "The Misguidance Counselor" (June 14, 1992), Clarissa begins the show with a sardonic statement: "Okay, time for another normal start of another normal day in the ever-normal Darling household." This episode goes on to spoof "normal" families, with the central narrative organized around an obviously ridiculous plan of the school's guidance counselor for Clarissa to "fit in." The process of "fitting in" is parodied as the guidance counselor enlists

Clarissa as part of the school dance committee, the cheerleaders group, and home economics class. There is a none-too-subtle critique in this episode of normative practices of femininity (evidenced by things like decorating a school auditorium for a dance, becoming a cheerleader, and taking a class in home economics that teaches skills such as cooking and knitting), as Clarissa finds herself unhappy with these practices and thus unable to "fit in." The program in general is very intertextual in that other television shows and films are often referenced and used as part of the plot: for example, at one point in this specific episode, the show parodies early family television shows such as *Ozzie and Harriet* by depicting a black-and-white television set featuring the show *Oh! Those Darlings,* complete with a head shot of Clarissa in nostalgic fifties garb, and the credit line "Clarissa Darling as Big Sis" underneath. Another episode also demonstrates this kind of ironic self-construction, where the opening line of "A Little Romance" (August 14, 1993) has Clarissa saying: "I think that it was either William Shakespeare or Sting who said, 'love is blind; love is madness; love is reason without reason.' Personally, I agree. Love is nuts!" This episode details the complexities of platonic relationships among adolescents, as Clarissa and her best friend Sam unsuccessfully "try" to be romantic.

John Hartley identifies *Clarissa* as an interesting example of a particular kind of potential civic behavior.[64] Locating the politics of citizenship within a variety of cultural artifacts and technologies within the "mediasphere," he argues that within media and commercial culture, we have moved through a series of different levels of citizenship, ranging from civic to cultural citizenship. The present moment is characterized by yet another form of citizenship, "DIY" (Do It Yourself) citizenship. DIY has a historical connection to British punk rock and has been recognized as a particular kind of alternative cultural production (especially in terms of girl power ideology) such as 'zines and riot grrl websites.[65] Interestingly, Hartley identifies the very mainstream *Clarissa Explains It All* as illustrative of DIY citizenship because the character of Clarissa is smart, in control of her environment, and she disrupts conventional modes of representation by talking directly to the camera. As Hartley argues, the character of Clarissa marks an important departure from conventional representations of young girls on television because she is the "undisputed centre of her show . . . a mainstream, fully-formed, 'adult' character, articulate, interesting, full of initiative, clever and congenial."[66]

Hartley continues by arguing that Clarissa is a particular kind of citizen, in a world of children's media that often excludes children as citizens, both ideologically and in practice. He identifies *Clarissa Explains It All* as a program that specifically attends to issues of citizenship for girls, and in that way the show is

10. Clarissa with her
mother, father, and
brother Ferguson, 1991.
11. Clarissa and her
mother, 1991.

disruptive of cultural mythologies of gender for young girls: the victim, the
unintelligent, the dependent.[67] Clarissa is quite clearly the opposite of all of these
personality characteristics. Not only that, the show itself is often organized as a
kind of *critique* of the constructed nature of cultural mythologies—of girls, of
boys, of romance, of popularity. In this way, the character of Clarissa represents
the kind of contradictions present in the broader politics of girl power: she is the
typical "powerless" adolescent girl in the sense of her position in a larger culture
that privileges both adults and males, but she is nonetheless a powerful figure
within commercial culture. Hartley describes DIY citizenship as bringing about a
kind of "semiotic self-determination" where representation of agency *becomes*
agency in a particular televisual society; in this way, Clarissa represents a *kind* of
girl power feminism that makes sense in this particular historical moment, and

under these particular conditions.[68] Importantly, though, Nickelodeon carefully constructs Clarissa *not* as feminist icon but just a "regular" kid. As Zarghami comments, "Clarissa was our first big success with girl protagonists. She ran from 1989 to about 1991. She was so successful, though, because her issues were not specific to girls but to all kids: school, friends and homework."[69] The network carefully maintains a "gender-neutral" stance—Clarissa's "issues were not specific to girls but to all kids"—while collecting cultural capital for being the channel that pays attention to girls. Without directly interrogating the practices of femininity that Clarissa found problematic in the series—or engaging with a critique of the power relations that support these practices—Nickelodeon was able to remain "neutral" and produce a profoundly ambivalent form of girl power.

Through its intertextuality, its unconventional methods such as narrating directly to the camera, and its casting as lead a kind of wacky teenage girl, *Clarissa* represents some of the important themes of girl power ideology. For example, in the episode "Can't Buy Me Love" (September 8, 1992), Clarissa opens the show with these remarks: "What's in and what's out: two harmless little questions that make otherwise rational people break out in hives." The recognition here of both the importance of fitting in socially, *and* the superficiality of that desire to fit in, mirrors the larger tensions of girl power ideology. The episode continues when Clarissa's brother Ferguson is befriended by the local "rich kid," predictably named J. Elliot Fundsworth III, and is asked to pledge to join an exclusive yacht club, the Young Americans Junior Yacht Club. Within this relationship, Ferguson is transformed from the solidly middle-class boy that he is to a pretentious snob, interested only in elite membership at the club. J. Elliot Fundsworth III, not surprisingly, is a fraud who befriends Ferguson only to gain access to Clarissa, on whom he has a crush. Although Ferguson is constantly at odds with Clarissa in the show, it is Clarissa who "saves" him from the clutches of the elitist, arrogant boy.

The episode is peppered with subtle (and some not so subtle) messages about class politics; although they are certainly not radical in that the episode focuses only on the very wealthy, there is nonetheless a pro-social message intended. More interesting, however, is the role that Clarissa herself plays as the savior of her brother, and the one who rejects the love interest of the selfish rich boy. She is clearly the lead character in the program, and each episode centrally revolves around not only her experiences as a young adolescent girl but also around the contradictions between political action and individual subjectivity that are inherent in current definitions of girl power culture. The last episode of the program, "The Last Episode," which aired October 1, 1994, depicted these contradictions on several different levels. The episode revolved around Clarissa's decision to go to college in Cincinnati, Ohio, to study journalism. Although her decision about college had ostensibly been made, when Clarissa wrote an article for a local newspaper about teen angst and malls (could there be a more illustrative girl power topic?), she was offered an internship at the *New York Daily Post.* She then was faced with choosing between college and career, a plot theme that carried on the show's explicit connection of gender identity with a kind of agency or citizenship by referencing a familiar feminist argument about the impossibility of women "having it all."[70]

Clarissa, because she is constituted as just "another kid," is an important icon for this particular historical moment, but she does not necessarily embody *feminist* empowerment. Her empowerment as a particular kind of citizen is assumed to be more generally connected to an increase in "empowerment" in the media and in the larger social world (in fact, "The Last Episode" is reminiscent of another media power player when Clarissa plays Murphy of *Murphy Brown* fame, in a spoof called "Murphy Darling"). And, like postfeminism itself, the agency of the character of Clarissa is reflective of a contradictory version of citizenship; the empowerment that it articulates for young girls does not include a model for how to *access* that citizenship except through representation. The tensions between representing girl power citizenship through the media and accessing that citizenship in a way that has larger implications for gender ideologies and practice define girl power.

Nickelodeon followed the success of Clarissa with other shows featuring girls in interesting lead roles, such as *The Mystery Files of Shelby Woo* and *The Secret World of Alex Mack.* Both of these shows, like *Clarissa,* feature an adolescent girl as a lead character. By the time *Alex Mack* aired, in 1995, Nickelodeon had become well-known in the industry for its commitment to gender-neutral programming. *Alex Mack,* a program that revolved around a thirteen-year-old girl with superpowers (gained through a chemical accident), clearly makes a statement about empowerment and girls as each episode focused on the contradictions between being a "normal" girl and one with power. Each episode of *Alex Mack* was a navigation through teen life—especially teen angst—through a framework of good (represented by Alex and her family) and evil (represented by the chemical plant that pursues Alex for experimentation). Alex's sister on the show, Annie, is an unqualified genius, thus depicting the power of being a smart girl alongside the supernatural girl. *The Mystery Files of Shelby Woo* was a youth-oriented action mystery television series that ran between 1996 and 1999. Starring Irene Ng as the title character, the series revolved around the adventures of a young teenage girl who lives with her grandfather. Shelby Woo works as an unpaid intern at the local police department and uses this context to develop her apparently unique insight, allowing her to help the police in solving mysteries. In this show, Nickelodeon reshaped a historically male-occupied role, a detective, and situated a girl as the lead role. The fact that Shelby Woo is Asian American, living with an immigrant grandfather, also adds to the complexity of the channel's commitment to girls. Nickelodeon framed both programs within the tradition of *Clarissa,* whereby, after the programs were successful, the network intimated that girls were rather "incidentally" in lead roles, allowing Nickelodeon to both claim the status of being the channel for girls while simultaneously arguing that it simply looks out for "all kids."

AS TOLD BY GINGER

As Told by Ginger (ATBG) was a Nickelodeon original animated production, which aired from 2000 to 2004. The show featured a main cast of five twelve- to thirteen-year-old girls, and generally revolved around the issues that surround this group in their school, Lucky Middle School. Although the program does feature three younger boys (all of whom are siblings of the main characters), the episodes are primarily concerned with issues that pertain to the girl characters. The characters are drawn in ways that challenge traditional forms of animation in several ways. Thematically, the show features characters who are often situated in oppositional ways to dominant norms: Ginger's mother, Lois, is a single mother who has clear feminist values; Ginger's boyfriend, Darren, is African American and thus challenges historical taboos (especially in children's programming) of interracial romance. Ginger herself is clearly very intelligent and writes poetry that is often featured on the show and frequently depicts feelings of exclusion and loneliness. One poem, "And She Was Gone," featured on an episode with the same name, opens this way:

> She chose to walk alone
> Though others wondered why
> Refused to look before her,
> Kept eyes cast upwards,
> Towards the sky.

> She didn't have companions
> No need for earthly things.
> Only wanted freedom,
> From what she felt were
> Puppet strings.

12. Ginger Foutley, from
As Told by Ginger, 2004.

The poem continues along these lines and clearly illustrates feelings of pressure to fit in socially, as well as a critique of how social norms contain and control girls—especially those who long for "freedom."

Visually, *ABTG* also challenges traditional forms of animation with its quirky style. Current fashion is very important on the show; unlike most animated characters who wear the same thing in every episode (think of Charlie Brown's t-shirt, Strawberry Shortcake's dress, or even SpongeBob SquarePants' underwear), the characters on *ATBG* wear "new" clothes almost every episode, always in the current styles. Indeed, on the official *ATBG* website, fans can click on different outfits of each of the characters to find the one they like best. This attention to style—and how important it is to middle-school girls—is at odds with Ginger's feminist mother and Ginger's heartfelt poetry. These contradictions exist side-by-side in the program, exemplifying the ambiguities that form the crux of postfeminism.

Despite Nickelodeon's claims to attract a "cross-over" audience, the audience for *ATBG* seems to be primarily girls; on various fan-sites of the show, there were a few obvious male voices on the message boards, but the overwhelming proportion of participants on the websites were girls. In fact, some of the girls I interviewed about this show commented on what they saw as the gender exclusivity of the program: when asked if boys would watch *ATBG*, they generally said no: "Because it's mostly about girls . . . if a boy watched *As Told by Ginger,* then it wouldn't be that good." Another girl claimed that "he [a boy watching *ATBG*] wouldn't understand . . . because it's mostly about girls, because the main part is Ginger."[71] The program has enjoyed some critical acclaim: it has been nominated three times for an Emmy award (animated series in less than an hour category)

13. Ginger and her friends in trendy clothes, 2004.

but lost to *The Simpsons* and *Futurama*. Like those other animated programs, *ATBG* also presents social commentary within each episode; the girl power issues that garner a kind of social power, such as popularity, cliques, the culture of "cool," are presented in this program within a context of critique. *ATBG* is at times self-reflexive, using parody and irony to critique social norms and standards about gender and class. The main theme of the show revolves around some of the very same issues that *Nick News* covers in "real life"; Ginger Foutley, the lead character, is accepted into the popular, "cool" clique at school but also hangs with her long-time friends, who are also represented as intelligent nerds. In fact, in one fan website, Ginger is described in the following manner: "Ginger Foutley is a regular kid—although maybe a bit more reflective than most—who's still trying to figure out who she is. The social structure of Lucky Junior High grosses her out, but she's also kind of obsessed with it. If she were part of the cool clique, she swears she would do things differently. Yet her bluff is called when Courtney, a princess of cool, decides Ginger can hang. With one foot in each crowd, Ginger constantly flip-flops between her loyalty to her old friends and her desire to be cool with a capital C . . . Welcome to junior high!"[72] The tension between wanting to "be cool with a capital C" in a commercially driven culture and a dedication to genuine female friendship is a marker of girl power. While this is certainly not a new theme in children's programming (the subject of the "cool crowd" seems to be a staple of programming targeted to the "tween" segment of the market), the refusal to resolve the issue makes *ATBG* unique.

In other words, most other children's programs that deal with issues of popularity seem to claim the moral high ground and come out for "genuine" friendship at the expense of the "obviously" more superficial popular social group. Yet

14. Ginger's "cool" friend Courtney, 2004.

ATBG plays with the tension more, even with characters other than Ginger. For example, Courtney Gripling, the "princess of cool," is cast in a Professor Higgins sort of role, a popular girl who wants to remake Ginger: "Totally self-absorbed and opportunistic, Courtney takes her position as Most Popular Girl very seriously. She prides herself on the diplomatic control and manipulation of her classmates. She's intrigued and baffled, however, by Ginger's backbone and real friendships. So she sets out to pluck the 'unknown' from the dregs of everyday life and make her a 'Popular Girl.' "[73] In this role, Courtney is at times more successful than others, but there is a general refusal to cast the characters universally as either superficial or genuine.

This tension is not simply a side theme of *ATBG*; rather, it forms the substance of almost every episode, often represented through a strategy of parody and self-reflexivity. There is a general subtext that mocks the distinctions between social groups and characterizes the groups as trivial, even while the show constantly focuses on social groups, thus legitimating them for the "tween" audience. For example, in one episode, "Family Therapy" (May 25, 2002), the contradictions between the superficial "cool" group and the genuine "real" group are brought into bold relief through the figure of Ginger's friend Macie Lightfoot. Macie, definitely not a member of the "cool" group, is riddled with neuroses and is an incredibly insecure, self-conscious character. In this particular episode, the program's theme revolves around the fact that Macie and one of the "cool" girls, Mipsy, both have birthdays on the same day. While Mipsy's birthday is announced at a school assembly and the "cool" girls immediately begin to plan a party (complete with a sushi chef flown in from Japan), Macie waits for what she anticipates will be a surprise party given by her parents. Unfortunately, her parents, both child psychologists, forget her birthday and need to be reminded about the date by Ginger. In an effort to compensate for their forgetfulness, they shower Macie with attention. However, they are so unconnected to their daughter that they don't realize that she is turning thirteen and treat her instead as if she were a five-year-old—they throw her a party with a petting zoo, they give her a swing set for a present, and give her a party dress more appropriate for a very young child. Macie originally responds to the positive attention, since she has received so little from her parents. The social commentary of the program—the child psychologists forgetting their own child's birthday, the hyperbolic character of Mipsy's birthday party, Macie's feelings of being neglected—positions it within the same popular cultural realm as shows like *The Simpsons* that offer ironic critique as part of the entertainment. *ATBG* is different from *Clarissa*—for one thing, it is produced at a very different historical moment, and the increased normalization of feminist rhetoric since 1991 (when *Clarissa* was first aired) has an obvious presence on the program. The issues of cliques, although always part of the landscape in adolescent culture, occupy a new position of salience in the early twenty-first century, where attention to girls has led to not only an increase in commercial products for this audience but also an increased public attention to the issues that characterize girl culture.

NICK NEWS

The issue of girl power is also addressed on Nickelodeon's award-winning children's news program, *Nick News*. *Nick News* is a half-hour weekly news program, shown every Sunday evening. Each regular edition of *Nick News* covers three or four topics per episode, and there is also a special edition *Nick News*, which devotes an entire show to one theme or special topic. *Nick News* is clearly different from *Clarissa* or *ATBG* because it is nonfiction; as a news program, it clearly addresses its audience as a different kind of "citizen" from the one the entertainment programs envision as their audience. As David Buckingham has argued, "for all its shortcomings, news journalism remains the primary means of access to the public sphere of political debate and activity."[74] The show is hosted by Linda Ellerbee, a public figure who is well known not only as a feminist but also as an important children's advocate.

According to Buckingham, the key to *Nick News*' success is the willingness of the program to be more "adventurous" with information and to "rethink politics" for children. *Nick News* at times achieves the goal of establishing the relevance of traditional politics, but it is also an example of the kind of tension present in girl power programming, a tension between a more "official" political rhetoric and the rhetoric of consumer politics. At times, *Nick News* does address children as "political actors," as Buckingham asserts. That is to say, children's voices, desires, and opinions are treated with respect and without condescension, and the program offers specific instruction on how to act politically—by writing to one's congressperson, by protesting social inequalities, or by simply learning more about what free speech means. So, for example, in one episode of *Nick News* (October 6, 2002), the first story involved cross burning, after a recent case in the southern United States. The program was significant in that it clearly articulated the complexities surrounding issues of free speech, and Ellerbee asked the children in the studio whether, for example, the Ku Klux Klan has a right to free speech, pushing the children to answer why and why not.

After this story, the show cut to a commercial break. At the return of *Nick News,* Ellerbee immediately began the program by discussing how one's dreams can come true—if one is an aspiring rock star. The program then went on to detail the story of O-Town, a manufactured boy-band that came into existence as a result of the reality television show *Making the Band.* The odd juxtaposition of these two stories exemplifies the specific tension found in girl power programming between a more typically political form of address and a more commercial address that emphasizes consumer choice. In fact, in a special episode of *Nick News,* "The Fight to Fit In" (December 2, 2002), Ellerbee specifically references the contradictions I am identifying more generally in girl power ideology: "Grown ups will tell you how easy it is to be a kid. Kids know better. There is, at your age—at any age really—a natural struggle between the desire to be part of a group and the desire to be an individual." The kids I interviewed also seemed to understand this tension: they uniformly found the O-Town story more interesting than the cross-burning story and certainly found it more relevant to their lives (these were middle-class, predominantly white children). In fact, most children I interviewed found *Nick News* "boring," "not very interesting," or "just OK."[75]

Nick News more expressly addresses girl power in several different ways: there are some special editions, such as "The Fight to Fit In," or "The Body Trap" (November 25, 2002), that focus on issues thought to be relevant to girl culture such as body image, girls' personal identity, as well as issues of inclusion in a male-dominated world (indeed, many of the "girl power" issues that are covered on *Nick News* explicitly reference the social world as largely male dominated, surely a recognition of the mainstreaming of feminist thought into children's consumer culture). In "The Body Trap," *Nick News* devoted an entire issue to problems related to body image, delivering a scathing critique of the popular culture industry's privileging of thin girls as ideals. Featuring not only Rosie O'Donnell as an "expert" but also graphic visual footage of a young girl suffering from anorexia, "The Body Trap" is an important counterargument to the hundreds of images of impossibly thin models visible in popular culture that so powerfully become the norm for young girls. The episode featured a group of children and adolescents, telling their personal stories about wanting to be thin, feeling stigmatized, and so forth. Although this kind of personalized, individual storytelling is important in terms of recognizing the problem, it also functions to distract audiences from larger social issues that are a result of "The Body Trap," such as gender discrimination or racism in the media.

Even in the regular *Nick News* schedule, girls are featured as important story subjects. For example, the fledgling National Women's Football League was covered in one episode (October 20, 2002), where the story made an explicit argument about the unequal playing field for girls' and boys' sports and argued that girls "are as tough as boys." Other episodes of *Nick News* dealt with the issue of cruelty and gossip among girl cliques. In an episode that aired on November 3, 2002, Ellerbee began the program: "Sugar and Spice and everything Nice, that's what little girls are made of . . . NOT!" In fact, Ellerbee continued, girls can be just as mean as boys, and even meaner. The episode then depicted several young girls recounting their stories of cruelty at school, featuring the author Rosalind Wiseman (of the aforementioned *Queen Bees and Wannabes*) on the voice-over stating that the "girl who has the most social power gets to do what she wants to the girl who doesn't." The episode also discussed the contradictions between societal expectations of girls—primarily that they be silent and passive rather than aggressive and active—and made the point that this expectation has led to a unique kind of cruelty that relies not on overt aggression but rather a more subtle, and arguably more insidious, type of malice such as gossip and secrets. Directly connecting girl cruelty to popular culture, *Nick News* argued that girls learn "that to move up they have to pull somebody else down" through glossy magazines, music videos, and other forms of popular culture that privilege a kind of brutal competition among girls. The segment ended with a discussion of Wiseman's "empower program," Owning Up, where she encouraged girls to stand up for themselves if another girl is being cruel. As *As Told by Ginger* suggests in an entertainment format, some of the more pressing issues of the early twenty-first century, at least when it comes to children, are issues that have to do with the dominant practices of femininity, self-esteem, and popularity in the social and cultural world. These topics have provided a broader cultural context for *Nick News* to address similar sorts of issues.

Finally, another way in which *Nick News* is an example of girl power programming comes not in the form of representation but in a more institutional way, through Linda Ellerbee herself. Ellerbee is a well-known feminist journalist who has been outspoken on the problems of sexism and ageism in the field of journalism. Her production company, Lucky Duck Productions, produces not only *Nick News* but also programs for Lifetime Television and WE: Women's Entertainment Network. Her work in journalism has garnered numerous awards, including several Emmys and the duPont Columbia award (*Nick News* itself has won three Peabody awards). Ellerbee is also a public speaker; she is a breast cancer survivor and speaks nationally on her experience. And she is well-known for her respect for both women and children and is the author of an adolescent reading series, "Get Real," about a young girl reporter. Henry Jenkins positions Ellerbee as an important figure in the world of children's media by virtue of her treatment of children as political and social agents, rather than impressionable beings in need of protection from the media. He argues that Ellerbee "creates television programs that encourage children's awareness of real-world problems, such as the Los Angeles riots, and enable children to find their own critical voice to speak back against the adult world. She trusts children to confront realities from which other adults might shield them, offering them the facts needed to form their own opinions and the air time to discuss issues."[76] As the producer of *Nick News*, Ellerbee is also a producer of children's culture—and in this specific case, a producer of girl power culture. Although *Nick News* is clearly not a DIY form of cultural production, or an alternative girl power 'zine, it nonetheless manages to function as an important producer of girl power ideology.[77]

Nick News claims specifically to empower children through the distribution of information. As Nickelodeon describes the show, "Every week *Nick News* keeps you in the know about the issues that are important to you, from personality profiles to interviews to polls and special guests . . . It's the news the way you want it, with help from kids everywhere!"[78] However, not only is it difficult to determine precisely what issues are "important" to all kids but *Nick News* has the same problem as most news programs: how to connect the issues on the program with the politics of a child's material life. As Buckingham argues, "young people need to be provided with opportunities to engage in political activity, rather than simply observing it from a distance—in other words, that they are entitled to be political actors in their own right."[79] *Nick News* is a program that, like citizenship itself, is fraught with tension about the various meanings of empowerment, and what it means to be a "political actor." The girl power episodes on *Nick News* create even more of a contradiction. On the one hand, the programs do encourage an awareness of the various issues surrounding contemporary gender politics. On the other hand, these very same gender politics are the products not necessarily of political action but of media visibility and the commercial realm. The issue of body image, for example, is an important feminist concern, and *Nick*

News acknowledges this but also approaches it from within the commercial realm of the media—a site that helps to produce dominant norms of femininity in the first place.

GIRL POWER AND THE CONTEMPORARY NICKELODEON CONTEXT

In 1991, when *Clarissa* debuted, it was important for the Nickelodeon brand identity that the cable channel was known for something different from the networks. The gesture to be more explicitly inclusive of girls was certainly a visible and powerful way to mark Nickelodeon's difference. Because in the early 1990s cable television was still "proving" itself, Nickelodeon's claim that it provided an empowering context for its female audience was crucial to its continuing success. Precisely *because* the broadcast industry denied the importance of girls, Nickelodeon reacted by embracing girls as part of its overt mission and philosophy as a channel that "respected" kids. Additionally, the larger cultural context of girl power and postfeminism framed the Nickelodeon discourse about reaching out to girls, so that there was multilayered support for early programming such as *Clarissa*, *The Secret World of Alex Mack*, and *The Mystery Files of Shelby Woo*.

How can the current context of gender representation and children's television be characterized? Nickelodeon took what could be called a political stance by including girls in its programming in 1991—what about in 2007? Are the same politics of postfeminism and the commodification of girl power still forceful in shaping children's programming? As I've argued, recent Nickelodeon rhetoric has backed off of the overt gender politics the channel seemed to embrace in the 1990s. The network instead adopts a "gender-neutral" stance, which translates (according to the network) as a commitment to neither boys nor girls specifically, but rather to "all kids." Rather than mark the girl protagonists of Nickelodeon shows as different because they are girls, or to insist on a critique of dominant power relations that constitute gender representation, Zarghami—now the network's president—insists on neutrality: "we care less about gender in our programs and more about kids." Why the refusal to be specifically interested in girls? After all, in the early 1990s the network became known in the industry and in the general public as media that championed girls and girl characters. Why is the network hesitant to take that same political stance in the current context? There are several reasons for Nickelodeon's shift from a specified political stance to a nonspecific, ambiguous perspective. The consumer context of girl power products has shifted from a somewhat narrow marketing niche to a normalized generalized brand. Additionally, the industry structure in which Nickelodeon is situated is shaped differently in the contemporary context, when cable channels resemble broadcast networks far more than they differ from them, given centralized media ownership, vertical integration, and an increasingly competitive cable environment.

The consumer context of children's media has changed in the early twenty-first century, precisely because of programs like *Clarissa* in the 1990s. As with so much of popular culture, the political "edge" of girl power shows of the 1990s has been appropriated as girl power becomes normalized into mainstream consumer culture (although it remains true that outside of Nickelodeon, children's TV producers remain committed to producing mostly boy-oriented programming and are often very resentful of Nickelodeon's success with girl power shows).[80] Yet, despite this cultural shift, it remains controversial (read: nonprofitable) to have overt feminist politics. It worked in the early 1990s, in a time of emerging, hip girl power, for a network like Nickelodeon to adopt a stance that was overtly pro-girl. But in the early twenty-first century, that stance had been depoliticized and utilized as a particularly effective niche-marketing strategy. Just as the earlier shift on the part of mainstream culture to adopt "feminist" values into commodity culture was an economically motivated move, so too is the strategy for Nickelodeon to back away from these same feminist values and frame the network's philosophy as "gender neutral" as a financially sensible one. The brand identity of Nickelodeon is about a general coolness, a hip channel for hip youth. In the early 1990s, girl power was cool and hip. In the early twenty-first century, gender neutrality (or gender ambiguity) is cool and hip. Both kinds of politics are crucial elements of the brand identity *before* they are employed politically, so the flip-flop from gender committed to gender neutral can be rationalized not as a contradiction or as hypocritical but rather as operating according to brand logic.

Nickelodeon fits into this contemporary cultural industry. John Hardman, for example, answered the question about whether Nickelodeon makes programs "just for little girls" by using slick marketing rhetoric, first claiming that the channel tries to reach as many bases as possible, and then discussing other shows that feature girls: "We also have a new program for Nickelodeon called *Rocket Powered* based on extreme sports. It's got surfing and skating. We found that young girls are very interested in that culture. So the program will have a lot of girls as active participants in the games."[81] This mix of political philosophy with marketing strategy, where the network is committed to creating representations of girls who are "not beautiful" but smart and capable alongside the market imperative to create "good selling products" is the crux of Nickelodeon's success in the competitive children's television market. Nickelodeon's efforts to include girls as lead characters may be understood as a lucrative market strategy to capitalize on the cultural fad of girl power, but programs such as *Clarissa Explains It All, As Told by Ginger,* and *Nick News* nonetheless provide a different cultural script for both girl and boy audience members, a script that challenges conventional narratives and images about what girls are and who they should be. Susan Douglas, writing about the Spice Girls, argues that "when adolescent girls flock to a group, they are telling us plenty about how they experience the transition to womanhood in a society in which boys are still very much on top. Girls today are being urged, simultaneously, to be independent, assertive, and achievement oriented, yet also demure, attractive, soft-spoken, fifteen pounds underweight, and deferential to men."[82] The Nickelodeon shows discussed in this chapter incorporate these kinds of tensions as part of their narrative logic and, in doing so, provide a context in which both girls and boys can question dominant narratives of gender.

Dow, when discussing prime time television shows of the 1980s and 1990s that were assumed to contain a "feminist" message, argues that while the gender ideology on shows such as *Murphy Brown* and *Designing Women* may not create policy change or affect material politics, those shows nonetheless represent a "kind" of feminism.[83] In other words, that these shows are being aired in the mainstream media (a place that historically has demonized feminism) does not mean they are antifeminist: "To use the word 'feminist' to describe them is not a mistake: within the limits of commercial television, they offer a version of feminist ideology. However, that ideology is one suited to television's needs, not to the needs of a feminist politics committed to the future of all women regardless of race, class, sexuality, or life situation."[84] This shift in the focus of postfeminism's engagement of power is precisely what produces ambivalence about gender politics. As McRobbie points out, the incorporation of feminist rhetoric in media outlets such as Nickelodeon "provide[s] commercial culture with a seeming licence, to speak on or behalf of young women, as though in the spirit of social responsibility."[85] Yet these "new markets" that are authorized by a postfeminist culture "allow for the expansion of the global market on the basis of strategic repositioning of women predicated however on an illusory freedom which permits more subtle modalities of gender re-inscription and re-subordination to be pursued."[86] Feminist "values" thus become the values of the commercial market— precisely the same market that has historically created misogynist and racist images of girls and women.

I see girl power shows on Nickelodeon as also representing a kind of feminism, one that is fundamentally about tension, contradiction, and ambiguity. Girl power programs such as *Clarissa* and *As Told by Ginger* are clearly situated within a postfeminist ethos, where empowerment and agency define girls more than helplessness and dependency. However, this empowerment is represented as an individual "choice" and at times resembles other commercial choices we all make. Nickelodeon is an important producer of a kind of feminism, but commercial and media visibility is an important part of what *legitimates* that feminism. The mixing of political addresses within the programming and advertising on Nickelodeon—both feminine and feminist, both social and individual—reflects the kind of dynamic postfeminists adopt as part of their subjectivity. Thus, the network itself speaks to its child audience in a mix of conflicting "feminist" voices.

The images young girls and adolescents watch on Nickelodeon—images of Clarissa Darling, or Ginger Foutley, or the "real" girls on *Nick News*—are empowering, at least within a specific context. They are diverse, and they represent a range of options and models, and in many ways these images are a refreshing and politically authorizing change from traditional images of femininity. While obviously the commercial shaping of girl power cannot be denied, girl power, like other forms of feminism, is about a particular kind of recognition. This is not simply a recognition that so-called women's issues such as sexual harassment, equal work for equal pay, and legal policies on rape and abuse are important issues that need to be addressed in the public sphere. It is also a recognition of women as contributing members of society now meriting a kind of visibility.

In this sense, the easy dismissal of "girl power" as a media-created new commercial avenue that has no connection with any kind of "real" politics is both inaccurate and misleading about the nature of "reality" in the twenty-first century. The charge by Second Wave feminists regarding the apparent lack of "real politics" of postfeminism may very well indicate, in part, a preoccupation with personal issues and individualism. But this sentiment not only romanticizes the feminist movements of the 1960s and 1970s as concerned only with the social and material spheres.[87] It also caricatures feminist politics of the 1990s as narcissistic and vacuous.[88] The media address of postfeminism and girl power ideology is about tension and contradiction, about the individual pleasures of consumption and the social responsibilities of solidarity. Nickelodeon, and the way in which the channel addresses its audience as "gender neutral," both creates and sustains these kinds of tensions. The imagined consumer citizen addressed and constituted by Nickelodeon buys girl power products, has a girl power attitude, and indeed is empowered through and within girl power—all the while remaining safely "gender neutral."

5 CONSUMING RACE ON NICKELODEON

In the spring of 2003, an advertisement appeared on Nickelodeon for the toy company Mattel's recent doll line, Flavas. This toy line features Barbie-type dolls characterized by ambiguous ethnic identities—with "neutral" skin color and vague facial features, the dolls could easily be Latina, African American, Asian, or white. What is clear, however, is that the dolls are "urban": they wear clothing that is hip and trendy, they carry boomboxes, and they are sold in boxes with a cardboard backdrop resembling a concrete wall covered in graffiti. On Raving Toy Maniac, a Web-based toy outlet, Mattel issued the following press release the week the dolls appeared in stores:

> EL SEGUNDO, Calif.—July 29, 2003—*Flava,* according to "Hip Hop-tionary: The Dictionary of Hip Hop Terminology" by Alonzo Westbrook, means personal flavor or style. With the nationwide introduction of Flavas (pronounced FLAY-vuhz) this week, the first reality-based fashion doll brand that celebrates today's teen culture through authentic style, attitude and values, Mattel (TM) has created a hot hip-hop themed line that allows girls to express their own personal flava. Born in the world of music and fashion, the hip-hop movement has evolved into a cultural phenomenon and celebrates fearless self-expression through freestyle dance, hip-hop music, street sport and signature fashions. Flavas, for girls ages 8–10, is the hottest doll line to embrace this latest tween trend encouraging girls to show their inner flava to the outer world. Starting this month, girls will be introduced to a crew of six friends—four girls and two boys—all sporting their hip-hop style.[1]

The Flavas marketing campaign featured not only ads, such as the one on Nickelodeon that featured hip-hop music and trendy dance moves, but also a sponsorship of the pop singer Christina Aguilera's tour, a singer who Mattel claims "personifies the idea of fearless self-expression." Despite the fact that the word "flava," the culture of hip-hop, and the idea of street style all signify race in contemporary U.S. culture, the racial identity of the dolls is never mentioned in the ads or the press release. While this could have been an interesting opportunity to explore issues of different skin color among African Americans, as there is a dark-skinned doll and a light-skinned doll, or racial issues in and between Latinos and African Americans, race in this context is just a "flava," a street style, an individual characteristic, and a commercial product. The racial ambivalence of the Flava doll correlates with some of the representations of race and ethnicity in contemporary children's television.[2]

Another recent media event worth noting within the context of race and television was the 2004 debut of a new "extreme" reality show. As is well documented, reality television shows such as *Extreme Makeover, The Swan,* and *The Biggest Loser* emphasize, among other things, liberal ideology: the triumph of the individual over a set of social, cultural, and physical "obstacles," such as idealized femininity, bodies that are too big by contemporary standards, crooked or yellow teeth, and the like.[3] The reality show *Gana la Verde* or "Win the Green" also emphasizes the triumph of the individual over "obstacles," by offering Latino immigrants the chance to compete for a green card, a crucial step on the way to American citizenship. The prize for the winner of *Gana la Verde* is one year of free legal advice from immigration lawyers, although clearly there is no guarantee of the green card. Despite this uncertainty, the show, which aired on smaller, Spanish-language television networks in Southern California and Texas, had a waiting list for contestants.[4] In order to win, the contestants must perform a number of extreme stunts, many of which are coded as "authentic" or "Mexican-themed," such as eating a tequila worm burrito. As one fan of the show commented, "There are things we do out of necessity, not because we want to. Eating worms for your papers is one of those things."[5]

I begin this chapter with these two examples because they demonstrate in interesting ways some of the features of current racial representation in media entertainment. Flava dolls and *Gana la Verde* both produce race within the specific context of late industrial capitalism in the United States, a moment which has been characterized in racial terms as "multicultural" or "post-race" society.[6] Within the contemporary climate, television and media products produce particular representations and narratives of race and ethnicity that are marketed as cool, authentic, and "urban." Certainly, the trope of the "urban" has long been associated with racial representation. However, while media representations of the "urban" in the 1980s and early 1990s predominantly signified the dangerous "other," in the twenty-first century, media-defined "urbanization" is an incredibly lucrative economic tool for marketing to broad audiences, especially white audiences. Thus, the "urban" itself is redefined in the twenty-first century. Rather than signifying treacherous inner-city life, populated by people of color, the urban in the contemporary context is connected to a particular notion of "realism." In turn, urban "realism" is associated with the ideological notion that contemporary U.S. society is a multicultural one, in which racial difference is no longer salient. As Gerard Raiti, writing for the children's media industry magazine *Kidscreen,* argues, "Creators and developers alike have started to recognize that national and racial boundaries are eroding, and that a realistic representation for children's programming means protagonists of all types. The '90s fallacy that all African-American programming needs to be urban has been refuted. When imagination meets realism, children watch because they are more astute than they are ever given credit for."[7] Raiti points to the notion that African American programming no longer needs to be "urban"—I agree, but not because racial boundaries are eroding. Rather, the definition of "urban" has been changed so that an urban style permeates *most* kids' programming and is not targeted simply to particular ethnic groups. The urban still has cultural capital in the kids' TV business, but it signifies a kind of racial ambivalence rather than a racial danger, precisely because it is presented to audiences as a commodity.

Within the current media environment, itself a product of a post–civil rights society, race thus functions as an ambivalent category, where on the one hand it remains an important issue in terms of representation—shown by featuring people of color more prominently (demonstrated by the Flava dolls) and crafting story lines that center race and race relations. On the other hand, the plethora of images of urban and "cool" people of color, in advertising, television programs, and music videos (among other popular cultural artifacts) implies that representational visibility no longer has the same urgency. Indeed, the implication is that race itself no longer matters in the same way it once did but is rather an interesting means to feature the authentic, cool, or urban—or as a theme in a reality show. This postracial television economy is the legacy of diverse programming such as *Sesame Street* and *The Cosby Show* but engages these earlier representations of race within new economic models, where the connection between enfranchisement and "positive" images of diversity no longer has the same meaning as it did in the media context of the 1970s and 1980s.

In this chapter, I explore how this racial ambivalence works within the context of Nickelodeon at the levels of programming, production, and the network's branding strategies. More specifically, I examine the various ways that Nickelodeon claims to empower its audience through discourses of race and ethnicity. At times, the network represents race through a conflation of race with

15. Arnold and his friend Gerald, from *Hey Arnold!*, 2004.

authenticity, where programs such as *The Brothers Garcia* and *Dora the Explorer* stress the importance of history and "roots" of ethnicities. In other programs, Nickelodeon's definition of diversity is much less specific and is more about a general political and cultural style that structures much of the programming as well as the network's brand identity. This representational strategy is evident in variety programs such as *Kenan & Kel* and in many of the channel's animated programs, such as *Hey Arnold!*, where Nickelodeon strategically uses a particular aesthetic racial style. This representational strategy commodifies and generalizes race as a trope that is urban and cool, without an obvious political reference. That is, in shows such as *Hey Arnold!*, which features a multicultural animated cast, set in an urban inner city, race is very seldom mentioned or directly referenced but is clearly important to the show's style and thematic elements. The use of diversity as a part of social identity, and as a more abstract narrative theme, is an important element in the network's claim to empower kids and to address the child audience as active cultural citizens. Diversity, for Nickelodeon, is part of the network's brand identity. Like other brands in contemporary culture, Nickelodeon targets aspects of personal identity such as race as a way to be inclusive; in fact, Nickelodeon's brand identity is crafted around the way in which the network is different from other children's media in how it "empowers" children through (among other things) the commitment to gender and ethnic representation.

The ability to claim that diversity matters to Nickelodeon has thus given the network a way to stand out as a "different" sort of network in the competitive field of children's television. In a 2002 report on diversity within children's television, the media advocacy group Children Now featured an article written by then–Nickelodeon president Herb Scannell on the network's success with diversity. As Scannell put it, "One of the questions we are frequently asked by the media and the advocacy community is why we've been able to present a more diverse screen when other networks are often criticized for their lack of diversity. I can only speak for Nickelodeon when I say that it really boils down to our core mission of serving all kids. While Nickelodeon is by definition a niche network, we actually seek to serve and attract the broadest audience possible within the universe of kids 2–14 years old. That means putting kids from all different backgrounds front and center: kids of all shapes, sizes and, most importantly, color."[8]

Scannell explicitly connects the channel's images of diversity with Nickelodeon's claims to "respect" kids, building up cultural capital with not only advocacy groups such as Children Now but also with parents, educators, and others in the television industry. Indeed, within the world of children's television, racial and ethnic identity works as a kind of currency, where it increases the political and social clout of a network to be able to claim that it is "diverse."[9] As cultural capital, Nickelodeon's mission to respect kids and provide a safe and secure environment connects specifically to representation. The network's claim to empower kids overtly references the historical invisibility and exclusion of people of color that has plagued television since its inception, and the inclusion of diverse casts and characters is explicitly recognized by the network as part of its mission to "respect" kids. As with the channel's commitment to girls, Nickelodeon pledges to air diverse programming and has created shows that feature nonwhite characters and developed programming that directly invokes racial or ethnic themes. At the same time, Nickelodeon's decision to create diverse programming is often discussed as "good business," distancing the channel from the political implications of embracing diversity. This contradiction shapes the crux of consumer citizenship, where political subjectivity is not necessarily the guiding principle for citizens; rather, accumulating cultural capital is a privileged method of forming subjectivity. The underlying question of this commercially driven commitment to diversity is this: where does this leave racist practices and minority groups? If a racially coded "urbanness" is rendered cool and is a part of the Nickelodeon brand, how does this deflect attention from continuing social and political problems of race, including eroding affirmative action policies, immigration policies and discourses, defunding of education, and police brutality, among other issues? This is ultimately the problem of consumer citizenship: representational practices offer what looks like a more inclusive, more democratic society—but one with no political referent or practice.[10]

In other words, in brand culture, when channels such as Nickelodeon *do* produce programs that feature and represent race and ethnicity in important ways, this production is rhetorically couched in terms that are not overtly political: "realism," respect, and good business. Race, in this context, fulfills a political function—increased media visibility and "positive" representations of race on television—but, through this visual strategy, distracts media audiences from political practice. My concerns in this chapter, then, revolve around this ambivalence: what are the consequences when race or ethnicity becomes cultural capital—a "competency" or a mode of consumption within the world of media entertainment? Moreover, when diversity is an explicit part of Nickelodeon's brand identity, where images and practices of diversity function more as smart marketing than progressive politics, does this mean that the channel's practice of hiring people of color in not only casting but also as directors, writers, and producers should be dismissed as more smooth branding?

TELEVISION, RACE, AND REPRESENTATION

In the anthology *Living Color: Race and Television,* Sasha Torres begins the collection by asking "what does race look like on television?"[11] As Torres, Herman Gray, Stuart Hall, and others have noted, this question, when it is asked, is frequently acknowledged as a particularly thorny one and is rarely answered or even theorized in depth.[12] The issue of racial representation on television has long been recognized as a "problem" that involves either the stereotypical portrayal of nonwhite characters or the sheer invisibility of these characters. However, issues of representation are always more complicated than this and frequently involve a number of dimensions: the issue of production, in the sense that the people behind the creation of television programming tend to be largely white; the issue of representation, in a contemporary context where it is hip to be "different" racially but in a way that signifies the politics of representation rather than representative politics; and the issue of the political economy of television representation, where development of diverse characters is still largely constrained by advertiser support.

The battle over representation on television, especially in terms of African American characters, was not a new fight in the later half of the twentieth century. Ever since *Amos 'n' Andy* first aired on television in the 1950s, advocates for nonracist television programming had lobbied various groups, such as the FCC and the networks themselves, for more "positive" representations of black characters. Indeed, cultural debates about "good" television and media activism were part of the general social upheavals of the 1960s in the United States, and airing "diverse" programming began to be recognized as cultural capital for networks (at least in the eyes of media advocacy groups). Despite the continuing presence of advertiser-supported programming, as the television scholar Aniko Bodroghkozy argues, television in the 1960s involved more than just "delivering the largest bulk audiences possible to corporate advertisers."[13] She demonstrates, through examining such programs as *The Smothers Brothers Comedy Hour* and *The Mod Squad,* that entertainment television continually engaged in an "ideological balancing act." As Bodroghkozy argues, "The products of the entertainment industry, in order to be popular, must engage at some level with the lived experiences of their audiences: they need to be relevant."[14] The combination of relevancy and commercial popularity is one that always characterized the U.S. television environment and remains an important element in the present context.

Bodroghkozy analyzes some of the more engaging television programs in the 1960s and 1970s that dealt with the contemporary climate of the civil rights movement and other ethnically motivated protest movements through representation and thematic elements. Children's television produced during this time also engaged with the political climate in innovative ways. As I've argued throughout this book, the media representations of children in the United States are predominantly framed by a discourse of lost innocence, and countless public debates occur over not only how to regain this innocence but also to identify what destroyed it in the first place. For obvious reasons, legislators, educators, and parents often name the media as the culprit. Yet just as clearly, the implicit recognition of the educational potential of the media has yielded some positive changes in the media landscape. Because of the often explicit pedagogical role that characterizes children's television, and the increased federal and public scrutiny to which it is subject, the question of diversity and multicultural representation has always been answered more readily and more effectively in children's television than in primetime TV.

The most famous success story regarding diversity in children's television in the United States is Creative Television Workshop's (CTW) *Sesame Street. Sesame Street* is a program (and production company) with a clear mission to merge political issues of diversity with the potential of television as an electronic classroom. As Heather Hendershot documents, one of *Sesame Street*'s earliest goals was to use television to "affect the socioeconomic disparity between blacks and whites," thus explicitly recognizing the potential of the medium to effect social and cultural transformation.[15] From its inception, *Sesame Street* has specifically engaged in politics.

Like so many other media forms, *Sesame Street* presents a kind of contradiction about race and diversity through its representations: the sheer visibility of African American and Latino characters has historically situated *Sesame Street* as an important exception to the dominant white landscape of children's television —as well as a model for other kids' programs to emulate. Yet the program's commitment to pedagogy as a "great equalizer" allows a kind of avoidance of the issue of institutionalized racism in the United States.[16] Cultural debates concerning the ideals of liberal pluralism and integration are always already grounded in racial blindness, which problematizes what "positive" representations should look like. And these debates are often played out around the child, at once innocent and a harbinger of the future, who often becomes the symbol of racial blindness (this despite the fact that most media representations of children are clearly racialized, featuring as they do white children).

Sesame Street's overt mission is to teach; more specifically, the program's intent is to teach about diversity and benign cultural heterogeneity through positive nonwhite representations. As I argued in chapter 2, much of the cultural capital of Sesame Street as "good" kids' television comes from the program's commitment to diverse representation (as well as its alliance with public television). This works to both create a "real" difference in children's television and to maintain the ideology that Sesame Street is "quality" television for kids rather than explicitly acknowledge that it is about race.[17] Even in a show that was specifically created to address the politics of racism in the United States, Sesame Street's political identity needs to be made palatable for a broad audience. It is this kind of colorblind ideology that structures much of children's television—in fact, creators of kids' TV often create characters that are animals or aliens precisely in order to sidestep the problematic issue of racial representation (although using animals or space aliens clearly doesn't always work—simply glance at Disney's The Lion King or Saban's television series The Power Rangers to see how animals such as hyenas or fighting super heroes are racialized).[18]

In early 1950s animation, for example, when cinematic archives were culled for "appropriate" animation for children's television and the child audience, this notion of creating a feeling of inclusion by refusing to directly engage with the question of racial representation led to an overwhelming white aesthetic. As Jason Mittell details, children's television producers searched these early film archives and made conscious selection of some "non-offensive" images over others within cartoons.[19] Much of this early film animation was created for an adult audience, and the flexibility of animation—where one can create a representational form based on imagination and fantasy as much as on reality—meant that animation was often intended as a kind of social commentary. Because of this factor, and because of the fact that cinematic cartoons provided much of the early fare for television animation in the 1960s and 1970s, considerable efforts were taken to remove racist stereotypical characters, racial references, and references to the war. As Mittell admits, while there is an importance to reframing televisual representations so as to not appear racist or overly stereotypical, there was such concern about creating the "wrong" ethnic or racial stereotype that the overall effect of this was to create animation with almost exclusively white characters.[20] The whitening of cartoons was also following historical trends of making media images "safe" for children. The fact that this kind of protection came in the form of transforming a potentially more diverse visual landscape into one that was primarily white and middle-class continues to dominate protectionist strategies of contemporary times, where children are protected from images and messages that are generally not middle-class and white.[21]

Despite the fact that programs such as *Sesame Street* challenged the whiteness that structured television, by the mid-1980s the television landscape was hardly diverse, either in terms of representation within programming or within the production of television shows. The regulatory environment of the 1980s as well as the general cultural climate nurtured by the conservative Reagan administration supported a predominantly white televisual universe. As is well theorized, one of the few exceptions, *The Cosby Show,* represented in microcosm the contradictory discourses about race and media circulating in the 1980s: *The Cosby Show* featured all African American characters, but each one of them "acted" white or performed whiteness in a particular way. As Herman Gray and Sut Jhally and Justin Lewis have noted, *The Cosby Show* was a good representative of the 1980s, where "diversity" was increasingly visible as part of the commercial world, but in a way that was easy to tolerate, palatable for the American public—a kind of "enlightened racism" as Jhally and Lewis coined it.[22]

In his study of African American representations on television, Herman Gray further extends the notion of the ideological balancing act regarding television and race. Gray astutely points out the complicated nature of representation and clearly argues that regardless of whether one sees the representation of race on television as "positive" (such as *The Cosby Show*), or more complex (such as *In Living Color*), the logic of representation needs to be situated within a larger framework of social, political, and economic forces.[23] Reaganomics and the ideology of the "free market," for instance, played a particularly important role in race relations in the United States in the 1980s, where nonwhite groups (specifically African Americans) were demonized as the primary justification for everything from dismantling affirmative action to trickle-down economics. As Gray points out, "As a contemporary sign of social erosion in post-civil rights America, the racialized concept of the underclass was perfectly suited for cultural and moral labor in a conservative-controlled discourse on poverty, morality, and entitlements. Lacking any meaningful economic and cultural ties—hence their strangeness and otherness—to the reconfigured conservative (and neoliberal) mainstream, the black urban underclass provided the perfect symbol with which to launch a full offensive against the welfare state and those it serves."[24]

This symbol of race—the black urban underclass—was represented visually on television and in film, where blacks, Latinos, and Asians were featured on both "real" news reports and within entertainment fare predominantly as criminals and/or degenerates. To provide "balance" for these demonized images of people of color, there were some positive representations of middle-class African Americans on television, although these too must be situated within the particular historical context of the 1980s. Television programs such as *The Cosby Show* and *The Fresh Prince of Bel-Air,* for instance, depicted one representation of blackness at the expense of others, so that the "positive" image of the black middleclass in these programs subsumed and rendered invisible other political and economic realities of African American communities. The trope of financial success and the family in these shows correlated with hegemonic norms, so that African American families constituted outside this norm were subsequently pathologized.[25] For Gray, then, the "struggle for 'blackness'" is one that involves challenging this dynamic as well as the distinction between "positive" and "negative" representations of race and refusing to situate race representation as a zero-sum game.

Yet it is the reductive categorizing of racial representation as either good or bad that industry executives seem to use as a map when creating programming. Racial representation *becomes* diversity, even if disconnected from actual diversity in American social and cultural life. Particular images of diversity are seen as "positive" and are thus "safer" than other, more complex images (and are used to contain more complex uses of diversity). The language of diversity has been used in a general way in popular culture, in politics, and in academic settings as an indication that difference is recognized and that the U.S. population is diverse. The media widely uses "diverse" representatives in advertisements and television programs and also promotes diversity by airing public service announcements containing "positive" messages about combating racial prejudice alongside warnings about guns and drugs. These images of diversity function as a way for the media to manage diversity—the media contains diverse representations and generally constitutes diversity as something safe, that all audiences can "take," as a way to lessen the threat of difference.[26]

But what are these "safe" images of diversity? Gray concretizes this definition of diversity by situating racial representation as a series of discursive practices that were particularly relevant in the 1980s. He identifies these practices as three interconnected strategies: assimilationist, or invisibility, where blacks are either simply not represented or represented as white people; pluralist, or "separate but equal," where blacks are represented on television, but as a discrete niche or target group; and multiculturalist, or diversity, where Gray sees the "struggle for blackness" taking place in complex and often contradictory ways.[27] The influx of racial representations in the 1980s media landscape did not necessarily reflect a political consciousness about the politics of race but was rather the result of a convergence of political and cultural dynamics, including the increase of niche channels on cable television, the rise of brand culture, the marketing tool of lifestyle demographics, and the conservative politics of the Reagan administration. In the 1980s, it became palatable—indeed, fashionable—to be multicultural and multiracial (within certain constraints and conditions). Black representation in 1980s media was part of an appropriation of discourses of "political correctness" as a specific element in brand identity development in a burgeoning brand environment, and it came to be an important factor in the specific brand development of Nickelodeon.

TWENTY-FIRST CENTURY REPRESENTATIONS OF RACE: THE NEW ECONOMY

Gray locates the impetus for *The Cosby Show* (as well as other programs that featured African American characters) within a context in which the cultural definition of "diversity" as a specific marketing tool was beginning to be realized in corporate America. Yet Gray's "struggle for blackness" is a different kind of struggle in the context of the early twenty-first century. To "struggle" for blackness assumes a kind of stable identity for blackness itself—it is something tangible and "authentic," worth struggling over. In other words, the struggle to which Gray referred was not simply about politics of inclusion within the media but more generally a politics of inclusion within all areas of U.S. cultural and civic life. In the current media moment, this struggle is taking place on different terms and in different contexts, such as cable television and Nickelodeon, and the connections to U.S. cultural life are formulated primarily within consumption practices. As a way to extend Gray's historical analysis, I see a slightly different practice occurring within the current television landscape, especially within the context of Nickelodeon, a practice which might be called "postracial," or "urbanization" in industry parlance.

A more overt connection of race with marketing dominated in the 1990s, especially marketing the "urban" to young, white middle-class Americans. Leon Wynter sees this more recent "movement" or shift in representation as resulting in what he calls "Transracial America," which is a "vision of the American Dream in which we are liberated from the politics of race to openly embrace any style, cultural trope, or image of beauty that attracts us regardless of its origin."[28] Of course, while the notion that through a process of urbanization we are liberated from the politics of race in the late 1990s and early twenty-first century is clearly an illusion, it is the case that this politics has been reframed within brand culture. Popular discourses of race and images of nonwhites become "street cred" in the contemporary marketing world, so that, for instance, when Nickelodeon programs feature diverse characters and themes, the station is not only entitled to claim itself as "the diversity station" but also to connect this claim with its other claims: that the channel "respects" kids and considers them citizens.[29] Nickelodeon, like other contemporary media companies, uses newly shaped economic models and an ethnically nonspecific "transracial" style as a way to appeal to increasingly diverse and segmented audiences without alienating specific groups. The "problem" of diversity in the current climate is thus no longer one of invisibility and, indeed, is no longer about "separate but equal" doctrine or pluralism. To the contrary, capitalism and brand culture, through the relentless narrowing of marketing niches by ethnic and racial identity, has *provided for* rather than prevented a kind of diversity. Contemporary marketers have efficiently capitalized on the connection of "cool" with images and narratives of the urban, so that popular culture is rife with what Gray discusses as the *proliferation* of difference.[30]

In a segmented political economy, Nickelodeon programs profit from this "postracial," hip definition of diversity by incorporating images of diversity in almost every program. For instance, the animated show *Hey Arnold!* features an urban cityscape, populated by a group of kids, including one African American, Gerald. Gerald is also known as the "Teller of Urban Tales" and is considered the knowledgeable source for legends and folklore of the neighborhood. Characters on other programs also embody the racialized stereotype of cool and hip. Libby, an African American character on *Jimmy Neutron: Boy Genius,* is mellow and calm and possesses all the latest electronic gear—pagers, cell phones, pocket organizers—and is constantly ringing or beeping. Suzie Carmichael, an African American character on *All Grown Up!* (a spinoff of *Rugrats*), is centered on music—she sings and dances constantly. These characters are drawn within the framework of particular racial stereotypes—the street-smart neighborhood sage, a fascination with flashy electronic accessories, a normalization between African Americans and music and rhythm. There are some exceptions to these conventional stereotypes, so A. J. on *The Fairly OddParents* is an African American boy who provides the brains in a friendship trio, and Darren on *As Told by Ginger* is African American and has a white girlfriend. But nonetheless, all these characters, situated as they are within a predominantly white animated cast, add "cool" to the programs and signify a "postracial" televisual environment.

The danger, of course, in labeling any kind of shift in discourse or practice "post" is that this prefix implies that whatever it modifies is somehow *over*—as I discussed in the last chapter, postfeminism entails not only that feminism is passé

16. Jimmy Neutron
and friends, from *The
Adventures of Jimmy
Neutron: Boy Genius*,
2005.

but also more obliquely that whatever goals feminism sought have been accomplished. To call this moment in late capitalism "postracial" is not to suggest that race or race relations are somehow irrelevant but rather to think seriously about recent shifts in capitalism that contain and market race and diversity in the media in new ways. The representation of race in current media is, on the whole, "positive" and is significant to how race is interpreted and navigated in cultural politics.[31] Racist and stereotypical representations of African Americans as thugs, or Latinos as gang members, for instance, are not as common within television programming, and when they do appear in programming, negative public commentary often follows. Yet the various ways that race and diversity have come to mean a market orientation toward the "urban" have further consolidated the ways in which race is produced as a particular commodity and functions to deflect social attention away from racist practices such as underfunded public schools and heavily policed immigration policies.

What has occurred in the more than twenty years since the first airing of *The Cosby Show* is that people of color have been increasingly included in the realm of media representation, but the connection between individual and group empowerment gained by media visibility and progressive change in poverty levels, unemployment, policy, and education continues to be elusive. "Race" as a political identity has been subsumed in dominant culture by the brand identity of the urban. This is not to romanticize a definition of politics as something stable and immediately meaningful—or, conversely, to vilify brand identity as exclusively superficial and ephemeral—but rather to insist on shifting the cultural frame through which youth empowerment is understood. Indeed, one of the interesting as well as disturbing consequences for the increasing mainstream visibility of identity politics and multiculturalism is not simply that people of color, gays and lesbians, and the working class "matter" publicly through media and policy presence but also that these groups became the target for corporate America in terms of cultivating specific marketing niches. Within this context, empowerment cannot be theorized as separate from market strategies but is rather a *constitutive* element in these strategies. Empowerment does not seem to be connected with social and political subjectivity, in that the number of people of color living below the poverty line in the United States continues to increase, unemployment is also disproportionately high among people of color, and institutionalized racism seems as institutionalized as it was in the early 1990s.

There is, however, no lack of the *image* of diversity within media culture: images of blackness and brownness function as lucrative commodities in the media marketplace, with little connection to institutions and the organizations of social life. Advertisements feature young, urban, hip people of color, sound tracks to ads and television programs often include urban music (such as hip-hop or rap), words associated with hip-hop culture such as "bling" and "dawg" are frequently used in family television, and multicultural casts in television for youth is more the rule than the exception. More specifically, the late-twentieth- and early twenty-first-century "New Economy," as Christopher Holmes Smith coins it, uses the tropes of the urban and hip-hop culture (represented most visibly by the hip-hop mogul) as means to designate a particular national perspective on diversity. Indeed, Smith identifies the 1990s New Economy as one in which "hip-hop evolved from being the symbolic anathema of the dominant commercial apparatus to serving as one of its most strategically effective symbolic instruments."[32] In the early twenty-first century, this evolution has continued, where "black cultural tastes have increasingly become—most notably through the commodification of hip-hop culture—extremely efficient devices for extracting profit from the consumption habits of America's youth. Ideas on how to identify and market black cultural knowledge and tastes have come to embody dynamic management solutions."[33] Nickelodeon's incorporation of "ethnic themes" in programming—racial authenticity, specific references from Latin America, tracing family history—is an example of this kind of strategy.

While the contemporary visual landscape certainly shares some similarities with the 1980s, when the economic and political context made it profitable to include particular representations of people of color within popular culture, the political economic landscape has clearly shifted. Race has become an even more important commodity within media culture, and the ironic construction of the authentic in this context is that it is sold as a mainstream consumer cultural identity, an identity that is mass-produced to sell products—not quite a

Benjamin-inspired definition of the "authentic."[34] Ethnicity, then, is a kind of marketing tool, used to sell products by tapping into consumers who are "ethnic-identified."[35] Race and ethnicity within current media culture are inextricably tied to dynamics of the market, where segmented marketing strategies and more localized ethnic ventures lead to a consumer-based valorization of ethnicity. The current moment is thus characterized by ambivalence rather than racial specificity, where an ambivalent racial category (the "urban") becomes dominant and is the entry point to a commercially defined "post-" or "transracial" society. As Eric King Watts and Mark P. Orbe argue in their essay about commodifying race on Budweiser television commercials, this racial ambivalence is experienced by media audiences as a kind of "spectacular consumption" that works in particular ways to contain race representations: "as the market economy seeks to regulate and integrate 'authentic' difference, white American ambivalence toward blackness is paradoxically both assuaged by its 'universality' and heightened by its distinctiveness."[36] This focus on the universality of racially specific images marks an interesting shift from the logic of clearly defined niche markets (i.e., the African American market, the Latino market, etc.) to one that is more racially ambiguous, yet still clearly "diverse."

This is demonstrated through Nickelodeon's connection of diversity with "realism," as the Nickelodeon executive John Hardman commented about the development of the program *Rocket Power*. *Rocket Power* is a show about a group of four friends in Southern California who participate in extreme sports—surfing, skateboarding, and rollerblading, among others. The show definitely revolves around a concept of "cool," exemplified by not only the sports and the California setting but also the characters themselves. As Hardman comments: "*Rocket Power* is very ethnically diverse. The show has Hispanic, Asian and African-American characters. We made a conscious effort to reflect the diversity of the people who do extreme sports in Southern California . . . We feel some sort of responsibility to be accurate."[37] A commercially defined notion of "accuracy" centers the politics of race at Nickelodeon—shows are ostensibly about "real life." It is not so much that this in itself is a problem but that the programs are animated fantasies and built on stereotypes and thus are not exactly about "real life" to begin with. Indeed, when Nickelodeon wanted to produce a spinoff of the popular program *Rugrats* using predominantly African American characters, this commitment to "real life" seemed not so adamant; as Hardman commented, "There are some African-American characters on *Rugrats*. The response Nickelodeon has gotten to those characters on the program has been phenomenal. Nick wanted us to put those characters in their own series. But we're not going to do that. They were created for *Rugrats*, and if we put them in their own series, they couldn't hold it on their own. Their flaws would show too much."[38] This is an odd statement—what does it mean that the characters "couldn't hold it on their own"? Perhaps these characters were not drawn with particular depth, but if the shows were about "real life," and there was an audience demand for a show revolving around African American characters, it is peculiar that this would be the response from the creators.

Yet this contradictory stance on "real life" and ethnic identity is not so peculiar in the contemporary commercial context. Within this context, in a Baudrillardian sense, identity is no longer the signifier of a product.[39] Rather, identity is the pure product that we consume, either as information or as image. While advertisements might be the most likely place to see this process, we also experience the image within commercial media, such as children's television. Specifically in terms of race and ethnic identity, the image of race is consumed, but without recourse to a referent of race that exists outside commodity culture. An example of this is the aggressive ways in which diversity is marketed as an "authentic" identity—so much so that, as Arlene Dávila has pointed out, commodity media culture "makes" a people.[40] As she points out in her book, *Latinos, Inc.: The Making and Marketing of a People*, contemporary identity politics is located within the commercial world more powerfully than other, more traditional places: the academy, "politics," education. Examining the advertising and television industries and how they create a "Hispanic" market, Dávila argues that the ostensibly "positive" shift in representing Latinos from "suspects to prospects" has not yielded a consequential shift in communities of Latinos in terms of income, education, or employment but has rather further marginalized the image of the "Hispanic" in the mainstream American imagination.

This is evident in an issue of the magazine *Diversity, Inc.* (the title clearly demonstrates the connection between racial identity and commodity culture), where LatinoEyes, a Latino advertising agency, suggests differentiating the Latino population into three different groups as the most effective way to market to U.S. Latinos: unacculturated Latinos, who are new immigrants and speak primarily Spanish; biculturals, who easily move from dominant white culture to a more specific, linguistically marked Latino culture; and acculturated Latinos, who most closely resemble the white mainstream and are most comfortable using English.[41] An offshoot of this last group are what the agency calls "retro-acculturated" Latinos, who are second- and third-generation Latinos in search of their "roots" and so seek "authentic" cultural artifacts, food, and the Spanish language. While this may seem to be an extension of the already incredibly narrow lifestyle demographics used by marketing firms to target specific audiences, the "retro-acculturated" Latinos could also have been groups involved in the Chicano nationalist movements of the 1960s and 1970s. Yet this is not the same group, for the political positions espoused by the latter—resisting the history of racism against Latinos in the United States, insisting on the various ways in which Latinos are an important element in a hierarchical economy, housing discrimination, and so on—form the referent for the political movement. For the Latino ad agency, the referent for the "retro-acculturated" is simply a commercial niche, a targeted market to whom selling products—and most definitely not liberation—is the only goal.

As is evident from Dávila's work, the "real" itself is a specific signifier for race and diversity, as it is produced and understood within commercial brand culture. Like Dávila, I also want to engage commercial culture as an important site for representational politics, within the specific framework of the early twenty-first century, where there is a curious paradox when it comes to racial representation: the more people are enfranchised, the more they are "included," the less the desire to change the structure becomes.[42] The simulation of inclusion thus becomes satisfying enough—the consumption of the image of diversity is a kind of politics within brand culture. Thus, programs that represent the brand identity of Nickelodeon do not operate according to the same capitalist logic as they once did—the "struggle over blackness" that Gray details seems almost nostalgic within the current political economy, rife with hip, cool images of blackness, brownness, and other "urban" images.

NICKELODEON AND RACIAL AMBIVALENCE

Nickelodeon has been very successful in producing variety-type comedy and musical shows for youth audiences age eight to fourteen. The programs are designed to be *Saturday Night Live* or *In Living Color* for kids, and feature multicultural casts, comedy sketches, and musical guests in a typical variety show format. The African American actors Kenan Thompson and Kel Mitchell had their debut on Nickelodeon's *All That* in 1995; following the show's success, in 1996 Nickelodeon's Kim Bass created *Kenan & Kel*, which ran until July 2000 and was a live comedy show. *Kenan & Kel* was about the relationship between the two lead characters and followed a typical comedic format where Kenan continually thought of new schemes and strategies to ease his way through life, and Kel continually foiled Kenan's plans. The show's theme song was performed by Coolio, a popular hip-hop singer at the time. The lyrics were decidedly "urban" and set to a hip-hop beat:

Everybody out there, go run and tell,
Your homeboys and homegirls,
it's time for Kenan & Kel,
To keep you laughing in the afternoon,
So don't touch that dial or leave the room,
'Cause they're always into something,
and you don't wanna miss it,
It's double K, like two to get greatness,
Kenan & Kel, or should I say Kel & Kenan
and you gotta watch Kenan, 'cause Kenan be scheming,
with a plan or a plot, to make it to the top,
but they're kinda in the middle
'cause they're always getting caught
This ain't The Hardy Boys, or a Nancy Drew Mystery,
It's just Kenan & Kel in your vicinity,
Like Siegfried & Roy or Abbott & Costello,
Magic & Kareem or Penn & Teller,
Somebody's in trouble? Ahh, here it goes!
On Nick-Ni-Nick-Nick Ni-Nick-Nick-Nick!

The song is replete with hip-hop lingo—"homeboy," "Kenan be scheming"—and hip-hop style—the repetitive "Nick" at the end of the song, the reverse parallels in beat structure to maintain the rhyme, and the overall flow of the song. The song also immediately sets the show apart as a kind of urban comedy—"this ain't The Hardy Boys." The typical comedy routine of Kenan and Kel has Kel, a tall, thin teenager, as the dim-witted part of the duo, and Keenan, a heavy-set, more cerebral (though not by much) character, as the one whose job is to "fix" Kel's mistakes and smooth over his mishaps. While some fans have called Kenan and Kel this generation's Laurel and Hardy, the duo has also been criticized as a new *Amos 'n' Andy*; indeed, it is not so difficult to read the sketches of the dim-witted Kel, continually rescued by the overweight, slightly smarter Kenan, or the two characters making fools out of themselves, as anything but reminiscent of *Amos 'n' Andy* or, at worst, a contemporary version of a minstrel show. Yet, at the same time, *Kenan & Kel* and other characters of color on Nickelodeon variety shows represent a kind of racial ambivalence. These shows do not simply follow an assimilationist paradigm, where they happen to be African American but otherwise perform whiteness. The cultural economy in which *Kenan & Kel* was produced had shifted from one in which an assimilationist paradigm continued to make sense; the style and consumer politics of the "urban" has redefined the television landscape so that the identity performance of actors such as Kenan and Kel is not one of whiteness but rather a commodified, brand-identified urban style. The cultural relevance of the show, the hip-hop theme, and the diverse cast makes it impossible to understand the program solely as assimilationist, because the actors are not performing whiteness but are rather performing a racial style.

Barry Shank, writing about race in rock and pop music, argues that the articulation and experience of race within musical forms is always a "bundle of contradictions which have been mobilized both politically and musically." He continues,

> The perception of race in rock and pop can take the form of recognizable musical sounds—certain rhythms, timbres, song styles and pitch structures; or it can be seen in the racial identifications of the performers or the audiences for the music; or it can be traced through the racially targeted branches of the music industry; or it can be acknowledged retrospectively as contributing to a certain racialized musical tradition. At each such moment when race does enter the perception of rock and pop, a renegotiation of the meanings of blackness and whiteness takes place, a renegotiation which is both musical and political.[43]

While children's cable television is clearly different from rock and pop music, I also see Nickelodeon programming as producing a "perception of race," which can be seen in the styles, sounds, the cultural relevance of the programs, the racial identification of performers, and a more general industry endorsement of Nickelodeon as the diversity channel. As with rock and pop, when race is a key factor in the production and consumption of Nickelodeon programs, a "renegotiation of the meanings of blackness and whiteness takes place" and a generalized concept of the urban stands in for historical specificity of racial identity and indeed functions as "race." The ways in which actors in Nickelodeon programs perform race on comedy and variety shows require an examination within the context of the history of images of race in the United States, especially in the realm of entertainment and visual culture. Minstrelsy, *Amos 'n' Andy*, the "black comedian," and other images in a visual archive of racist images all contribute to the contemporary definition of race produced by Nickelodeon programs. It is thus against this history that Nickelodeon's programs are then recognized as progressive—and it is also against this history that Nickelodeon "respects" its audience as empowered citizens.

Within the Nickelodeon context, my question about the network's commitment to "diversity" concerns how this commitment is linked to Nickelodeon's claim to "empower" kids. Is the fact that diverse programming is more frequent on Nickelodeon mean that the children watching—white kids, African American kids, Latino kids—are empowered by the representations? As I've argued throughout this book, the current invocation of youth empowerment is a strategy that makes sense only within the logic of the commercial brand. The social construction of race as hip or cool also makes sense within this logic. So, young audiences see many more images of people of color within popular consumer culture than even ten years ago, and the representations signify a different cultural landscape; there is a clear change from seeing people of color on television as primarily "menaces to society" to seeing images of African Americans, Latinos, and Asian Americans as symbols for a hip generation.[44]

Given both the normalization of the "urban" as a dominant style politics and social parlance in American youth culture and increasingly diverse cultural and ethnic demographics, it is not surprising that the television industry (both broadcast and cable) has responded with changes in casting and rhetorical strategies about "diversity." Nickelodeon, consistent with the network's claims to be a "different" network for kids, has led the field in terms of diverse casts and crews for its programming, yet it has also maintained an ambivalent political statement about diversity. For example, in 2000, Nickelodeon joined with the National Council of La Raza to survey the demographic composition of young television audiences. In this survey, Nickelodeon and the National Council of La Raza determined that children are more ethnically diverse than the rest of the population.[45] Moreover, according to this study and others, African American and Latino children watch more television than white children.[46] The alliance with the National Council of La Raza could have produced an interesting debate about serving a particular "public interest," but Nickelodeon addresses this audience diversity by creating representations that are pan-ethnic and often racially nonspecific—more "urban" than local or regional. This strategy fits with the network's vague claim to be "for kids only"; television that is "for kids only" allows diversity to be translated into a generalized kid aesthetic rather than a specific political or progressive platform. Thus, the rhetoric of "kids only" renders racial specificity invisible even as "kids only" claims to be all-inclusive.

This strategy is translated as a gesture of "respect" for kids, as it represents "realism" rather than an unattainable ideal. The question of inclusion for Nickelodeon is turned on its head: the network claims that it *is* empowering children, so that the question of *how* children are empowered is never asked. For instance, when asked about diversity on Nickelodeon programs, John Hardman answered in a way that clearly separated ethnic identities into different marketing groups:

Look, each group has a different take on ethnic issues. The Asian kids are not as concerned about representation as the other groups. They accept that Asians aren't represented and when they are, it's often stereotypical. With Hispanics, English-language programs are not as big of an issue as you might think. They know they have Spanish-language television and they sometimes watch with their parents. They don't expect English language networks to broadcast in Spanish. African Americans, on the other hand, expect more representation. They have some conditioning to it. There's more sitcoms out there directed at African Americans. The market has made more of an effort to produce and market shows to them. Kids are hip to that so they expect more.[47]

African Americans have had some "conditioning" to the issues of representation, and, at least according to this Nickelodeon executive, the kids who are the audience for Nickelodeon "expect" more representations of African Americans. Clearly, this expectation is based not only in the historical "conditioning" of African Americans but also within the commercial presence of the urban in the New Economy. This is not an indication that the shows are not "really" diverse, but rather that diversity itself needs to be redefined within the contemporary media economy as part of brand culture. Images of race and ethnicity sell products, so that when it becomes good for business to reflect "reality," more diverse images are produced.

For Nickelodeon, the distinction between being "good for business" and being respectful to kids is blurry, at best. As one Nickelodeon executive claims, "In developing shows, we always start from the standpoint of what's good for kids . . . We talk to kids all the time. We do our research. And through it all, we usually get the sense that kids like seeing themselves, their friends and their world on TV. And their world happens to be highly diversified."[48] Here, the Nickelodeon executive relies on a strategy of colorblindness—the network does not actively *seek out* diverse characters, according to this statement, but rather simply stands behind the noble standpoint of "what's good for kids." However, unlike the ways in which a colorblind politics has worked historically in the United States, when whiteness is privileged as the norm and the invisible, the consequence of Nickelodeon's stance on colorblindness is a coincidental urban landscape: Nickelodeon programming is often diverse, simply because the world of kids "happens" to be "highly diversified."[49] Another Nickelodeon executive, Paula Kaplan, commented on the network's ambivalent stance: "What we do differently here is that we are open-minded and try to be flexible as to who is right for the part . . . It's more work, but people get excited about seeing great acting . . . And we want to make sure we are reflecting what is in a kid's life. The world is a big melting pot now, and what we do is try to reflect their lives."[50] Again, in this statement, the network executive refuses an overtly political stance about diversity and instead relies on a discourse of "reality"—the network simply reflects reality. More importantly, however overused, the image of the melting pot as urban and hip is economically important: diversity is a *market*, not a political position. Industry executives back away from claiming a "conscious decision" about diversity, or at least not a *politically* conscious decision, as deferring to a constructed definition of reality as a politically safe strategy. Rather, it is about "good kids' TV." For instance, Nina Jacobson of Buena Vista Motion Picture Group (which includes Disney) commented that the company recognized that "our movies should reflect the reality of our cultural world."[51] Or, as Scannell points out, the channel is not dedicated so much to diversity as to "good characters and stories."[52] Here, the implication is that kids don't see diversity; rather, they just relate to characters they like and "good acting."

In another interpretation of diversity, Scannell framed Nickelodeon's perspective on this issue as one that is about "good television": "One of the other oft-cited excuses people have for not having a diverse screen are the business pressures, i.e. ratings and advertising sales. We believe that being good for kids is good for business, and that diversity is good for kids. If you want a business case for diversity, look no further than Nickelodeon. We have been the number one rated network in cable for six straight years, and I believe strongly that the diversity on our screen has been a big reason for that success. Kids are comfortable with diversity. It is in their lives everyday."[53] While the network was (and continues to be) outspoken in its commitment to alleviating asymmetry when it comes to gender identity, when it comes to issues of race, Nickelodeon frequently relies on a conventional notion of racial invisibility or colorblindness despite the continual presence of ideologies about race: race shouldn't be the "main subject" of programming, and the network's commitment to diversity wasn't some "PC" notion of what is "good television." In Scannell's words, "We wanted to have our shows reflect the world that today's kids live in, and that is a world rich with cultural diversity."[54] Constructing diversity as "reality" is problematic not because it is a material inaccuracy. Rather, this rhetorical strategy evacuates the political potential behind diverse programming and thus maintains an ambivalent stance on diversity. This conflation of market strategies and increased representation of people of color leads to a profound ambivalence about race for Nickelodeon. Indeed, Scannell recognizes that the world is full of "cultural diversity," but the construction of Nickelodeon's programming as merely reflective rather than politicizing indicates a redefinition in how diversity is understood in the contemporary media environment.

I don't mean to trivialize the channel's claim of cultural diversity, but I do want to examine it more closely. Why does the network remain ambivalent about racial diversity in its programming? Why is it acceptable within the industry to feature programming that specifically highlights girls and features girl issues as primary concerns but to refuse a similar kind of specificity about race? In other words, when Nickelodeon decided to create the program *Clarissa Explains It All* in 1991, it did so explicitly to challenge the dearth of strong, intelligent girl characters, in direct opposition to other children's television that privileged boys. But when Nickelodeon creates *Kenan & Kel*, or *Hey Arnold!*, or even the ostensibly more political *The Brothers Garcia* (created by Jeff Valdez, founder of SiTv), these programming choices are framed by the network as a kind of "sign of the times" rather than a direct challenge to the whiteness that has historically structured television programming. There is, then, an inherent contradiction in the way in which Nickelodeon executives discuss the channel's position on race. For instance, Cyma Zarghami, then senior vice president of programming, commented when asked whether the channel "looked for" diverse actors for shows, "We try to celebrate all kids including their diversity. We want all kinds of kids. *Shelby Woo, Kenan & Kel, Alex Mack* have diverse casts. *Gula Gula* is the first preschool program with African American hosts. These programs aren't just for kids of color, but they show all different kinds of kids. Right now, Shelby Woo is the only Asian-American lead on television. There's a lot of traditional myths that we have tried to break and now a lot of other people are following suit."[55] In this statement, Zarghami demonstrates both the commitment of Nickelodeon to challenge historical racial stereotypes on kids' television ("there's a lot of traditional myths that we have tried to break"), and the simultaneous disavowal of the politics concerning "breaking myths" ("we try to celebrate all kids"). Part of the ambivalence about race contained in Nickelodeon's rhetoric has to do with the history of race relations on television itself, where we witness a resilient ambivalence about not only what race should "look like" but also a more general uncertainty about whether an outspoken commitment to diversity will gain channels the proper (in the minds of both the audience and the advertisers) kind of cultural capital—or alternately, a public backlash.[56] Within the context of children's television, this ambivalence becomes even more complicated: in many ways, children's television has been much more progressive than prime time television in terms of representing diversity, in large part because of the presumed role of kids' television as a particular kind of symbolic educator.

Part of Nickelodeon's ambivalent stance on diversity also has to do with the nature of representation itself. Despite continuous searching for "positive" representations, as Stuart Hall reminds us, there is no "good" or "bad" representation: all representations are culturally situated, and all rely upon social mythologies about what is currently the authentic nature of identity.[57] Because an important part of Nickelodeon's rhetoric is that children *are* in fact diverse, Nickelodeon is able to claim that race isn't a major "issue," even as the channel simultaneously receives political clout for being the "diversity station." It is not surprising that Nickelodeon adopts a rhetoric of diversity to support its "kids only" ideology. Despite the fact that Nickelodeon is diverse not only in terms of casting but also in terms of hiring production crews that are nonwhite, the company relies on a familiar meritocratic argument: roles on television shows are given to the "best" actors, regardless of race. This creates Nickelodeon's position on race as a non-position; as the Puerto Rican actress Christina Vidal, who plays the lead character on Nickelodeon's program *Taina*, commented, "Ethnicity is not thrown in everyone's face—it's not like there are subtitles and rice and beans on every show . . . It gives everyone a chance to see Latin people in a different light—like 'they are just like everybody else.' Once in a while we add some flavor and culture so people can see that, but it is not so far left field that they can't relate to it."[58] Of course, framing ethnicity in this way functions as a reassurance that whiteness remains dominant—it is whiteness to which the "everybody else" Vidal mentions refers. Race and ethnicity is "flavor," but not so much that whites cannot "relate" to it.

NICKELODEON'S PAN-ETHNICITY: *DORA THE EXPLORER*

The popular preschool program *Dora the Explorer* is a good example of this kind of "pan-ethnic" strategy. As one article puts it: "Finally the idea emerged to have the star be a little girl with a sidekick partner, but it wasn't until a Nickelodeon executive attended a Children Now diversity seminar in 1998 that the doors opened for Dora. Did someone say abre?"[59] *Dora the Explorer* is part of the preschool Nick Jr. block and so has a slightly different relationship to the Nickelodeon brand identity of the upstart rebel who operates according to Us versus Them ideology. Rather, *Dora* is a program built on pedagogical research concerning the use of television to educate preschoolers. In every episode, the narrative revolves around solving a puzzle or mystery (such as how to find the frog's voice, or how to save a baby jaguar). The program itself is structured to be a computer game, so that there is a cursor that "clicks" on the right answer when Dora asks the audience for help. There are pauses in the program, where Dora looks at the audience, waiting for them to reply to her questions about the daily mystery, thus encouraging a kind of active interaction on the part of the preschool audience.[60]

17. Dora the Explorer
and her sidekick Boots
the Monkey, 2004.

The emphasis on audience interaction is, of course, typical for many contemporary children's television programs, where creators have researched the pedagogical potential of television. It also speaks to a more general cultural shift—signified by postfeminism, among other things—that recognizes media audiences as active, savvy consumers. Textually, the tropes of postfeminism and urbanization are evident in the overall aesthetics of the show, including featuring an intelligent girl as a lead character and celebrating a kind of racial "authenticity" through the physical representation of Dora, the names of the other characters on the show, and the general representational style of the program. Dora is Latina and speaks both Spanish and English. Other human characters on the show are also Latino, including Dora's parents, Mami and Papi, her grandmother Abuela, her cousin Diego, and the newest addition, Dora's twin baby siblings. Most of the other characters on the program are animals and are also often racialized: Benni the Bull, Isa the Iguana, Tico the Squirrel. The home in which Dora resides with her parents is Spanish-style, an adobe building with a red tile roof. While the plot themes of the show are often developmental and pedagogical, the narrative of *Dora* also frequently references Latino culture, traditions, and styles, although not necessarily in an ethnically or geographically specific manner. A Christmas episode features a Mexican parade called a parranda, the rain forest is a frequent destination on Dora's adventures, and salsa music is a typical accompaniment to episodes. One episode is based on a Puerto Rican legend, involving Dora and a coqui (a frog) who has lost his voice and cannot sing unless he gets back to his island. As with every episode, Dora saves the day: she helps the frog, and he eventually finds his voice and his way back.

The weaving of the Puerto Rican legend into the show, and, more specifically,

18. Dora's twin baby siblings, 2005.

incorporating themes of migration and exile culture as the primary narrative of the episode, along with Latino dances and music, are ways to employ the strategy of being racially specific but ethnically nonspecific. This strategy, as a part of postfeminism culture and the celebration of "difference," functions as an effective way to both target and create a particular community of consumers. *Dora the Explorer* represents Nickelodeon's commitment to diversity. Dora is "pan-ethnic" intentionally, so that as a Latina she has a wide appeal for her young audience. In an article titled "Adorable Dora is Opening the Doors of Diversity," the producers of the show comment specifically on her pan-ethnic representation, "With Dora, Nickelodeon found a heroine that appeals to kids of all ethnic backgrounds" . . . [producer Gifford] recalling one Chinese child who said, 'She's just like me; she speaks another language.' The creators purposely do not specify Dora's ethnic background, preferring that she have a pan-Latino appeal, and revised her original green eyes to brown after content supervisor Dolly Espinal pointed out that a majority of Latinos have brown eyes and that it was important to celebrate that."[61] The difference embodied by the character of Dora allows for an ethnically informed style politics, yet it is a difference that is not necessarily acted upon. Challenging racist stereotypes by creating a new one fitting for the current political and cultural economy, *Dora* operates (at least in part) as part of a strategy motivating a commercially defined notion of diversity. As Dávila has pointed out in her study about marketing aimed at Latinos, "To sell themselves and their products, those in [the advertising] industry have not only drawn from existing stereotypes . . . but have also positioned themselves as the 'politically correct' voice with which to challenge stereotypes and educate corporate clients about Hispanic language and culture."[62] Nickelodeon's self-identity as the "diver-

19. Dora, Boots, and her twin siblings, 2005.

sity station" utilizes a similar kind of strategy, where the channel gains political clout by featuring diverse representations to its young audience.

Within the current market environment, a dual process of challenging and reinforcing racial stereotypes in the media is necessary in order to maintain an "ethnic" niche for the market.[63] Yet, in programs such as *Dora the Explorer* that also confront stereotypes as they simultaneously reformulate them for a shifted market, the stereotype that is reconstituted is one that is not necessarily intended for an ethnic niche market but is rather meant to appeal to a broader (more "global") audience. Using this strategy, Nickelodeon can claim that the network is "committed" to diversity, despite the fact that this progressive ideology works as a more general market imperative. This strategy works hand in hand with postfeminist politics, where Dora as a strong smart female character is clearly a product of a culture that recognizes the importance of "positive" gender representations yet also does not call attention to any kind of "feminist" politics other than the politics of representation. Thus, the challenges to dominant stereotypes *Dora the Explorer* poses are framed within normative social conventions so that the challenge is contained and made palatable for a media audience. What this means, at least for Dora, is to utilize Latino "themes" as part of the program, but in a safe way, so as not to alienate Nickelodeon's predominantly white, middle-class cable audience.

Dávila argues that stereotypes work "by restricting the range of interpretations and therefore facilitating the evaluations that reproduce and valorize the social distinctions at play in the greater society. Even when individuals may interpret these images and ideas differently or imbue them with idiosyncratic meaning, these renditions are by necessity framed within dominant social conventions."[64] The dominant social conventions to which Dávila refers are those that create the generic "Hispanic" market. Examining Hispanic "themes" in ads, Dávila argues that these themes interpellate the audience using particular strategies: authenticity, assimilation, "positive" comparison to whites based on apparent inherent Latino qualities (such as the ability to eat a habanero chili pepper). Regarding Nickelodeon, it is less about these kinds of overt comparative strategies than about incorporating "diversity" into the shows.

In the case of Nickelodeon, demonstrated by *Dora the Explorer*, diversity is part of the construction of the identity of the empowered consumer citizen. Indeed, Chris Gifford, the co-creator and executive producer of *Dora*, claimed he had "empowering children in mind" when he created the show.[65] The construction of Dora as a "global citizen," where her ethnicity is specific but her appeal is racially nonspecific, makes her what the consultant Carlos Cortes calls "a crossover phenomenon and the product of a slow evolution in television."[66] This "evolution" of television is indicated by the construction of ethnic markets such as the Hispanic market Dávila theorizes, an increasingly diverse body of consumers, and the emergence of a cool, more "multicultural" approach to making television shows that corresponds with a general youth market. Another interpretation would examine this "tolerance" from the point of the global market, where diversity is depicted according to an "It's a Small World" mentality, where ethnicity is appealing to all, and threatening to none.

THE BUSINESS OF DIVERSITY

Nickelodeon's position on diversity has important consequences for the network's finances as well. Regarding the channel's stance on diverse programming, Ellen Seiter and Vicky Mayer have argued that Nickelodeon executives "seemed to follow a party line aimed at widening their potential advertisers and marketers, reiterating in all interviews that their shows were really about character and interesting story lines."[67] Indeed, there is an "express disavowal of the politics of representation," on the part of the network, despite the important presence of race on shows such as *The Brothers Garcia* and *Dora the Explorer*. Simply including nonwhite representation—or making a conscious effort to do so—is seen as "preaching to the kids." It becomes "moral" rather than entertaining if the network is perceived to have a particular political agenda regarding race and diversity. Indeed, as soon as it looks like a diverse character or plot line is planned *because* of diversity issues, media companies back off, indicating a disavowal of the fact that having a historically white televisual landscape *is* in fact a political agenda. As Katherine Sender has argued about the making of the gay market in the United States, the separation of business from politics is important for marketers: "By separating business from politics, marketers appeal to a liberal-utilitarian economic model in which financial decisions can be made free of political motivations or ramifications, and where marketers can reach new consumers and generate increased profits independently of any impact this activity might have on social relations or cultural politics."[68] In the case of Nickelodeon, the case is slightly more complicated, because the channel *does* claim to have an overt agenda: to respect kids. Nevertheless, what does it mean to legitimate diversity as a marketing strategy, where one's identity as a "kid" is already constituted as part of a marketing strategy? For Nickelodeon, it is a marketing strategy to construct its audience as "kids," so why not Latino kids? What is the difference? And how is this difference negotiated when there does seem to be an overt agenda to include ethnic representation? In the preschool program *Go Diego Go!*, for example, the main character is Diego, Dora's cousin (the show is a spinoff from *Dora the Explorer*). Thematically, the show focuses on animals, as Diego is committed to saving animals that are in trouble (this may mean endangered animals or simply a jaguar that gets stuck on a mountain). Each show focuses on a particular animal, and one of the show's "rules" is that the animal must be from Latin America. The show incorporates Latin American folktales and mythology about animals as part of each episode, so that the narrative as well as the characters is ethnically based.

Nickelodeon's marketing strategy allows the channel to maintain its ideological stance and commitment to being a network for kids, but at the same time it indicates that the network does not have to be "about race"—race is simply something that "happens" in a kids' world. Nickelodeon conducts research—primarily in the form of focus groups—on kids to determine what "they like" in terms of television programming. These focus groups also provide data in order to make decisions about diversity; as Bruce Friend, then vice-president of worldwide research and planning for Nickelodeon, said when asked about minority kids in focus groups: "We oversample a bit with minorities. We've had some distinct groups of minorities as test groups. We skew the norms in terms of their representation in the population. But the multicultural focus groups give us different kinds of information. We ask them how Nickelodeon fits into their lives. We don't have a problem with representation and thus need the focus groups. It's the opposite. We're very strong in this area. We want to further our understanding of our appeal. We recognize our audience is not homogenous."[69] As this comment indicates, the executives at Nickelodeon promote an antiracist agenda (where they "skew the norms" so as to get a more multicultural focus group), but this comment also reflects the complexity of producing images that are antiracist to a nonhomogenous audience: any time a representation of race is produced, it reflects a stereotype or a narrativizing of a cultural myth about race—even if ostensibly "positive."[70] So Nickelodeon employs several different strategies of representing race: race either is represented as hip or cool, as a kind of aesthetic style, or it is represented through the lens of authenticity, with "real" tropes of race structuring the narrative of a program. The inclusion of explicitly racial images on Nickelodeon programming coincides with the exclusion of a specifically racial agenda, so that inclusion functions as a kind of exclusion. Nickelodeon advocates a commitment to the "every kid," a kid who is nothing spectacular, nothing exceptional; as Zarghami recalls, "Historically, we used to do a show which showcased kids with special talents. For example, Sam, the seven-year-old pianist. But then we found that these shows did more damage to kids' self-esteem than help. It was then that we decided to make shows about normal kids."[71] Clearly, the intention behind the strategy to "make shows about normal kids" is obviously not malicious, but it runs the risk of consolidating an idea about the "normal" child—the white child who is most likely to be watching Nickelodeon. When the channel's self-identity is about a particular idea of "normal," it becomes difficult to see how "normalcy" itself is grounded in a racial politics.

When media corporations such as Nickelodeon produce programming that structures representations around a market-driven racial code of cool and hip, it is a reflection of Naomi Klein's discussion of the ways in which the current corporate climate produces a "market that thinks it is culture."[72] Dávila reminds us that this dynamic works in the opposite direction as well, where advertising agencies and media corporations produce "culture for the market."[73] This dynamic between producing "culture for the market" and creating a "market that thinks it is culture" structures much of Nickelodeon's brand identity. The framing of racial identity as an important element of the Nickelodeon brand accomplishes several things. For instance, this kind of frame situates racial empowerment through representation as another layer in the Nickelodeon-defined concept of youth empowerment. Empowerment as defined by Nickelodeon not only entails offering the means to cultural citizenship through the brand but also enables access to a liberated notion of personal identity politics—gender and race—as a crucial factor in brand development. And in fact, many of the Nickelodeon fans that I interviewed identified Nickelodeon as a station that is committed to diversity, an identification which is critical to enabling empowerment. For instance, when I asked her about diversity on Nickelodeon, one eleven-year-old girl said, "I think Nick Jr. probably does a better job than Nickelodeon itself. Because Nick Jr. tries—I think they try to expose kids to different races and stuff before they're out there with all these different people."[74] Clearly the assumption here is that "difference" indicates nonwhite people—the preschool audience that watches Nick Jr. is thus exposed to difference—"before they're out there with all these different people." Nonetheless, this Nickelodeon fan saw the channel as doing something important in terms of diversity—although others I interviewed felt that PBS was more successful with diverse characters. As one eleven-year-old boy commented, "I think PBS does a better job . . . [because of] *Sesame Street*. Because *Sesame Street* always has kids with disabilities and they talk to people and talk to kids on the show. And like half the people will be black and half the people will be white. And some people have disabilities. And you'll have kids from all over the place. You'll have Asian kids and they'll have Native American kids and stuff."[75] While Nickelodeon might not have the same amount of cultural capital as PBS in terms of diversity, the channel certainly is noticed more than broadcast television. In one conversation exchange between four fifteen-to-seventeen-year-old girls, they all commented on Nickelodeon's impressive record when it comes to diversity—although some noticed diverse programming more than others. They recalled shows that they watched when they were younger that featured minority characters:

J: And that was even like when we were little. So they had, I mean, stuff back then.

K: They've done a lot with black actors like Kenan and Kel.

C: And even if the main character was white, it still . . .

J: The cast was always mixed.

K: There was always like a blonde person, it was equally distributed.

C: But even on that show, they had all white friends.

L: I can't see that separation, it didn't stand out to me, but now that I think about it. I can't say that I was five and thinking, "Oh look, I'm so glad they had a black person, or a Hispanic person."[76]

Clearly, there is no consensus in this group as to whether Nickelodeon was successful in its claims of diversity, but nonetheless the group felt that the channel did put forth considerable effort to be diverse. Indeed, as the young audience member who thought that Nick Jr. provided good "exposure" to diversity continued, "Like they start to teach kids some Spanish and Dora—not much, but just like sometimes they say a little Spanish and tell you what it means. And then *Little Bill*, it's like everyone in his family is African American."[77] Undeniably, *Dora the Explorer* has received attention for both the show's intrepid Latina heroine and the use of Spanish as part of the preschool program's curriculum. Another show, targeting more of a tween audience, is *The Brothers Garcia*. Rather than employ a strategy that privileges pan-ethnicity, *The Brothers Garcia* utilizes authenticity as its entry point into diversity.

THE BROTHERS GARCIA

The Brothers Garcia debuted on Nickelodeon in the fall of 2000 and was created by Jeff Valdez. The program, which made television history as the first English-language sitcom with an all-Latino cast and creative team, revolves around a family of six—mother, father, three sons, and a daughter—who reside in San Antonio, Texas. According to Valdez, he primarily created the program as a way to demonstrate to investors that English-language programming for Latinos could work in the marketplace.[78] Conventional industry wisdom held that linguistically segregated programming was the most effective way to appeal to the increasing number of Latino viewers in the United States. Spanish-language networks such as Univision and Telemundo held the great share of audience ratings for Latino viewers. Through the creation of SiTV, a media organization dedicated to English-speaking Latino audiences, Valdez aimed to tap into this market, and Nickelodeon, given its relationship to "diversity" as a crucial part of its brand identity, was a logical training ground.[79] Thus, the concept for *The Brothers Garcia* was from the beginning about the use of diverse imagery to capitalize on what was seen as an untapped market: English-speaking Latinos in the United States. Scannell, when asked about the motivation for *The Brothers Garcia*, commented: "The show really came from [Valdez's] passion and was based on what he knew . . . He had a goal bigger than creating a show. First, he knew there is a lot of creativity in the Latino community in the United States. Second, Latinos weren't seeing themselves reflected in programming, and third, there is a large group of people attuned to Hispanic culture who primarily speak English."[80] The program was structured around two primary discourses which shape its overall narrative: one, the legitimation of the English-speaking Latino market; and two, the appeal of the "authentic" in Latino-themed programs.

To demonstrate the way in which these dynamics of market authenticity and ethnic authenticity work to constantly reinforce each other, it is useful to examine a particular episode of *The Brothers Garcia*. This episode (which was actually a full-hour—instead of a half-hour—program) is titled "Mysteries of the Maya" and begins with the youngest Garcia son, Larry, reading "La Familia Garcia"—a story of the family history. The Garcia family can apparently be traced to Mayan culture, and as an effort to "rediscover our roots in Mexico," the father of the Garcia family (a history professor) decides to take the entire group on a trip to discover their origins. The episode continually plays with distinctions between authenticity and commercially defined "culture": the Garcias travel to Chichen Itza to see ancient Mayan pyramids only to stay at "Maya Land," a kitschy tourist destination complete with reenactments of Mayan conflicts and dances. The family is met by a Mexican guide who speaks with an American hip-hop–derived dialect (he refers to Professor Garcia as "Yo! Mr. G!," for example), who appeals most to the two older brothers who are characterized as girl-crazy, branded teenagers. The two older boys are clearly what the ad agency LatinoEyes would call "acculturated Latinos"; they constantly refer to American popular and brand culture, they have an active *disinterest* in "discovering their roots" (at one point disputing with their younger brother about attending a narrated tour of the pyramids or watching MTV *Cribs* on the hotel television), and they are much more interested in traveling to the tourist destination of Cancun.[81] The villain of this episode, Don Cortez, is played by Cheech Marin and is also clearly within the "acculturated Latino" identity category. Not only is Don Cortez not interested in preserving "roots" and heritage; he is actively involved in stealing Mayan artifacts and selling them for profit. He runs a tourist service, Cortez Tours, as a front for finding new—and valuable—artifacts. His Latino identity is both overstated and mocked as he speaks with a false, exaggerated accent, saying things such as "I deedn't mean to es-startle you."

Larry and his father, on the other hand, exemplify the "retro-acculturated" Latinos: searching for signs of family roots, the two climb pyramids, investigate ancient Mayan caves, and eventually play primary roles in the mystery of the episode, when an ancient Mayan prince (a far-removed cousin of the Garcias) comes back to life to find his soul mate. In this way, the program gestures toward the authentic, where Larry is depicted throughout the episode as clearly the intellectual in the family, carrying a book of legends to every destination and constantly pointing out cultural referents to the family's national heritage. The father, Professor Garcia, dresses in "explorer" clothing: khaki shorts, straw hat, even a leather whip. At one point, his wife refers to him as "Indiana Garcia," referring to the popular character of the anthropologist Indiana Jones from the *Indiana Jones* movies.

The gender dynamics of this program adhere to dominant ideologies about gender roles in the family: the wife and daughter are clearly interested in "feminine" things, while the boys and the father concentrate their interests on ideas and events that are gendered masculine. The emphasis on brothers in the program's title clearly erases the daughter, Lorena, from the representational scene altogether, although she is featured in nearly every episode. Her primary role as a character is to demonstrate her desire and knowledge for telenovelas; indeed, she interprets the plot of every episode according to its similarity to a telenovela script. The highly stylized and refined gender construction of Lorena extends to the mother of the family as well, who works outside the home, running a beauty salon (called "Casa de Beauty") and is unambiguously charged with typical household duties such as child care, cooking, and cleaning.

The program, and this episode in particular, is interesting because of the way it represents the complicated negotiation involved in cultural discourses of the "authentic" versus the commercially contrived. This negotiation exists as a kind of productive tension throughout the show, in a way that situates consumer culture and its connections to personal identity as affirming and pleasurable, as simultaneously a notion of the "real" is constructed throughout the episode as untouched and more authentic than consumer culture—even if this "real" is accessed precisely through consumer culture. This is present in many different moments of the episode, ranging from the obvious differences between the Maya Land theme park and the Garcias' own quest for Mayan roots (a difference that is remarked upon often and disparagingly by Professor Garcia), to the characterization of the ancient Mayan prince's soul mate—a woman he eventually finds, working at Maya Land as a tour guide, dressed in a contrived version of "authentic" Mayan clothing. Chichen Itza is juxtaposed against the touristy landscape of Cancun, and the visual scenery of the episode cuts from shots of ancient pyramids and caves to long stretches of beaches, with a visual focus on young women in bikinis (indeed, while in Cancun, Lorena becomes sunburned while relaxing on the beach, to which her mother comments, "You don't have that Mayan skin").

Finally, the use of the Spanish language in *The Brothers Garcia* functions, much as it does in *Dora the Explorer,* as an explicit marker of authentic identity. The family uses Spanish words and phrases throughout, and in places Larry and the Mayan prince use an ancient Mayan language. There is some play with subtitles in this episode, where, when Yucatec is spoken, it is sometimes translated into English ("Let's cruise," for example), and sometimes in Spanish (where "Vamanos" is used). The markers of authentic identity—the search for roots, Mayan culture, the Spanish language—are in constant tension with contemporary consumer culture such that an ambivalence is produced about ethnic identity. This ambivalence is created through the tension between legitimating a quest for origins and subsequently validating those origins as "authentic" and the validation of popular consumer culture as the key to personal identity. *The Brothers Garcia* often conflates popular consumer culture with "American" culture, thus contributing to a racial and ethnic hierarchy where some version of American culture holds the place in the center, against which and to which all other "cultures" are then measured and compared. The television reviewer Richard Vazquez comments on this kind of assimilation:

> The only difference between this family show and another is that the family is brown, they speak with accents that aren't exaggerated, and occasionally the Garcias use a Spanish phrase in a context where it can be understood. The Garcias don't live in a gang-infested neighborhood, nor are they running from immigration. Nobody is likely to be shot unless it is a "very special episode." The show, in the long run, may prove to be the Latino Cosby Family—normalizing Latinos as people. This family just happens to have salsa with meals, listen to different music, and speaks Spanglish. They're just a family with hard working parents who are in love, and precocious, mischievous kids.[82]

The efforts by Valdez, the industry, and Nickelodeon to create racial and ethnic representations as "just like everyone else" can be read in a way similar to the way *The Cosby Show* has been read by Gray: this characterization constructs Latinos in *The Brothers Garcia* as *all* Latinos and thus renders invisible the cultural politics of many Latino communities, involving poverty, unemployment, discrimination, and racism. Yet the show is different from *The Cosby Show,* in its gestures toward the real and the authentic as well as in the more general construction of race as a commodity post-Cosby. In this way, the references to Latino culture are not simply peripheral but rather inform the aesthetics, cultural politics, and personal identities that shape the program. For example, the family itself, as the subject of *The Brothers Garcia,* is positioned as a trope for Latino culture. The family is devoutly Catholic; episodes frequently contain references to Catholic saints, grace is said before meals, and religious symbols adorn the walls of the Garcia house. Catholicism is a strong (if complicated) cultural component of many Latino communities, and the presence of religion on the program is clearly about making that connection for the audience. The language, the food, the telenovelas that Lorena watches on television, the reverence the family has for Abuelita (Grandmother), as well as other tropes and narratives, provide a political and representational landscape that denies the ambivalence of "this is just an American family that happens to be Latino" even as it supports this ambivalence through its reliance on race and ethnicity as particular sorts of commodities.

NEW SCHOOL DIVERSITY

Contemporary capitalism, as part of global culture, and the motivation for the increase in brand culture curiously embrace diversity through increasingly segmented, "diverse" marketing niches. This kind of diverse capitalism is part of postfeminism and girl power as a new gender politics and, as I will discuss in the next chapter, as camp and irony in popular culture, functioning not as a counterhegemonic visual and narrative strategy but rather as a dominant mainstream trope within representational politics. But this articulation of capitalism is a bit trickier to pinpoint in regard to race, because dominant understandings of race are really a last vestige of "old school" modernity—even if the dominant way of experiencing race is truly a new school phenomenon.[83] Multiculturalism within current capitalism is about brand identity and consumer culture, where advocacy is not focused on changing what is already there but rather about how to include more of one group or another, how to increase access to the same system—but not to change the system itself.

What characterizes contemporary commercial culture, then, is what Ann duCille, in her discussion of black Barbie dolls, calls "mass produced difference." Precisely because Barbie has historically held the place in the children's consumer world as the white ideal with her blond hair and blue eyes, duCille theorizes the complicated nature of representing difference by focusing on the production of the black Barbie. Arguing that any change in this hegemonic construction of femininity is potentially progressive, duCille also points out that on the other hand, "this seeming act of racializing the dolls is accomplished by a contrapuntal action of erasure. In other words, Mattel is only able to racialize its dolls by blurring the sharp edges of the very difference that the corporation produces and profits from. It is able to make and market ethnicity by ignoring not only the body politics of the real people its dolls are meant to represent, but by ignoring the body politic as well—by eliding the material conditions of the masses it dolls up."[84]

This love/hate relationship with diversity and difference is not simply a response by white audiences but is also a factor within media corporations. It is important to be "different" in the contemporary competitive brand culture, so that a network's or program's identity stands out. But this "difference" needs to be managed in a particular way so that racial and cultural hierarchies remain intact; as duCille puts it, difference that is mass-reproduced ends up being just another interchangeable fashion. The ambivalence that this representation of diversity contains thus works to simplify race for Nickelodeon, a channel that truly is the "diversity channel" within the landscape of children's cable television —but it is a diversity that is brought to market-segmented audiences as an easily identified commodity.

6

IS NICK FOR KIDS?
IRONY, CAMP, AND ANIMATION
IN THE NICKELODEON BRAND

Animation is the intrinsic language of metamorphosis, and
the literal illustration of change and progress.
—PAUL WELLS, *ANIMATION AND AMERICA*

Go SpongeBob! Go SpongeBob! Go Self!
—*SPONGEBOB SQUAREPANTS*

He's not very masculine for a male character. And he's soft.
—ALFRED FUNG

It's really funny, and it's really unrealistic, and all the characters are sort of weird and funny. And so when they're all
put together it makes a fun show.
—M., AN ELEVEN-YEAR-OLD BOY

In the year 2002 Nickelodeon profited from over $500 million of
merchandise themed with characters from the wildly popular animated program *SpongeBob SquarePants*. *SpongeBob SquarePants* features the eponymous wacky sea sponge as well as a foolish but affable
starfish named Patrick; Squidward, a cranky squid; a pet snail named
Gary; and Sandy, an effervescent muscular female squirrel, all living under the sea in a village called Bikini Bottom. The *SpongeBob
SquarePants*–themed merchandise includes the usual suspects: lunch-
boxes, plush dolls, key chains, kids clothing, school supplies, and even
macaroni and cheese with SpongeBob–shaped pasta. But it also includes items obviously geared for a more mature audience: Bikini
Bottom thong underwear, men's boxers, neckties, men's t-shirts that
say "SpongeBob NudiePants" and "SpongeBob PartyPants." In 2004,
Paramount Pictures produced *The SpongeBob SquarePants Movie*,

which had some critics claiming that with its kitschy humor and campy references (David Hasselhoff plays a "life-guardian angel," for example, who runs on
the beach *Baywatch* style, with muscles gleaming and in slow motion), the movie
was intended more for the eighteen-to-thirty-four-year-old audience than for
children. *SpongeBob* has recently come under fire by conservative Christian
groups, where one Christian website warned families about the *SpongeBob* movie,
claiming that the film contained "cartoon rear male nudity, repeatedly," "pinch-
ing of banner staff between nude buttocks," and "suggestion of sadomasochism in
transvestitism."[1] In January 2005, Dr. James Dobson, founder of the conservative
Christian foundation Focus on the Family, claimed that the cartoon was used to
legitimize a "group that will corrupt children with a homosexual agenda" when
SpongeBob was featured in a video made for grade schools by the We Are Family
Foundation, in which the foundation makes a pledge of tolerance and respect for
all people, including those with sexual identities different from one's own.[2]

Clearly, *SpongeBob SquarePants* is not *just* for kids. The show is the most
watched program currently broadcast on Nickelodeon, but aside from the usual
kid-friendly daytime hours, the program is also aired at 11:30 p.m. on Nickelodeon, and at 11:00 p.m. on the network's sister station, MTV. And while the
show's creator, Stephen Hillenberg, insists that the program is designed to appeal
to children between two and eleven years old, current Nielsen Media research has
demonstrated that, like the audience for the movie, 22 percent of the show's
regular audience is between eighteen and forty-nine. Yet another indication of an
adult fan base is recent attention to the ostensible sexual politics of the program.
The show's appeal has made current headlines in the popular press because of the
apparent sexuality of the main character; an article in the *Wall Street Journal* in
October 2002 set off a predictable media frenzy when it claimed that there was
"something about SpongeBob that whispers gay."[3]

The adult following of *SpongeBob SquarePants* calls several elements of children's media into question, especially on a network like Nickelodeon. Nickelodeon has built much of its successful marketing campaign around the idea that
"Nick is for kids!," featuring programming and narratives that base their appeal
precisely on the idea that adults find them difficult to decode. As discussed in
earlier chapters, the idea that "adults just don't get it" has cultural currency not
only within programming but with advertisements on the network and its ancillary products, such as the Nickelodeon website. The channel's divisive generational strategy has been one of its most effective strategies to address kids as
citizens—Nickelodeon is a network for children where kids are authorized in
particular sorts of ways. As I've argued throughout this book, however, this
generational divide often masks the channel's transgenerational address. In fact,

as Heather Hendershot has shown, the broader transgenerational appeal of Nickelodeon taps into a desire on the part of adults to "be" a kid, thus deliberately playing with the boundary between adult and child. As Hendershot puts it, "according to the Nickelodeon logic, if adults are sometimes not stuffy, just as children are sometimes not innocent and naïve, it proves (or disproves) nothing about the 'essential nature' of adulthood or childhood; it proves only that adults and kids can play at being each other."[4] Supporting this kind of play is an important factor in the Nickelodeon brand, and the network has been efficient in creating its widely acclaimed original animated series (such as *SpongeBob Square-Pants*) to deliberately make boundaries between adult and child indistinct.

Another way that the current generation of U.S. youth is hailed as citizens is through a particular kind of comedic address. Irony is a dominant trope within contemporary television, and it assumes a smart, media-savvy audience. Nickelodeon animation (and its appeal to both adults and children) is central to the network's brand identity of ironic humor and irreverence. The slippery quality of Nickelodeon's address and its openness to multiple readings by different audiences is particular to the contemporary media economy. This economy, alternately cheered and lampooned as kitschy and ironic, and in fact distinguished by the dominance of the brand and ironic consumption, demands a product that resembles subversive popular culture. As I've argued, the present cultural context of "cool" nourishes popular culture which critiques the mainstream and dominant material conditions through a kind of rebellious social commentary. Yet, despite this rebel feel, contemporary popular culture is shaped and framed by market imperatives—indeed, the rebel feel that is so important to Nickelodeon's brand identity *is* a market strategy. In this chapter, I argue that Nickelodeon's animation style—particularly the use of parody and irony—is yet another way the channel imagines its audience as consumer citizens. To demonstrate how this marks Nickelodeon as a "different" network in the competitive world of children's television, I trace the history of television animation within this media economy, contrasting Nickelodeon animation (Nicktoons) with earlier forms of television cartoons. Nicktoons stand out in the television landscape because they are double-edged in meaning, appealing to different generations by employing an ironic social commentary. Yet the critical edge of this commentary needs to be read against the context of the postmodern media economy, where a kind of cool subversion is not so much social critique as a crucial part of a dominant market address.

Within this frame, I examine in this chapter three of Nickelodeon's original Nicktoons, *The Ren & Stimpy Show* (1991–92), *SpongeBob SquarePants* (2000–), and *The Fairly OddParents* (2003–), as emblematic of the double-coded program, one that functions most effectively through the network's aesthetic theme of animated irony and commodified kitsch. These shows, to some degree, illustrate the various ways in which animation can stretch the boundaries and limitations of representation. This "stretching" becomes a signature of the network and its particular kind of humor. Specifically, the irony and kitsch that characterize these shows become part of the Nickelodeon brand itself—a distinct way in which the network recognizes itself as well as a clear signifier for its audience. Nicktoons are notable in the children's television context where so many cartoons are produced based on licensed toy characters and function almost entirely to sell ancillary products. Nickelodeon cartoons, in contrast, often critique the very context in which they are aired, poking fun at toy gimmicks and consumer culture.

In order to contextualize the multiple codes of meaning within Nickelodeon animated programs, specifically in the ways that kitsch, irony, and camp characterize the network's cartoons, it is necessary to first examine the more general dynamic of animation itself as it functions within the Nickelodeon universe. The differences (and lack thereof) between creator-driven animated shows and toy-based programs, the targeted audience for cartoons and debates about the theory of "double-coding" within animation, and the inclusion of irony and camp to make "smart" cartoons as signatures for Nickelodeon are all important to consider when trying to make sense of the appeal of shows such as *Ren & Stimpy*, *SpongeBob SquarePants*, and *The Fairly OddParents*. Nickelodeon went from edgy irony in *Ren & Stimpy*, a show that seemed designed more for a particular subculture of "animatophiles" than children *or* adults, to a more straightforward slapstick, camp humor in *SpongeBob SquarePants* and *The Fairly OddParents*, whose fan base is more mainstream. This trajectory in the style and substance of Nickelodeon animation corresponds to a similar trajectory of the market that evolved over the 1990s, where the emergence of brand culture appropriated (and contained) the language of irony and camp as important ways to sell products to young consumers. The theory of double coding, where a program has at least two levels of "code" to its logic so that it appeals to different audiences, such as adults and children, or heterosexuals and gay people, has significance for this argument, although I ultimately argue that the assumptions structuring the theory of double coding in media texts are destabilized in the current economic environment. The multiple meanings of visual culture surely still exist, such as "gay window dressing" where, as Danae Clark, Katherine Sender, and others have argued, one motif in a television show or an advertisement appeals to a mainstream audience, while another attracts a gay "reading." Yet the distinctions between the multiple audiences are both more ambiguous and less ambiguous in the current market environment, depending on the marketing strategy.[5] I locate a camp style in children's television programming but also want to re-situate camp within a particular kind of consumer context, as a specific way to address children as consumer citizens. Camp children's shows, like "girl power" programs and Nickelodeon's use of diverse imagery and narratives, harness a political ideology—gay identity politics, queer theory—and commodify it as an aesthetic practice. As with other cultural forms, Nickelodeon's campy style is about contradiction—the contradictions that similarly function as the logic for consumer citizenship.

ANIMATION: FROM CREATOR-DRIVEN TO TOY-BASED AND BACK AGAIN

In the 1980s, Nickelodeon created a name for itself in cable television through its live-action shows. A typical programming schedule in 1987 might include programs such as *Pinwheel* (1979–89), *You Can't Do That on Television* (1981–93), *DoubleDare* (1986–93), and *Mr. Wizard's World* (1983–2000). These shows all used live actors, and most incorporated Nickelodeon's philosophy of "Us versus Them" as part of their thematic logic. *You Can't Do That on Television,* for example, introduced green slime to the Nickelodeon audience (it was poured over the head of anyone who said "I don't know"), and *Mr. Wizard's World* was a science show where a teacher, Mr. Wizard (played by Don Herbert), taught kids scientific tricks and experiments using household materials without condescending to kids or sounding too "teachery." The network carried some animated programs, but because it did not own an animation studio at that time, these shows were primarily imported from non-U.S. studios: *Belle and Sebastian* (1984–87) was French, as was *The Little Prince* (1983–88); *The Mysterious Cities of Gold* (1983–) was a Japanese/French production, and *The Adventures of Little Koala* (1987–92) was a Japanese anime import. These shows, since they were created outside Nickelodeon, were not explicitly designed to contain brand narratives and the aesthetic style of Us versus Them that characterized the network. In 1991, however, Nickelodeon launched its own animation package, Nicktoons, which consisted of three original programs, *Doug, Rugrats,* and *The Ren & Stimpy Show.* The success of these programs motivated Viacom to continue to fund animation studios, and Nickelodeon has since become as well known for its creator-driven cartoons as its live-action comedy sketches.[6]

Of course, there is a long history of early-twentieth-century cinematic animation in the United States that predates the advent of televisual animation and the association of animation with children and children's culture. While there are unmistakable influences in television animation of this cinematic history, my concern here is with the trajectory of television animation, specifically in the cultural distinctions that are drawn between auteur-based animation and toy- and license-driven animation. However, it is necessary to note that early cinematic animation was created for an adult audience and was often seen as cutting social commentary.[7] Because of the flexibility of the form of animation, where creators are not bound to the physical boundaries of human representation, the fantasy and imaginative worlds of animated programs routinely provide a social critique of the "reality" of material life.

Yet the economic structure of broadcast television, and the imperative to target specific audiences to sell to advertisers, represents a shift in the cultural position of animation and a force of containment on its imaginative and critical potential. The flexibility of animation in early film culture was limited within television so as not to offend audiences and affect ratings.[8] In the later 1950s and early 1960s, cartoons were eventually relegated to what Jason Mittell calls the "great Saturday morning exile."[9] Part of this change has to do with the institutional structure of television compared to film: during this time, television had clearly been recognized as a powerful symbolic force that needed to be regulated in order to be a true broadcast medium. As William Boddy and Lynn Spigel have argued, increased commercial censorship of television programming in the late 1950s and early 1960s had to do with several factors, including the increasing reliance on advertiser sponsorship, the quiz-show scandals, the conservative political climate of postwar United States, and a progressively more volatile cultural climate that paid a new kind of attention to racial and ethnic stereotypes in televisual representation.[10] The resulting television programming from this contextual mix was primarily shows intended to appeal to "most of the people, most of the time," mediocre programming that prompted 1961 FCC chairman Newton Minow's "vast wasteland" speech (in which he refers to cartoons as one of the worst offenders).[11]

It also resulted in recreating the definition of the function of animation; once considered to have a transgenerational appeal, television cartoons were relegated to the least attractive time slot on television, Saturday morning. Because the Saturday morning audience was children, and the industry assumptions about children were that they were both an uncritical audience and that they enjoyed watching repeats, this time spot became a financially lucrative one for broadcasters. Advertisers were just beginning to understand the economic value of reaching the children's audience, and as Mittell argues, "As the genre continued to be dominated by theatrical retreads and prime time failures, production costs were negligible for most Saturday morning cartoons—networks and producers could maximize returns on their productions by endlessly rerunning one season of a program like *Top Cat* or *The Alvin Show* making the generic time slot a comparatively low-risk venture with high potential for long-term profits."[12] Cartoons were consequently "harmless entertainment" and the media content was shaped to fit the audience.[13] The form that animation eventually took within television was based (at least in large part) on an economic imperative to attract the appropriate audiences for advertisers.

Animation was generally separated into distinct categories—cartoons for kids were safe and nonoffensive, while cartoons for adults retained the edge, the social commentary that characterized cinematic cartoons. These two categories did occasionally intersect in particular cartoons, such as in some Warner Brothers cartoons (*Bugs Bunny* and *Road Runner,* for instance), as interesting, transgenerational forms that include commentary about the Cold War, gender relations, and corporate culture. The overall association of animation with children, however, accomplished a number of things: it firmly established animation as a genre for children, and thus specifically *not* for adults; it debased animation as a "quality" genre precisely because it was thought to be for children; and it did not garner the economic backing that other television shows received because, at that time, the children's audience as a market had not reached the kind of three-in-one potential it enjoys today.[14] Mittell points out that "the ways in which these texts, both recycled and original, were situated through scheduling and cultural circulation, demonstrate how these practices came to link the genre to a set of shared assumptions that have remained associated with the cartoon genre to this day."[15] The various ways in which the television industry censored cartoons to make them appropriate fare for children constituted the foundation for the cartoon genre for years to come, and contemporary cultural and political debates over sexuality and violence in cartoons directly relate to this history of defining this genre as one that is as "innocent" as its intended audience.

As a way to guarantee that cartoons would remain formulaic (and thus appealing to children), the production process of animation shifted from one that was primarily creator-driven to one that was simply put through the "cartoon mills," where a team of people could cheaply and quickly put together a cartoon based on prescribed ideas and normative representations.[16] This overtly commercial context of animation, where cartoons made explicitly for children were created according to market logic, was intensified in the 1980s. With the loosened regulatory environment of the Reagan FCC, toy-based cartoons began to characterize the television animation landscape. Indeed, the 1980s are often characterized by critics as the worst moment in animation history because of the influx of toy-based programs, and by the television industry as a great marker of the development of the kid market, also because of the enormous boom in licensed characters in the toy industry.[17] With deregulation, old rules about limiting the number of minutes spent on commercials within children's programming blocks no longer shaped the structure of kid cartoons, and programs that could be characterized as "30-minute commercials" came to dominate children's television. For these shows, characters were designed as toys first with the TV program to follow as a seamless way to sell toys to the kid audience.[18] Because these programs were generally perceived by critics to be entirely commercially based (as opposed to artistically, or creator, based) they continued the association of cartoons with low cultural legitimacy and capital.[19]

ANIMATION AT NICKELODEON

As I detailed in chapter 2, Gerry Laybourne (president of Nickelodeon from 1989 to 1996) was particularly passionate about her dislike for toy-based programs in children's television. Her decision to support creator-driven cartoons at Nickelodeon was a crucial move for the network's overall signature and philosophy. Indeed, given the network's insistence that it was a "different" network, it is not surprising that Nickelodeon had a specific philosophy regarding animation as part of its brand identity.[20] Linda Simensky, in charge of the animation department at Nickelodeon for seven years, discusses Nickelodeon's reputation in the industry as being very committed to rejecting toy-based properties: "Even when they had these properties, they still had the reputation as the place where they can't make them take your toy-based properties. Toy companies came to Cartoon Network and said if you don't run our shows we're not going to advertise on your network, and they basically bullied them into running *He-man* and *Transformers* and stuff like that. You couldn't do that with Nick—you couldn't walk in there and tell them that."[21] According to Simensky, Nickelodeon committed itself early on to rejecting animated shows produced by a "cookie cutter process" and thus made the decision to support creator-driven animated shows, with new and original characters and storylines.[22] Although clearly this was in the interest of attracting an audience to the Nickelodeon brand, the network's rhetoric framed its philosophy on creator-driven animation as part of its claim to "respect kids." As with so many other market strategies deployed by Nickelodeon, the channel's stance on creator-driven animation felt like a rebellious, anti-establishment move within the children's television industry. By insisting on creator-driven animation in the licensed-toy environment, Nickelodeon was seen as "bucking the system," thus highlighting the ethos of empowerment championed by the channel at a historical and commercial moment where rebellious upstart companies were quickly gaining cultural capital. In this way, the channel's commitment to creator-driven cartoons was as much a part of its claim to "respect" kids and treat them like citizens as was Nickelodeon's promise of positive gender and racial representation. These stylistic and narrative strategies that came to characterize not only Nickelodeon programming but the channel's overall brand identity are reflective of a cultural economy in which children are situated as significant consumer citizens.

Nickelodeon was only able to be perceived as bucking convention because of the particular institutional structure in which it was embedded. The cable network had the luxury of trying out these animated programs as *experiments*—which meant that they could fail. As I detailed in chapter 2, because the cable industry was still so new, and relatively unregulated, *everything* Nickelodeon did was new and different. Simensky states that, in typical Us versus Them fashion, Nickelodeon "would do the opposite of what conventional wisdom dictated" in making new animated shows, which went through a pilot program (quite unusual for animated programs, when networks tended to just buy blocks of episodes without trying them out before an audience first).[23] Thus, Nickelodeon could afford to "dismiss" conventional wisdom regarding creator-driven animation; indeed, the whole concept of a television channel dedicated to children's programming flew in the face of conventional ideas of what could succeed on television. Again, this philosophical—and moral—stance ostensibly taken by Nickelodeon was part of constructing children as consumer citizens: appearing to *refuse* to submit to the whims of the market was both a real refusal and a way to construct a *new* market inhabited by an "empowered" audience. As Simensky said regarding this issue, "The whole adults versus kids, Us versus Them thing, really did pervade everything, every aspect of the network. In the course of development, one of the things I would look for was: did the show have a certain Us versus Them quality to it—there was branding in the shows, it wasn't just in between the shows, the shows had to feel like Nickelodeon shows."[24] The "Nickelodeon shows" required a Nickelodeon audience—one that responded with savvy and sophistication to animated shows that were intelligent and ironic.

Yet it was not only that the cable industry provided a kind of freedom to áexperiment that shaped Nickelodeon's decisions about original animation. Although the current landscape of televisual animation remains primarily characterized by "process-driven" animation rather than creator-driven, in the early 1990s the cartoon began to slowly move out from its Saturday morning exile and loosen its connection with merchandising and toys, thus attracting more of an adult audience. More specifically, the lines drawn between adult cartoons as edgy and interesting, and kid cartoons as bland and formulaic, began to appear more ambiguous. The 1990s witnessed a revival in interest in cartoons for adults, as well as a renewed commitment on the part of media studios to create both films and television that had a transgenerational appeal. In the film world, for example, Disney was creating animated films that, for the first time in decades, enjoyed box-office success, critical acclaim, and a multigenerational audience. The company's 1991 film *Beauty and the Beast* was the first animated film ever nominated for an Academy Award for Best Picture, and the other films produced during this time—*The Little Mermaid, Aladdin,* and later Pixar's *Toy Story*—firmly reestablished Disney as a powerhouse in animation. On the television screen, the animated shorts shown during *The Tracy Ullman Show* on HBO became the Fox network's *The Simpsons,* the first prime time animated series since *The Flintstones* in the 1960s. Since that time, Fox has also produced *King of the Hill* and *Futurama;* Nickelodeon's corporate sibling MTV has produced successful animated programs for young adults such as *Beavis and Butthead* and *Daria;* the variety program *Saturday Night Live* often includes "adult" cartoons such as *The Ambiguously Gay Duo;* and the raunchy, edgy, and intensely ironic *South Park* has become an important source of revenue for Comedy Central. And Cartoon Network has recently launched a late-night programming block of adult cartoons, called Adult Swim, featuring edgier, more politically oriented cartoons, as well as nostalgic fare. These examples demonstrate a shift in the landscape of television animation—a shift that not only acknowledges the double meaning in cartoons for kids and adults but also indicates a shift in how child audiences were imagined. The kids who were understood in terms of "innocence"—an innocence that corresponded with the bland formulaic quality of most cartoons—were reconsidered in terms of citizenship and empowerment within the context of brand culture.

IRONY AND CAMP: DOUBLE CODING IN POSTMODERN ANIMATION

Paul Wells has argued that the cinematic animation of the early twentieth century characterized modern American tastes, social mores, and cultural values. Additionally, he argues that the artistry of the animated form served as a point of entry for critiquing these same tastes, mores, and values.[25] The renaissance in prime time animation is similarly symbolic of the current cultural climate in the United States. Rather than intensely modernist, however, animated programs such as *The Simpsons* and Nickelodeon's animated programs are more postmodernist in both form and content. Indeed, an important element of the artistry of cartoons involves the genre's ability to be self-reflexive; in an era of postmodern visual culture, reflexivity takes "the form in postmodern style of referencing context or framing in order to rethink the viewer's relationship to an image or narrative. One postmodern narrative style is to refuse viewers the opportunity to become absorbed in the narrative and lose themselves, to forget their role as viewers."[26] Cartoons seem especially capable of appropriating this visual style, in that the representational form itself is so flexible.[27]

Because of the changing aesthetic landscape, as well as shifting conceptions of the audience, the fixed status of television animation as a children's genre is destabilized within the current culture. The boundaries of media audiences for programs such as cartoons are no longer (if they ever really were) easily divisible by generation. What assumptions are made once "double coding" (appealing to both adults and children, but in different ways) is an *explicit* part of animated programming? This question is significant in theorizing children as consumer citizens, as part of this definition has been the fundamental difference between adults and children. The idea of the double code generally assumes that particular aesthetic styles such as irony and camp that are present in cartoons appeals to adults, and that more straightforward visuals and sound effects are attractive to the less sophisticated audience of children.[28] This strategy has functioned effectively to attract a wider audience for a variety of media, so that divisions and stylistic differences that seem to be generational often appeal on a transgenerational level.[29] As the Nickelodeon executive John Hardman commented about Nickelodeon's very deliberate use of this strategy: "We've always tried to play to a large audience. We try to develop programs that get the parents to watch as well. Our programs have different levels for kids and adults. Now everyone else is trying to create programs with different levels so families watch together."[30] Indeed, an effective approach for many television programs has been to not only address adult audiences as children but also to address children as mature adults. This kind of dual strategy, as Kinder puts it, "provide[s] an illusory sense of empowerment both for kids who want to accelerate their growth by buying into consumerist culture and for adults who want to retain their youth by keeping up with pop culture's latest fads."[31] This is clearly part of the contemporary market logic of cool, working *rhetorically* by stressing the generational difference between audiences, and functioning *actually* to increase the breadth of the potential market.

This dual strategy constitutes a media environment of consumer citizenship, where empowerment is defined within the confines of the market. This appeal functions effectively as a marketing strategy so that Nickelodeon attracts two audiences by appealing precisely to the divisions between them. Indeed, the contemporary commercial context of television has also made divisions between audiences based on generation much less distinct, as thematic issues such as race, gender, and sexual orientation have become much less controversial and much more lucrative as marketing ploys for different generations. Specifically, the contemporary young consumer citizen is characterized, at least in part, by a finely honed sense of irony. It is not simply that the current youth generation is perceived to be disaffected or cynical about culture, however, but also that irony has a particular logic within the overall narratives of commercial popular culture. As marketing becomes more and more sophisticated, irony becomes its own marketing niche, reflecting its savvy audience. Films such as *Reality Bites* set the tone in the early 1990s for an ironic pop culture, as did television ads for "youth" products such as Sprite, which deliberately used celebrities to endorse products, while pointing to the fact that celebrities were selling products.[32] Increasingly jaded and cynical young characters found their way into films such as *Cruel Intentions* and *Murder by Numbers*, and recent television shows such as *One Tree Hill* and *The O.C.* portray high-schoolers as sophisticated and contemptuous.

Irony is an important part of the identity of contemporary youth culture and is a key element in the current environment of consumer citizenship. In fact, Naomi Klein characterizes the presence of irony in the current context as "ironic consumption": "Not only were [youth audiences] making a subversive statement about a culture they could not physically escape, they were rejecting the doctrinaire Puritanism of seventies feminism, the earnestness of the sixties quest for authenticity and the 'literal' readings of so many cultural critics. Welcome to ironic consumption."[33] Klein's cynicism about the use of irony as an effective marketing tool can in part be related to the notion that irony as politics is a much more personal kind of politics than a more activist, public politics. Within the cultural economy of consumer citizenship, citizens flourish, find voice, and are "empowered" through these individualistic, consumer-based practices. "Empowered" consumer citizens are those who are defined by power relations within the confines of consumer culture. The consumer culture that Klein characterizes as "ironic consumption" seems to evacuate politics from the landscape in one sense because of the intense focus on personal identity and consumption habits. Yet, in another important sense, as Jeffrey Sconce reminds us, "All irony may confuse issues of tone and perspective, but no form of irony is truly disengaged from its material."[34] Indeed, the notion that media texts are split into different meanings for different audiences, where irony and camp are strategically used to "conceal" meanings from the mainstream, has been noted as an important part of audience identification in gay communities. This is what is implied with the "double code," a strategy defined by Sender as implicit advertising appeals that, "through the use of coded representations which appear innocuous to heterosexual readers . . . can be interpreted as 'gay' by bisexual, lesbian and gay readers."[35]

The key here, however, is that the messages are in fact *hidden;* what happens when historically concealed messages—concealed precisely because of the rejection of gay identities by dominant culture—are made into commodities, an integral part of the mainstream? Sender discusses the dynamic of gay visibility within consumer culture, positing that when commodity culture is overtly involved in the construction of the double code, "it has the effect of depoliticizing the radical tendencies of [queer] activism."[36] The issue here revolves around who is "getting" the message—if it is *everyone,* straight or gay, youth or adult—can it still be a "double" code? Nickelodeon banks on the idea that it can be, but a double code that is inherently about a broader market, signaling consumer citizenship rather than access to a politicized subjectivity. Indeed, the brand identity of the network revolves around this precise notion—that there are some (Nick kids) who get it, and others (adults) who do not.

Part of the Nickelodeon brand, then, entails an appreciation on the part of the audience for a unique "Nickelodeon humor" that is specifically crafted as a double code. This was evident in almost all of the interviews I conducted with kids who watch Nickelodeon shows—especially those fans of *SpongeBob Square-Pants* and *The Fairly OddParents.* For instance, one eleven-year-old boy said, "*SpongeBob* has some humor that's like adult humor. But not inappropriate humor, just humor that adults think is funny, too."[37] Another eleven-year-old girl made the point to me that Nickelodeon was different from the Disney channel, because of the humor contained in the programming: "I think Nickelodeon is a bit better . . . They have more stuff for like adults and grownups, and more humorous things."[38] One other nine-year-old fan confirmed this notion that the appeal of Nickelodeon is in part due to the fact that the programs contain humor for both adults and children: "[The main point of *SpongeBob* is] to be funny for grownups and kids . . . Like one reason is that kids get it, grownups get it, they start laughing."[39] In the contemporary context, part of attracting Nickelodeon's youth audience meant to incorporate this sense of irony into its animated programming. The trick is figuring out how to incorporate the strategy of irony to have a rebellious feel, without letting on that this particular kind of rebellion is precisely what is being sold through the brand. Commenting on the presence of irony in cartoons, Simensky had this to say: "I think it's a cartoon way of life . . . It comes from a creator and a team of people with a similar sense of humor being able to make the jokes they want to make—not having their shows go through a factory process where everything gets blended. It's being able to tell the jokes you want to tell. Irony is a big part of cartoons, where you expect this . . . and wham! This other thing happens and that's where the surprise comes from . . . And a good cartoon is about surprise—it is about the unexpected."[40] However, the unexpected, as it is referenced in irony and camp, has become an important part of *mainstream* popular and consumer culture. A campy, ironic style has emerged in media culture as the dominant, rather than a subversive, address. In 1993, David Bergman wrote that although camp is quite difficult to define, most scholars writing on the subject agree on four different points: one, camp is a style that is predominantly about artifice and exaggeration; two, camp exists in tension, not in agreement, with consumer (or mainstream) culture; three, people who interpret things as campy are people outside the mainstream; and four, camp is affiliated with homosexual culture.[41] While I think that there are certainly moments of contemporary camp that share these four elements, it is also the case that the cultural and historical context in which Bergman was writing has changed. Bergman argues that there was an intellectual hostility to camp in the 1970s that gave way to a scholarly embrace of the subject in the 1980s, due to a variety of factors, including the rise of queer theory and poststructuralism in the academy, the increasingly visible presence of gay activists, and the escalating knowledge about AIDS in mainstream culture.[42] Predictably, the cultural context of the 1990s and early twenty-first century has shifted yet again, and new economic, political, and social factors affect the way in which camp is both produced and interpreted. Indeed, as I have argued, this new cultural and political-economic context was fundamental in not only shaping the particular self-identity of Nickelodeon but also in providing a means through which youth consumer citizenship could be articulated.

Despite the vagaries of both culture and camp, Susan Sontag's essay "Notes on Camp" continues to be acknowledged—albeit often as a point of critique—as a crucial narrative outlining the slippery theoretical definition of camp.[43] In this essay, Sontag situates camp primarily as an aesthetic style, evacuated of politics, functioning culturally as frivolity and superficiality. Camp, for Sontag, is about artifice, and artifice in turn about an almost child-like sense of make-believe: "Camp sees everything in quotation marks. It's not a lamp, but a 'lamp'; not a woman, but a 'woman.' To perceive Camp in objects and persons is to understand Being-as-Playing-a-Role. It is the farthest extension, in sensibility, of the metaphor of life as theatre."[44] As Gilad Padva, David Bergman, and Andrew Ross, as well as numerous others, have pointed out, Sontag misses the political complexity of the quotation mark and that which it represents; Bergman notes that it is precisely the constructed nature of camp (a construction that is signified by quotation marks) that contains its politics: "as a style of exaggeration and artifice that brought to bear the artificiality of all those categories that we are so deeply invested in as 'normal': gender, femininity, masculinity."[45] It is within the incongruities of camp, the contradictions and the missing narratives, that its politics is found. Camp is most associated with sexual identity because, in part, the contradiction most exploited by a camp style is that of gender, between the masculine and the feminine. As Jack Babuscio argues, "Irony is the subject matter of camp, and refers here to any highly incongruous contrast between an individual or thing and its context or association. The most common of incongruous contrasts is that of masculine/feminine."[46] Camp thus has been the mechanism to reveal the constructed—and often ironic—nature of the categories we invest in as "normal," such as sexuality or gender. An exaggerated representation of masculinity in a film, for example, would appeal to a heterosexual man invested in the "normalcy" of his own gender, as well as to a gay man invested in the artificiality of hegemonic masculinity—for the gay audience, the representation of masculinity is the "wink" in the show's message.[47]

The semiotic openness of cartoons, the sheer artificiality of this representational form, destabilizes the fixity of the double code and exploits its potential for camp irony. However, the complex nuances of the media seem to characterize the current landscape more accurately than a theory of the double code, precisely because of the political-economic context I've discussed.[48] Theorizing the ironic or camp quality of cartoons allows for a side-stepping of the rigidity of the double code, because irony and camp refuse to be considered as either only style or politics but are rather always both. This is one problem with Sontag's formulation with camp; in her focus on this identification of camp with style, Sontag collapses the two without acknowledging how style is *politically* informed by camp.[49]

Camp is both activist and consumerist; these two categories are not mutually exclusive but rather inform and shape each other constantly. To locate a camp style in children's programming is not to empty camp of its political and/or erotic meaning but to resituate it within a particular kind of consumer context. The change in the pattern of youth consumption also changes the aesthetic, reflecting a kind of consumerist politics that, like "girl power," harnesses a political ideology. Camp and irony historically have signaled a subversive, and political, practice. But like postfeminism and the use of diversity, in this historical moment where brand culture is the primary means through which subjectivity and citizenship are understood and experienced, camp and irony become practices of consumer citizenship. In the current manifestation, these aesthetic styles encourage a focus on individualism and consumption habits as political activity. Situating camp and irony as key markers of consumer citizenship within the context of Nickelodeon doesn't depoliticize *SpongeBob SquarePants*, but it is a different kind of camp from, say, gay camp novels, or drag queens.[50] In contemporary consumer culture, where subversive identity positions are commodified as niche markets, the distinction between the two positions engaged by the double code is less sharply drawn. A viewer's recognition of the distinction itself becomes not a marker of marginalized identity but rather an indicator of one's commitment to brand culture.

Indeed, a common theme of current branding strategies is to incorporate irony into their presentation, so that the pitch of companies often includes a kind of self-mocking, a reflection of the ironic viewer they are trying to cultivate. It certainly is true that irony has become, because of brand culture, the signature emotion for a youth generation, but the commodification of irony also occasionally results in an interesting social commentary. What happens to the edginess of irony when it is used as a crucial part of a brand? When a corporation plays on the crassness and obvious commercialism of marketing as a way to market a product, what does that do to irony as a powerful form of counterhegemonic critique? I argue that both formulations of irony—as social critique and as slick marketing tool—exist simultaneously in a similar way as consumer citizenship, which forms its logic on both the power of a demographic market and the construction of political subjectivity within that market.

NICKELODEON'S CREATION AND CONTROVERSY: *REN & STIMPY*

In 1991, the animator John Kricfalusi's *The Ren & Stimpy Show* was included in the first original Nickelodeon animation block, Nicktoons. *Ren & Stimpy* is a cartoon about an asthmatic, mean-spirited Chihuahua named Ren Hoek and a friendly-but-stupid cat named Stimpy. Initially, *Ren & Stimpy*'s irreverent style, nostalgic aesthetic feel (a flat background, and few "special effects"), and use of irony seemed to fit ideally with the brand identity of Nickelodeon. The very premise of the show was self-reflexive; *Ren & Stimpy* "looked back to the subversive aspects of cartooning, not merely to express personal perspectives but to critique the conservatism of made-for-television cartoons."[51] The program took full advantage of animation's representational flexibility, so that it was just as likely to feature Ren's bloodshot eyes literally falling out of his head as it was to see a living fart on the show. This kind of "disruptive play" appealed to both kids and adults and thus embodied the double code that challenged Nickelodeon's Us versus Them philosophy—both "us" and "them" were addressed in the show. Yet, contradictorily, the program validated the Us versus Them brand identity by positioning itself as different from other kids programs. As Rebecca Farley notes, *Ren & Stimpy* creates this disruptive play by playing with the animation itself, through the "grossness and vulgarity" of the characters themselves (which stood out in bold relief in comparison to the broadcast networks' toy-based animation,

20. Ren and Stimpy,
from *The Ren & Stimpy
Show*, 1991.

featuring creatures such as *The Care Bears*). As Farley puts it: "If . . . Disney's
'relentless striving for cuteness' helped create and nurture the 'family' audience,
the look of *Ren & Stimpy* literally signified its active disinterest in such an
audience."[52] The visual appearance of *Ren & Stimpy* challenged the smooth
cuteness of other televised animation—the characters were, as Farley puts it,
"spectacularly ugly." Kricfalusi disrupted other conventions of television animation as well: the figures of Ren and Stimpy were continuously distorted and
disfigured, and the two characters (Ren especially) generally mistreated each
other as a plot of each episode.

For example, in one episode of *Ren & Stimpy*, "Stimpy's Invention," Stimpy
tries out a number of different inventions on Ren, including a phone made out of
cheese, a remote-control razor that he uses to shave off Ren's fur, and "stay put
socks," which are socks full of glue so that they do not fall down. Ren becomes
incensed at being used as a guinea pig for Stimpy's silly inventions and shouts
"You filthy swine! I will kill you!"—not exactly a line one might find in *The Care
Bears* or *Strawberry Shortcake*. Stimpy decides to invent something to make Ren
happy (and tries out many experiments along the way, using animals such as a
duck and a beaver as subjects, clearly playing off of the politically progressive "no
testing on animals" caveat that accompanies so many contemporary products)
and invents a "happy helmet." The helmet, placed on Ren's head, comes with a
remote control, with a dial to control how happy Ren will be. Stimpy gleefully
turns it way up, while all the while Ren is furiously resisting being happy. Kricfalusi here exaggerates the forced smile on Ren's face, the bloodshot eyes as he
tries to resist happiness, and finally his capitulation, as he mumbles "no . . .
got . . . to . . . fight . . . it" until he loses the battle: "Stimpy, I'm so happy . . . must

21. Ren and his "happy helmet," 1991.

22. Stimpy's "Happy Happy Joy Joy" album, 1991.

go do nice things." Ren is then shown cheerfully ironing Stimpy's underwear and cleaning steaming excrement from Stimpy's cat box, all the while saying things such as "I must do wonderful things for my best friend Stimpy." The episode culminates in Stimpy dancing with Ren to Stimpy's favorite record, "Happy Happy Joy Joy," where the voice on the record says, in a threatening voice, "I don't think you're happy enough. I'll teach you to be happy. I'll teach your grandmother to suck eggs."

The transgressing of boundaries of taste and convention in *Ren & Stimpy* is playful; "Stimpy's Invention" consciously mocks the authenticity of "being happy," so that the unofficial anthem of *Ren & Stimpy*, "Happy Happy Joy Joy" is provocatively ironic. Indeed, the mocking of the earnestness of both a conventional sense of happiness and, more obliquely, children's television shows is

23. Mock advertisement for "log" on the *Ren & Stimpy Show*, 1991.

24. The simplistic "motto" for log pokes fun at TV ads directed to children, 1991.

clearly evident in this episode. The contemptuous scorn of children's television that was such a part of *Ren & Stimpy* was both its brilliance and ultimate downfall on a network like Nickelodeon: despite the network's self-conscious construction as a rebel and an upstart within the world of children's television, the reality was that Nickelodeon was the leader in children's television, and it was not in the network's best commercial interests to expose *this* particular irony. The failure of *Ren & Stimpy* reflects a central contradiction within consumer citizenship: since the definition of this kind of citizenship only makes sense within the market, too much critique of this market (and the social and economic conditions from which it emerges) is a form of symbolic annihilation—within this scenario, the consumer citizen that Nickelodeon celebrates no longer is sustainable.

One of the most innovative characteristics of *Ren & Stimpy* is its self-reflexivity;

not only are the characters themselves reflexive but the show constantly remarks upon the structures and constraints of television, especially children's television. The show regularly critiqued children's television as part of the narrative and featured, on every episode, some kind of satiric in-house advertisement. For instance, Ren or Stimpy is depicted mocking the gimmickry of children's ads with "Breakfast Tips," which derides the ridiculousness of including toy prizes in children's sugar-based cereals, or the series of ads marketing a toy log, which was really just a log. As Farley points out, this kind of reflexivity within the show "was an especially daring transgression, mocking the long and heated debate over advertising in children's programming."[53] Again, the idea that the show was mocking conventions, while aired on a network that was firmly ensconced in a corporate media environment, owned by one of the largest media conglomerates, was the biggest irony—and one that ultimately Nickelodeon could not incorporate as part of its brand identity. Rather, the audience for *Ren & Stimpy* was not the mass audience appealed to by major media corporations but was more of a cult following, including not so much the adolescent audience that tunes in to Nickelodeon but a more specialized subculture of what Mark Langer calls "animatophiles."[54]

THE CREATOR: JOHN KRICFALUSI

Once Nickelodeon committed to a much larger budget for original animation and sought to find the right programs for its irreverent message and its Us versus Them ideology, the next step was finding the right artists to create the programming. Kricfalusi had an impressive track record, working with Ralph Bakshi and Jim Hyde on *Mighty Mouse: The New Adventures* and then opening up his own animation studio, Spumco. As Langer notes, given Kricfalusi's experience, it was not difficult to understand why Nickelodeon thought he was a good match for the "Nickelodeon feel"—he was ironic, irreverent, and seemed to revel in challenging the system—all the same things for which Nickelodeon was known.[55] However, the various ways in which Nickelodeon defied the system were not exactly counterhegemonic; in other words, Nickelodeon produced a different kind of programming in a television landscape that was bland and formulaic, but the network remained a corporate entity—the ways in which it was a "different" network only registered as different within the context of corporate culture. Kricfalusi, on the other hand, was not interested in being a corporate player. As Langer points out, "Kricfalusi constantly made reference to the detritus of American culture and deliberately violated norms of good taste. While some 'gross-out' comedy is not unusual in children's broadcasting, a company like Nickelodeon has to engage in a difficult balancing act in which it is necessary to please children without offending parents. Kricfalusi was not similarly inclined."[56] Kricfalusi, after a series of disputes with the network over program deadlines, was eventually fired after the first year of production in a well-publicized conflict. Using the same rhetoric Nickelodeon uses about adult culture, Kricfalusi claimed that the network "just didn't get it," and the conflict is often read as a battle between the individual artist and the corporate entity.

Of course, the strategic use of "they just don't get it" clearly resonates within this context when so much of the appeal of *Ren & Stimpy* was in its "smart sensibility" where some audiences "got it," and others did not. The fact that Kricfalusi believed that his corporate bosses at Nickelodeon also "didn't get it" clearly gains him cultural capital within a certain audience.[57] Kricfalusi and Nickelodeon both imagined a different kind of citizen as audience. The "creative differences," then, cited as the reason for firing Kricfalusi was not simply a predictable alibi for something deeper and more insidious: the difference between the two really was about a kind of creative product—but more importantly, for whom that creative product was intended.

Interestingly, *Ren & Stimpy* remains the Nickelodeon program that receives the most scholarly attention. Although the network and its programming certainly receive its fair share of mainstream press coverage, the amount of scholarly interest in the network has been (until recently) minimal, except for work analyzing *The Ren & Stimpy Show*.[58] The "high art" status of *Ren & Stimpy* seems to be produced from a number of different angles: adults nostalgic for an animation feel of earlier cinematic cartoons; the way in which *Ren & Stimpy* deliberately dismissed the "kids only" rhetoric of Nickelodeon by including many "adult" references; the cult following of the program; and perhaps most importantly, the rejection of the show by Nickelodeon, a move that revealed the corporate ideology of the channel as not quite as rebellious as it claimed to be. Nickelodeon wants to be hip, but not that hip; while dedicated to "respecting" and empowering its audience, the channel defines respect and empowerment within the terms of the general market. Nickelodeon wanted anything but the narrow cult following sought after by Kricfalusi; rather, it sought to be ubiquitous in American households, with not a detached audience but an engaged one—and one that, importantly, believes in the "system" so that the notion of "empowerment" has a particular kind of hegemonic (as opposed to counterhegemonic) logic.

This does not mean that the programming on the network cannot contain irony or camp as part of the textual address. The irony in Nickelodeon programs cannot mock the network (or for that matter, children's television) so derisively, because this challenges the way the channel defines consumer citizenship. Within the corporate environment of the network, the self-mocking of Nickelodeon programs is conducted in a more earnest and playful, rather than an intensely critical, way (and thus works as part of its marketing). Since *Ren & Stimpy*, a number of cultural factors have shifted and changed, so that the tropic qualities of the show—irony, camp, self-reflexivity—are still part of Nickelodeon's brand identity, but the political economy of brand culture has appropriated these techniques as part of commodity culture. Thus, the discourses of irony and camp are more in the vein of self-reflexive marketing, so that the brand identity of Nickelodeon as cool and irreverent is both further established and made more mainstream.

SPONGEBOB SQUAREPANTS

The highly publicized battle between Nickelodeon and John Kricfalusi refer- enced, among other things, a kind of "selling out"—or, as his followers insist, a refusal to sell out, on the part of Kricfalusi, to the safe corporate politics of the network. For the animatophile subculture, Kricfalusi represented a kind of artis tic authenticity in the face of the slick commercialism of Viacom's channel; he was unmistakably the activist David to the network's commercial Goliath. The way that this program appealed to different political groups, rather than groups assumed to have naturalized, essential boundaries (such as child/adult or gay/ straight), forces a different reading from one that insists on a simple double code. The struggle between creator and network was interpreted in several different ways: a fight between the atomistic individual and the greedy corporate entity; as an aesthetic issue, as Langer points out, where Kricfalusi is creating for a particu- lar audience of animatophiles that doesn't happen to be Nickelodeon's audience; and as a cultural shift, where the political economy and social standards of the time authorize the mainstreaming and commodification of a camp aesthetic.[59]

Less than a decade later after *Ren & Stimpy* debuted, the network had slightly shifted its aesthetic frame of camp and found a much more suitably (for the network, at least) campy program: *SpongeBob SquarePants*. This program clearly connected more meaningfully to a contemporary audience of young consumer citizens and allowed Nickelodeon to retain an "edgy" feel while not alienating the channel's demographic (or their parents). *SpongeBob* has come under some of the same public critiques as *Ren & Stimpy* did almost ten years earlier: the humor was seen to be illogical, the characters unrealistic, and, most visibly, the main characters of the show, SpongeBob and the starfish Patrick, were inter- preted by some as involved in a homosexual relationship—just as Ren and Stimpy were often read as involved sexually. The animation of the show is clever and

25. SpongeBob
SquarePants and
his best friend
Patrick the Starfish,
from *SpongeBob
SquarePants*, 2003.

sophisticated, with the program taking place in Bikini Bottom, with a kitsch landscape complete with houses made out of pineapples and Tiki heads reminiscent of Easter Island. Because of the way that animation already stretches "real" representation, the character of SpongeBob is even more flexible in its performance: although he is a sea sponge, he resembles the typical domestic sink sponge—yet he can transform his shape into anything that makes sense at the time: the state of Texas, the letter S, a flower. Perhaps most importantly, SpongeBob exists in a liminal generational stage—neither child nor adult, he performs a kind of playful act on the show, camping it up at every opportunity.[60] As Simensky says about SpongeBob, "He's kid-like in that way that kids might have that innocent naïve thing going on and a kid might say something that's completely honest and funny, and sort of ironic for the situation. *SpongeBob* has a certain quality to it—and the people making it—that's their sense of humor. Because it is so creator-driven and so creative-driven, you can't separate the people behind it from the cartoon. So that goes a little bit beyond creator-driven into this idea that people working on the show have a whole lot to say in the humor of the show."[61]

The adult fan base of *SpongeBob*, as well as the campy, kitschy nature of the program, has resulted in a semiotic reading, by some, of the show as a "gay show." SpongeBob is sometimes pictured holding hands with his best friend, the pink starfish Patrick, "he is flamboyant, defiantly cheery, emotional, gregarious, and sometimes break[s] out in song with his male companion Patrick and muscular female friend Sandy Squirrel."[62] The show's curmudgeon, Squidward, is a squid who enjoys bubble baths and listening to classical music (and in fact, Planet Out.com, a website targeted to a gay male audience, remained equivocal about

26. SpongeBob and
Patrick, 2003.

SpongeBob's sexuality but claimed "his neighbor Squidward, a fussy queen who
plays the clarinet, is another matter entirely").[63] Patrick and SpongeBob watch a
favorite superhero television show on the program, "The Adventures of Mermaid Man and Barnacle Boy," which is reminiscent of other male buddy programs that are popularly recognized as either camp or containing a gay aesthetic,
from *Batman and Robin* to *Saturday Night Live*'s "The Ambiguously Gay Duo" (a
spoof on the apparent gay coding of superhero programs).

Unlike Jerry Falwell's homophobic diatribe against another children's television character that was often read as gay, Tinky Winky from the BBC's *Teletub-
bies,* the media attention currently garnered by *SpongeBob SquarePants* seems
more generously spirited. Falwell's outrage over "innocent children" being subjected to the gay identity of Tinky Winky of course begs the fundamental question: if children were so innocent in the first place, how would they be able to
"read" a character as gay *or* straight? In keeping with Nickelodeon's method of
addressing its audience as active, politically engaged citizens, the creators of
SpongeBob SquarePants don't make this assumption about the innocence of their
audience and instead admit to the campy quality of the show. For instance, Tom
Kenny, who voices SpongeBob, was interviewed on a late-night talk show (already an indication of the show's transgenerational appeal) and was asked about
the sexuality of the show's main character. He denied that SpongeBob was created as a gay character but did say that "all the main characters are hiding
horrible secrets of their own."[64] The mainstream media have generally reported
the "story" of SpongeBob's sexuality with good humor. As Heather Hendershot
has argued, the show "parodies masculinity and features the most 'out' gay
character on children's television" but does so in an "innocent," playful manner;

she continues, "*SpongeBob* is loved by adults for its 'childlike' naivete, but the show is also quite 'childlike' in its playful interest in bums (tits are of less interest) and, more generally, in the performance of gender."[65]

SpongeBob "performs" gender in a way characteristic of the cultural and media context in which the program emerged. More specifically, by 1999, camp and irony was not a marginalized, subversive rhetoric that was contained in a "wink wink nudge nudge" kind of style, where certain audiences would "get it," and others wouldn't. Rather, by this moment, everyone "got it" and camp and irony was normalized within media consumer culture. Ellen DeGeneres came out, both publicly and on her television sitcom, in 1997; *Will and Grace*, a sitcom that features two openly gay men as lead characters, was a huge success; the "lesbian episode" was talked about as a particularly common rite of passage among young college women; and ironic, jaded female heroines such as Buffy the Vampire Slayer and MTV's Daria populated the television landscape as exemplars of savvy, postfeminist chic. *SpongeBob* was quite different from *Ren & Stimpy*. It is not mean-spirited or sharply sardonic and critical but rather sweet and play-ful. However, it is also campy, and occasionally ironic.[66] The sexual nature of SpongeBob's and Patrick's relationship is not always contained and hidden, and the other characters on the show also generate an ironic reading: SpongeBob's pet snail named Gary (who meows); the boss, Squidward, who is more stereo-typically figured as a "queen"; and the primary female character, Sandy, who is definitely more an example of lesbian style than hegemonic femininity. The visual and stylistic characteristics of *SpongeBob* are reflective of the arguments I've made throughout this book about consumer citizenship: a particular knowl-edge base of the audience is assumed, a sophistication (both economically and sexually) is relied upon.

Rebecca Farley says about play, "Play can be thought of as a mode of com-munication emphasizing disruption, imagination, expressivity and (above all) fun."[67] For Farley, the way in which prime time animated programs such as *The Flintstones* and *Ren & Stimpy* attract an adult as well as a child audience lies not in a double code built into the programming but rather in how these programs incorporate play as a primary mode of representation.[68] Because the playfulness of animated shows is present in both the aesthetic form of the programs, in the way that animation stretches the bounds of reality and exaggerates and modifies representation, as well as in the content, where the scripts deliberately play with normative conventions and typical situations (both domestic and public), it challenges an argument about double coding that relies precisely on this kind of separating form from content. As Roger Silverstone notes, play disrupts these kinds of categories altogether: adult from child, as well as form from content. As

Silverstone puts it, "Play brings the child out in the adult; and the adult out in the child. Play enables the exploration of that tissue boundary between fantasy and reality, between the real and the imagined, between the self and the other. In play we have a licence to explore, both our selves and society. In play we investigate culture, but we also create it."[69] As Silverstone implies, play involves a kind of transgression, but it is more contained than the edgier, more critical play of a show like *Ren & Stimpy*. Because the current political economy involves commodifying precisely this kind of playful transgression, transforming ironic play into a market *strategy* rather than a *challenge* to the market, popular culture produced within this context similarly incorporates irony and play. The consumer citizen whom engages this playful, ironic text is also part of this market strategy. *SpongeBob* is what Silverstone might call a product of postmodern culture, which is defined by continuous transgression and challenging of social and symbolic boundaries: "In architecture and in literature, but most especially in the hybrid forms of the electronic media, through parody and pastiche, the world becomes real only in its reflections. But the mirrors are fun-fair mirrors. They reflect only to distort . . . In all these and other places the media are playing, playing with each other and playing with us. And we in turn play with them. Their lack of seriousness is serious. Their seriousness is disarming. Their disarming is ironic. Their irony is compulsive, celebratory."[70] SpongeBob SquarePants is just this disarming, celebratory character who is also serious and ironic. The ideological address of the program is ambiguous; it at times seems sharply critical, but it never feels "anti-establishment." One sixteen-year-old girl I interviewed was more specific about the playful appeal of *SpongeBob*: "It's a good show . . . I think it's partly a trend, but it's a little bit more. It's like an escape. If you're having a rough day you can escape to Bikini Bottom where everything is like good. And you can have a little half an hour of happiness before you get back to your day." This "little half an hour of happiness" is the celebratory transgression of boundaries to which Silverstone refers; *SpongeBob* thus provides a nonthreatening, humorous escape for (at least some of the) audience.[71]

In one episode, "Mermaid Man and Barnacle Boy II," the opening scene depicts SpongeBob watching television in his pineapple house in Bikini Bottom, waiting for his favorite show, "Mermaid Man and Barnacle Boy," to begin. As he is watching, he is eating Mermaid Man and Barnacle Boy cereal and waiting for the Mermaid Man and Barnacle Boy toy that comes with the cereal (the Branded Mermaid Munchers). SpongeBob wins a prize from a Mermaid Man and Barnacle Boy contest and anxiously awaits the mail (which comes almost instantaneously) for its arrival. The scene is a clear ironic—and critical—commentary on the fusion of children audiences, commercial television, and consumption habits that characterizes the dominant children and media relationship. The Branded Mermaid Munchers take aim at cereal brands (and their indistinctness from each other) and the way networks manipulate and buy their audiences. Like other brands produced during this historical moment, this metanarrative critiquing children's commercial culture also works to *legitimate* children's commercial culture by creating a brand identity that appears to be empowering for its audience of consumer citizens. This episode continues by highlighting the antics of SpongeBob with the real Mermaid Man and Barnacle Boy as they fight crime in Bikini Bottom. The two superheroes, however, are elderly and arthritic—Mermaid Man's back cracks as he strikes a pose to impress SpongeBob—and they both live in a home for the elderly, complete with communal lunch and entertainment room. The episode is filled with campy bits: SpongeBob wears only his underwear, because he wants to give the illusion of tights (since all superheroes wear tights, of course); the sexual relationship between the two elderly superheroes is ambiguous but clearly co-dependent; and the rendering of animated sound effects, while reminiscent of *Batman and Robin*'s "Wham!" or "Blammo!," is slightly more self-mocking and tongue in cheek: "Lame!" or "Cardboard!"

In other episodes, the camp qualities are even more apparent. In "Brother, Can You Spare a Dime?" SpongeBob feels sorry for his friend Squidward, who is fired from his job and ends up homeless. SpongeBob takes him in and ends up becoming his personal servant—he feeds him, bathes him, and reads to him. In one scene, Squidward insists on SpongeBob wearing his "uniform," and Sponge-Bob returns wearing a typical "French maid" uniform—short black dress, frilly white apron, little hat. When SpongeBob turns around, his underwear is revealed, as the dress has no back. SpongeBob is often seen in drag, like other campy icons ranging from Tony Curtis to Mr. Smithers on *The Simpsons*. Like those other characters, SpongeBob is "performing" gender in the sense that Judith Butler discusses it: rather than simply a role he takes on and off at whim, the cross-dressing of SpongeBob becomes his gender in the sense that it is a constant performative style. His character is obsessed with showing his underwear, a gesture both to the target audience of young males but also to the transgressive sexual politics that is hinted at throughout the show. As Hendershot points out, "SpongeBob's last name might as well be 'Underpants' not 'SquarePants,' since he truly delights in his tighty-whities."[72] The dependability of SpongeBob's underpants is clearly part of the camp element of the show, while it is also a visual reminder of SpongeBob's masculinity. Indeed, SpongeBob's masculinity is often questioned in the show—he is depicted as a wimp, a crybaby, and a nerd, among other decidedly "unmasculine" traits. Sandy the female squirrel is clearly stronger and more muscular than SpongeBob. Hendershot argues that

SpongeBob's ambiguous masculinity demonstrates that "it is fun . . . to be a sissy-boy, and, occasionally, parodically masculine or feminine, and, at other times, seemingly asexual."[73] However, the display of his male underpants seem to be there as a reassurance to the audience that the sponge is, in fact, a man. The contradictory nature of the camp style in relation to gender and subversion within *SpongeBob* functions as part of consumer citizenship—the politics of gender subversion that *SpongeBob* references are reframed as a signature of the Nickelodeon brand where everyone is in on the joke—the creators, the audience, and SpongeBob himself.

THE FAIRLY ODDPARENTS

Another recent hit on Nickelodeon is *The Fairly OddParents.* The show continues the network's tradition of being creator-driven. Because of this, the program resembles other Nickelodeon programs: there is little explicit violence, the show revolves around one kid, Timmy, who is quite ordinary, yet everyone around him is crazy, the program is ironic and campy and often contains subtle commentary about contemporary social life. Timmy is reflective of the consumer citizen imagined by Nickelodeon. That is, *Fairly OddParents,* like *SpongeBob Square-Pants,* offers an ambiguous ideological message: at times it critiques the corporate conditions within which it is created, but the commentary works ironically to legitimate the show (and thus Nickelodeon) and its narrative. Perhaps the most explicit social commentary is the campy theme of the show itself: the program is about ten-year-old Timmy, whose parents are simply too busy for him—they worry about him and love him but are constantly at work and are obviously neglectful. An illustration of this is in the surprisingly critical opening to each episode, which depicts Timmy's parents as two cardboard cut-out characters, standing in the doorway of a suburban home, smiling and waving. To compensate for their neglect, Timmy's parents hire a babysitter, the evil Vicky, who is not concerned with Timmy's welfare at all. This could clearly be read as a statement about the status of many children in contemporary U.S. society, living in a single-parent or dual-parent, dual-income household, where a babysitter is present more often than a parent. The fact that the babysitter is created as mean-spirited, a young girl who doesn't care about Timmy, could also be read as a commentary about women in the work force, and the "consequences" that are paid by making that "choice." Timmy is not destined, however, to be an ordinary latchkey kid—instead, he has very unusual godparents, the fairies Cosmo and Wanda, who grant him his every wish, so long as he articulates it.

The series was created by Butch Hartman, an animator who had worked on

27. Timmy Turner and one of his "fairly odd parents" from *The Fairly OddParents*, 2005.

Nickelodeon previously. Hartman explicitly credits the success of *SpongeBob* as "opening the door" for something such as *The Fairly OddParents;* in a newspaper interview, he said, "I owe a lot to 'SpongeBob.' They paved the way with a really wacky style of comedy."[74] Interestingly, *The Ren & Stimpy* show, a show that much more clearly "paved the way" for a wacky style of comedy, is completely erased here. In fact, the article goes on to say, "The playful spirit and escapist fun at the heart of Nickelodeon shows like 'SpongeBob' and 'Fairly Odd Parents' never lapse into the edgier high jinks of 'The Simpsons,' 'South Park,' or Cartoon Network's satirical late night 'Adult Swim.' "[75] The creative and economic moment of the early twenty-first century, when both *SpongeBob* and *The Fairly OddParents* are produced, is a moment in which the "wacky style" of humor and animation of these programs has been mainstreamed and no longer attracts a kind of subcultural, or even an animatophile, following. Rather, the fans of these shows are fans of primetime animation in general: these programs are aired to an audience well seasoned by the commodification of irony, the mainstreaming of camp, and the general lack of earnestness (except as parody) in animated shows that appeal to both kids and adults.

The Fairly OddParents consciously supports and continues to create the overall mission of Nickelodeon. For instance, Nickelodeon has explicitly avoided animated shows about superheroes because of the violent overtones, the connections with the toy market, and the ways superhero programs (such as *Batman* or *Spiderman*) have historically catered explicitly to boys.[76] As Cyma Zarghami, then senior vice-president of programming at Nickelodeon, commented, "Historically, when you have superheroes, then the potential for violence comes along with it. We try to stay away from violence. We also celebrate normal kids as

28. Timmy from *The Fairly OddParents*, 2005.

special in their own way. Typically, those programs are also boy driven. That's not to say we will never do a superhero program. But if we do it, we'll do it in a Nickelodeon way." One example of doing superheroes the "Nickelodeon way" is *The Fairly OddParents,* which takes this a step further, explicitly mocking the superhero genre, with a series of episodes that have to do with Timmy's favorite superhero, the Crimson Chin. The Crimson Chin has superpowers in his exaggerated chin, and his voice is performed by the late-night talk show host Jay Leno, who also possesses a famous chin. His body is overmuscled and huge, and he talks only in the "action phrases" that are part of the toy action figure of Crimson Chin. In one episode, "Chin Up!," the program mocks superheroes in general by setting the scene at a comic book expo, where, as Timmy explains, he and his friends can dress up and "prove they're not geeks!" Timmy goes to the expo to meet Crimson Chin, who shows up on stage as an overweight, unshaven, middle-aged man. He trips and falls off the stage, and his crimson outfit, which is too small to begin with, reveals the crack of his butt. Timmy, extremely disappointed with this version of Crimson Chin, wishes that the "real Crimson Chin" would appear. When the "real" superhero arrives, it is only to find out that he is a made-up character, an imaginary being. When this is explained to Crimson Chin, he goes into a deep depression, where he tries to "deal with the fact that I don't exist—that I'm FICTIONAL!" Although Timmy wishes him back into the comic book, as opposed to the "real" world of the comic book expo, Crimson Chin remains in a fetal position, crying for " thirty-six pages." Timmy tries to save him, only to be greeted with "oh you're the 'real' boy who showed me that I'm a big fat lie." The episode continues in a very self-reflexive way, both mocking and praising comic book culture by having the characters in the show move within the "panels" of the book, deliberately disrupting any kind of narrative trajectory or logic. Timmy mocks superhero culture—at one point, when he calls Spatula Woman's spatula (apparently her weapon) a "thingy," he says to himself, "Hmmmm . . . I gotta work on my heroic dialogue." The most evil villain is Bronze Knee Cap, who hurts people by kneeing them in vulnerable places, again critiquing the hypermasculinity and hyperbolic violence of superhero cartoons. The episode involves a storyline about the real and the imaginary, the authentic superhero and the fake superhero—and mocks and satirizes those boundaries even as the actual show, *The Fairly OddParents*, clearly supports them. This episode ends with the Crimson Chin thanking Timmy, saying, "You saved me from myself . . . Man, that was schmaltzy! Who'd you say writes my material?" To which Timmy answers, "Some forty-year-old guy who lives with his mother."

The series often creates this kind of ironic, self-reflexive dialogue. Another episode, "Channel Chasers," mocks all forms of animation as Timmy "travels" through different animated genres and morphs into a variety of animated forms, from the Muppets on *Sesame Street* to nostalgic Christmas animated shows such as *Rudolph the Red-Nosed Reindeer* to 1970s-style characters such as Scooby-Doo to characters resembling Pokémon. In this episode, Timmy runs away from his "home" by traveling through time in television—explicitly commenting on the increasing sophistication of both technologies and audiences. Like the episodes about Crimson Chin, this episode constantly references popular and consumer culture as well as other television shows. One eleven-year-old boy I interviewed went into great detail when I asked him about *The Fairly OddParents*: "It's so funny . . . yeah, and in one [episode] they have Arnold SchwartzenGerman and he's this German guy and he talks like Arnold Schwarzenegger and then there's this other one where they have this guy named Sylvester Calzone, like Sylvester Stallone or whatever."[77] In another episode, "Boy Toy," the show revolves around the relationships between boys and girls and consciously satirizes the toy market that is rigidly segmented into boy toys and girl toys. In this episode, Timmy becomes tired of his Crimson Chin action figure (it is last year's model) and thus wants to destroy it. The episode is peppered with references to the silliness of action figures, especially focusing on the kind of physical action the dolls can do (a Timmy doll in this episode has "thumb-sucking action") and action phrases. In fact, as Timmy articulates, one reason why he becomes so bored with his doll is because his "action phrases stink!" The Crimson Chin action figure says things like "I have goats in my pants!" and "Of all of my muscles, my brain is one of them!" The episode ends when Timmy gives his doll to a girl, who happens to be his evil babysitter Vicki's kid sister. Timmy wishes for the Crimson Chin doll to have twelve thousand I Hate Vicky action phrases, including "Evil Red Heads

29. Timmy, in the episode "Channel Chasers," is drawn in the style of the animated series *Fat Albert*, 2005.

30. Timmy in a rescripting of the classic Christmas Peanuts special, drawn in the style of the animator Charles Schulz, 2005.

make boy bands say EEEEUUUWWW!" The self-reflexive tone of *The Fairly Odd-Parents,* the way the show mocks television and commercial merchandise, the implicit commentary on the "oppression" of kids living in an adult world—all are part of a definition of consumer citizenship, where political ideologies that critique the political and cultural economy are harnessed to work for Nickelodeon —perhaps the "uber-product" of this same political and cultural economy.[78]

Simensky, while discussing Nickelodeon animation, commented that other networks—especially Disney and Cartoon Network—have consciously imitated Nickelodeon in the general tone of their animation. The "cutting edge" that characterizes so many of Nickelodeon's programs has been so normalized that many new programs on different channels have that "Nickelodeon feel." In fact, it is no longer specific to Nickelodeon; as Simensky says, "[In the early years], Nick had this house style. Some shows now (like *Fairly OddParents*) look like they could be on any of the networks. As successful as they are, I think that Nick has watered down their look some. Imitation, combined with sharing of people, and what you're getting is less of a clear sensibility for each of these networks."[79] The trajectory from *The Ren & Stimpy Show*, which was too risky for the risk-taking Nickelodeon, to *The Fairly OddParents*, which looks remarkably like *The Power Puff Girls* on Cartoon Network or *Recess* on Disney, is not simply one of animation style or aesthetic but also involves a commercial context where irony and camp are normalized and regularly employed as marketing strategies. The question at this point regards the process of interpreting this mainstream style: is the commodification of camp, in Susan Sontag's words, "the betrayal of camp," where to talk about it literally means to kill it? Or is Naomi Klein accurate in her cynicism concerning consumer culture, where she maintains a tight distinction between consumerism and citizenship? I argue here that this distinction is disrupted precisely by the creative productions of media outlets such as Nickelodeon, where the line between play and seriousness, irony and earnestness, and consumerism and citizenship is deliberately blurred and therefore made all the easier to interpret from the logic of a consumerism that makes everything saleable.

CONCLUSION:

KIDS RULE: THE NICKELODEON UNIVERSE

Timmy: Who gets to run the country!
Kids: Kids!
Timmy: Who gets to say what's cool!
Kids: Kids!
Timmy: How can I put it bluntly?
Kids: Kids!
Timmy: Now it's kids who ruuuuuuuuuuule!

SONG FROM *THE FAIRLY ODDPARENTS*

Imagine a family taking a vacation in Orlando, Florida—home of mega–theme parks Universal Studios and Disney World. Rather than reside in a hotel that functions primarily as crucial down-time from the theme park activity, the family stays in Nickelodeon Family Suites, a Nickelodeon-themed hotel. Children have their own suites in this hotel, decorated with television characters like SpongeBob Square-Pants and Dora the Explorer. In fact, the family can eat breakfast with SpongeBob and Dora and later find other characters, activities, and shows designed to appeal to Nickelodeon's target audience of five-to-fifteen-year-olds. According to one reviewer, who called the hotel "Spring Break for tweens," "Even my preschooler forgot about the nearby theme parks the moment he saw the swimming pools. A buffet full of kid fare and a kids' spa add to the appeal. Or, in the words of a boy just outside our guest room window, 'Hey! He-e-ey! I'm *in* Nickelodeon!' "[1] Indeed, in particular ways, many U.S. children are always "in" Nickelodeon: it is a children's cable television channel, but it is also clearly more than that. The Nickelodeon brand certainly originates in the commercial success of the corporation's television shows, but the Nickelodeon name no longer seems to need television to market itself. In 2004, not only were sixteen out of the top twenty-four children's television shows Nickelodeon shows but Nickelodeon Enterprises, which is made up of consumer products, websites, publishing, and recreation, brought in $3.9 billion to its parent company, Viacom.[2] As one reporter commented, "Nick TV shows play in 100 countries. With Viacom's recent $160 million acquisition of Neopets, a global online entertainment network, Nickelodeon becomes the biggest player in the kids-online-entertainment business. Is there anywhere Nick won't go?"[3]

The concept of being "in" Nickelodeon, as a way of life, catalyzes the complexities within consumer citizenship itself—complexities between identity and politics, between rebellion and corporate co-optation. I've argued throughout this book that consumer citizenship, especially when it comes to the youth population, needs to be approached theoretically as not a question of *either* consumerism or citizenship but how consumerism and consumption habits inform and shape a dominant notion of citizenship. Children have been historically excluded from traditional definitions of citizenship for a variety of reasons, but in the contemporary context of brand media culture, it no longer makes sense to sustain this exclusion. If a contemporary meaning of citizenship includes a sense of community as well as individual agency, then the relationship the current youth generation has with media needs to be considered as a potentially productive site for the forging of citizenship. The interaction of children with media is not confined to the television; media use has expanded to the Internet, cell phones, video games, text-messaging. Children are just as likely (if not more) to congregate together and establish communities at myspace.com and other "friend" networks as they are to hang out at a mall or at the movies. Advertisers are aware of the many different media platforms that now exist for children's entertainment, as well as how kids are accessing these programs. Importantly, Nickelodeon has not simply been a part of this burgeoning media culture but rather has played an instrumental role in creating, disseminating, and legitimating it. Reimagining citizenship is thus called for, but not as a nostalgic longing for a past vibrant political culture and a yearning for those identities that apparently inhabited that culture, and not based upon a naïve assumption that commercial culture is the *only* site for social change and political identity making. Rather, a reimagining of citizenship is required that situates citizenship as residing and taking on meaning within these contradictions. To imagine citizenship as existing outside the commercial world is not only unrealistic but, more importantly, it is limiting. Indeed, the distinction between consumerism and citizenship is spurious from the ground up—in the United States there is no citizenship outside consumption, and part of the pleasure of consuming is that the act itself constitutes one as a citizen, someone who "matters" in this particular body politic and historical moment.

This book is my attempt to make sense of the status of this kind of "mattering" for a U.S. youth population. What are the consequences of understanding television as a safe haven, a trusted friend, a refuge in a world of adult turmoil? Some of these consequences are that citizenship is ultimately defined as a series of private acts, individualized as consumption practices. It may well be that these kinds of private acts constitute the definition of citizenship, but what that means is that we not only reimagine the identity category of citizenship but we also need to reimagine what citizenship *does* for us, the practice of citizenship. The practice of consumer citizenship allows individuals to make particular choices in specific circumstances; in the case of a children's cable channel, it constitutes youth audiences as always being "in" Nickelodeon.

As media use expands among children, the actual television programming on Nickelodeon becomes just one entertainment option among many. In an essay about the changing uses of television with new technologies such as TiVo (digital recording devices) and interactive games on TV, William Uricchio recalls Raymond Williams's notion of "flow" and suggests that the notion of flow needs to be adjusted to the current televisual landscape, as does the workings of ideology itself.[4] I've argued throughout this book that Nickelodeon stakes out a particular claim in the media lives of children, one that promises "empowerment" and "choices" in a world that is structured by rigid adult rules and uncertain fears and anxieties. Nickelodeon offers children a "safe place," away from those fears and anxieties, where children can constitute a particular kind of consumer citizenship within the confines of the brand. This is one way to adjust Williams's notion of flow—Williams was remarking upon the ways in which the seemingly disparate elements of programming, advertising, and channel promotional spots all flowed together seamlessly, as a way to capture a viewer's attention and encourage capitalist consumption without the viewer being aware of it. Flow, for Williams, was a form of ideology. However, as Uricchio points out, when flow expands beyond the roots of television, then the definition of ideology needs also to be developed in different ways.[5] In the case of Nickelodeon, the flow of the channel extends far beyond television programming, to merchandising, new media forms, alliances with federal policy makers, even to a *SpongeBob SquarePants* bed in a Nickelodeon hotel. The ideology of Nickelodeon, however, is not one of mere consumption; rather it centers on *how* to construct citizenship within the sphere of consumption. Clearly, the Nickelodeon "way of life" is not simply about buying merchandise; as I've argued, the channel has been very important in terms of pushing the conventional boundaries of representation on children's television and has played a key role in the practices of "girl power" and an urban aesthetic within U.S. youth culture.

Because children—specifically between the ages of eight and fourteen years—have been recognized as one of the most lucrative commercial markets, it makes sense to analyze the ways that children are targeted as particular kinds of consumer citizens in the current media environment. Indeed, with the increase in media use and media options among children, commercial media is a factor in every part of a contemporary child's identity. Commercial brand culture has become expert in cultivating a particular youth appeal and incorporating the politically alternative within the commercial mainstream. Nickelodeon, in this sense, is the quintessential successful brand, because it taps into ideologies of community membership and belonging so seamlessly through its rhetorical and representational strategies. Lisa Sun-Hee Park, writing about how Asian Americans feel "compelled to prove their 'Americanness'" through acts of consumption, argues that "consumption . . . is a communal, political activity and an important expression of one's identity."[6] For Nickelodeon viewers, consuming the brand—becoming a member of the "Nickelodeon Nation"—is a kind of political activity, where membership and belonging are defined and determined by a kind of capitalist loyalty to a network. The network, in this case, stands in as a kind of authority and functions as a means through which children can demonstrate their "patriotism" to a televisual nation.

By shifting the focus from children as potential political citizens to children as empowered consumer citizens, this book represents my effort to challenge, or at least interrupt, a dominant discourse that structures the way the relationship of children with the media is publicly understood. As I have argued, although recent scholarship on media and audiences has intervened in this debate in decisive ways, historically the discursive frame regarding children and the media has remained dependent on a conventional paradigm of active versus passive, where children are either impressionable passive viewers or empowered active agents. This bifurcated discourse continues to both create and limit not only cultural understandings of children and media; it also impacts institutional and policy decisions on how media should (or should not) be regulated for the child audience as well as restricts the various ways in which media interaction is understood as potentially empowering for youth. Nickelodeon's claim to be a network "just for kids" is one of the ways in which the network acknowledges the connection between political subjectivity and consumer identity: it is not simply a place that is defined exclusively for kids; it also capitalizes on the enormous commercial potential of its child audience.

Part of Nickelodeon's strategy in capitalizing on its audience has been to make the claim that it—Nickelodeon—"empowers" children in a particular way. Empowerment within the context of media culture is clearly not a relatively simple matter of "possessing" power, or being a member of the dominant group, or even exercising resistance to the dominant group. As I demonstrate in the various chapters in this book, empowerment is ideologically complex and involves contradictory dynamics. This is especially the case when empowerment is connected to children; children are positioned outside the formal venues where power is often conferred in the voting booth, or by a legal system that relies upon a historically (and racial- and gender-) specific definition of consent. Within commercial media culture, empowerment often means any number of things: visibility or representation within the media; access to media production; ownership of media corporations; the economic capital associated with lucrative market segments; individual empowerment to "reject" media (or media texts) within a liberal capitalist political economy. Thus, part of examining the ways in which children are constituted as both consumers and citizens within the current media context means taking seriously the ways in which both these identity categories carry with them a particular kind of power. And rather than insist upon the intrinsic division between the "citizen" and the "consumer," or to lament the loss of that division, it makes more sense to theorize the *possibilities* of understanding oneself as a citizen—especially a child citizen—within the current U.S. political economy. The first step in this kind of theorizing, it seems, is to refuse romanticizing the "real" at the expense of the "commercial" when thinking about what comprises consumer citizenship. Nickelodeon is a particularly useful site in which to practice this kind of theorizing. I have attempted to refuse the distinction between the "real" and the "commercial" when considering current configurations of citizenship, as citizenship is most profoundly understood within the confines of the commercial.

Nickelodeon's strategy at targeting children as consumers through a discourse of empowerment and agency has provided a model for other cable niche channels, especially those dedicated to child audiences. Indeed, it seems almost passé in this moment of brand culture to closely examine corporate strategies that use notions of hip, cool, and the urban as ways to commodify particular lifestyles and sell youth products. Yet Nickelodeon set the stage for this kind of marketing to children and thus became, as Heather Hendershot has argued, a cultural as well as a brand phenomenon.[7] Quite simply, Nickelodeon changed the children's televisual landscape and ushered in a new way of marketing to kids that appealed to both children and adults, even while emphasizing the differences between them. Nickelodeon claims that it "pledges allegiance to kids"—and it does. However, the appropriation of political rhetoric in this claim—pledging allegiance—is about both politics and consumerism simultaneously. Nickelodeon, in short, is a media demonstration of the politics of being a consumer in a brand-dominated culture.

The changes to the televisual landscape heralded by Nickelodeon include some very important disruptions—Nickelodeon regularly features girls as key important characters, and the casts on almost all shows, both live-action and animated, are multicultural. When the channel was relaunched from a "green vegetable channel" with no commercials to a "kids-only zone" in the mid-1980s, Nickelodeon programming set out to buck the system—a system that generally remained safely within the confines of conventional television: low-risk, formulaic, stereotypical, featuring primarily white boys as heroes. In this way, Nickelodeon demonstrated to the television world that the conventional industry wisdom dictating that the only safe bets for kids' TV were "LOP" (least objectionable programming) shows was in fact a fiction, a compromise of quality at the expense of profit. Of course, the fact that Nickelodeon emerged in the burgeoning cable industry, where for a brief moment it seemed as if all bets—not just the safe ones—were off, was a crucial reason that the channel was able to emerge as a renegade.

However, it seems as if the critical edge that characterized Nickelodeon in the 1990s has been co-opted and reframed as slick corporate strategy in the early twenty-first century. The contemporary Nickelodeon looks very similar to Cartoon Network, PBS Kids, even the Disney Channel. Nickelodeon fans of the early days who were first addressed in terms of empowerment and "respect" seem to notice: in 2007, there are numerous fan websites that tout the value of "old school" Nickelodeon programming, often featuring message boards where nostalgic fans lament the state of Nickelodeon programming today, longing for the shows of the 1990s. Not surprisingly, the channel has attempted to appease these older fans by launching a new cable channel, Nicktoons, which airs "old" Nickelodeon cartoons and programs. However, it is a mistake to characterize Nickelodeon in a clearly bifurcated manner, divided into the original, more critically engaged channel and the newer, slicker corporate channel; this assumes that the original Nickelodeon was not interested in profit and cultivating a new vast market of kids. Nonetheless, as Hendershot speculates, Nickelodeon "may well be a victim of its own commercial success" as it increases its global scope and media holdings and is part of an enormous multimedia conglomerate.[8]

As the Nickelodeon brand continues to expand, the channel represents an important step in the overall Viacom strategy to take its audience "from the cradle to the grave." In the midst of this cluttered branded landscape, it becomes more difficult to sort out how the channel is really providing children with "a network of their own" as Geraldine Laybourne promised years ago. Rather, it seems more as if U.S. kids are always "in" Nickelodeon—as part of the brand itself. In this book, I have attempted to tease out the tensions involved in citizenship, media audiences, and consumerism, presenting a unique and, I hope, compelling argument about how children interact with and attempt to resolve these tensions in a particular political economy, cultural setting, and media environment. The time when Nickelodeon "bucked the system" seems to have passed. The rebellious, upstart network is not so much an alternative to the multimedia conglomerates as it is the primary media source for U.S. youth. Indeed, the programming, industry practices, and rhetoric of the channel do not pose a challenge to the "system"—for Nickelodeon *is* the system in the current media environment.

1. "WE, THE PEOPLE OF NICKELODEON"

1 See, for example, BBC News, "US Right Attacks SpongeBob Video," http://news.bbc.co.uk/1/hi/world/americas/4190699.stm (accessed March 11, 2007).

2 Ibid.

3 American Heart Association, "Nickelodeon, Clinton Foundation and American Heart Association Announce Partnership to fight Childhood Obesity," October 20, 2005, http://www.americanheart.org/presenter.jhtml?identifier=3034761 (accessed March 11, 2007).

4 Ibid. Herb Scannell served as president of Nickelodeon from 1996 to 2006. When he stepped down, the parent company of Nickelodeon, MTV Networks (a division of Viacom) announced a restructuring, under which Cyma Zarghami is now president of Nickelodeon. As of December 2006, Nickelodeon is grouped under MTVN Kids and Family Group, which includes Nickelodeon, Nick at Nite, Nick Online, Nick Movies, Noggin/The N, Nicktoons, and more. See David B. Wilkerson, "Nickelodeon President steps down," *MarketWatch*, January 4, 2006, http://www.marketwatch.com/news/story/nickelodeon-president-steps-down/story.aspx?guid=%7BF233C3F5%2D8034%2D46F4%2DAB06%2DEF7D22C3752F%7D (accessed March 11, 2007).

5 Despite these impressive figures, there has not been much academic attention to Nickelodeon. A notable exception is the recent anthology edited by Heather Hendershot, *Nickelodeon Nation.*

6 Statistics from Viacom, http://www.viacom.com. See also Hendershot, *Nickelodeon Nation.*

7 Viacom, http://www.viacom.com (accessed December 2005).

8 Hendershot, *Nickelodeon Nation,* 1.

9 Linn, *Consuming Kids;* Schor, *Born to Buy;* Milner, *Freaks, Geeks, and Cool Kids;* and Quart, *Branded.*

10 See, for instance, Seiter, *Sold Separately;* Seiter, *Internet Playground;* Hendershot, *Saturday Morning Censors;* Sammond, *Babes in Tomorrowland;* Cook, *Commodification of Childhood;* Buckingham, *Death of Childhood;* Livingstone, *Young People;* and others.

11 Schor, *Born to Buy;* and Klein, *No Logo.*

12 Singer and Singer, *Handbook of Children and the Media;* Cantor, *Mommy, I'm Scared;* and Bryant and Anderson, *Children's Understanding of Television.*

13 Kinder, "Home Alone," 77.

14 As is well known, Habermas argues that in eighteenth-century Europe, a bourgeois

public sphere emerges through a newly organized civil society. This public sphere is, according to Habermas, a "domain of private autonomy . . . opposed to the state." The public sphere is occupied by what he calls "educated" citizens (generally white, property-owning men) and serves as an important forum in which "rational critical public debate" over a variety of cultural and political issues takes place. Habermas argues that within the public sphere, rational debate provides an important mediating tool to negotiate the interests of potentially conflicting social groups and allows for the social construction of oneself as a political subject, or citizen. Habermas, *Public Sphere.*

15   A primary question underlying the constitution of the Habermasian public sphere is one of location: *where and when* is this public sphere? Habermas gestures back to a "golden age" where salons and the political press offered democratic venues in which elite individuals could discourse over ideals of rationality, rights, and political freedom. Nancy Fraser has pointed out how we need to rethink Habermas's vision of a public sphere because of its inherently exclusionary nature—women, for instance, do not have a place in a Habermasian public sphere because of its privileging of the masculinist narratives of "rational" discourse. Fraser, "Rethinking."

16   For more discussion of this, see Greenstein, *Children and Politics;* Dixon, *Catching Them Young;* Connell, *Child's Construction of Politics;* and James and Prout, *Constructing and Reconstructing Childhood.*

17   See, for instance, Rousseau, *Emile;* and Locke, *Two Treatises on Government.*

18   Greenstein, *Children and Politics.*

19   Ibid.

20   See also Greenstein, *Children and Politics;* and Flanagan, "Youth Political Development." Greenstein argued that while the mass media was important to children, the political socialization of children occurred perhaps more powerfully within formal education and the family, where political information, such as affiliation with political leaders, the workings of the government, the importance of voting, and ideas about political authority, were most likely to be of pedagogical priority for children. Greenstein's 1965 book represents one of the early ventures in political socialization and was one of the first studies of children's early political development in the United States. In *Children and Politics,* he examined conceptions of political authority held by children between the ages of nine and thirteen, the development of political information and party attachments, and differences in political learning based on social class and gender. Greenstein's work is recognized for its argument that significant aspects of an adult's political behavior have their genesis in the child's early political learning. Although work in the political social-ization of children was supported in the late 1960s and early 1970s, for more than two decades, research on the the processes whereby children are "trained" to be U.S. citizens, or to become members of political communities, has not been a prominent theme in scholarship. Perhaps this has to do with the idea that, as has been convincingly pointed out, the public sphere no longer exists (if it ever did), at least not in the way Habermas imagined.

21   Berlant, *Queen of America,* 6.

22   Miller, *Well-Tempered Self.*

23 Canclini, *Citizens and Consumers*, 43 (emphases in original).

24 See Anderson, *Imagined Communities*.

25 See Berman, *The Politics of Authenticity*.

26 Miller, "Introducing Cultural Citizenship." Aihwa Ong, taking cultural citizenship a bit further with the concept of "flexible citizenship," argues that contemporary notions of citizenship represent "a strategic making-do that seeks access to as many rights as possible while falling prey to as few responsibilities as possible." This idea of flexible citizenship captures some of the dynamics of the contemporary moment because it invokes both a traditional political identity (accessed through rights) and a consumer identity (the adjudication of social responsibility). Cited in Miller, "Introducing Cultural Citizenship."

27 Recent scholarship on media and audiences has demonstrated that there have been important developments in conceptions of the audience, from challenges to traditional work, ranging from the Frankfurt School and researchers working on the "effects" of the media on audiences, to celebrations of "active" audiences busily interpreting the media from a limitless field of reading strategies, to theories on the various ways in which particular media interpellate women, people of color, lesbians, and gay men. See, for example, Fiske, *Media Matters;* Hall, "Encoding/Decoding"; and Gross, *Up from Invisibility*.

28 I am indebted to Elizabeth Bird's discussion of how best to study an "audience" and what the media offers in terms of identity strategies. Bird discusses the complicated ways of understanding the role of the audience in a media-saturated age and argues specifically for the use of what George Marcus has called a "multi site" ethnography. This kind of ethnography requires not just a recording of the voices of the "subjects" being studied but a more interdisciplinary, intermethodological approach that questions the idea that there is a "subject" to be studied in the first place rather than a range of embedded and interconnected practices that are part of constructing subjectivity. Despite the richness of Bird's study, she maintains a particular divide between certain elements within culture, even while questioning others. Bird, *Audience in Everyday Life*.

29 Ibid., 182.

30 For further discussion of this, see Jenkins, *Children's Culture Reader*.

31 Greenstein, *Children and Politics*.

32 Dávila, *Latinos, Inc.*, 11.

33 See Jones, *Entertaining Politics;* van Zoonen, *Entertaining the Citizen;* and Canclini, *Consumers and Citizens*.

34 Cook, *Commodification of Childhood*, 15.

35 For more on the news, see Schiller, *Objectivity and the News;* and Schudson, *Discovering the News*.

36 Clearly this is the primary assumption shaping Rousseau's theory (in *Emile*) of the tabula rasa.

37 Buckingham, *Making of Citizens*, 59.

38 *Nick News*, which, in addition to its primetime slot on Nickelodeon, was, in 2004, syndicated in more than 92 percent of the country, won the Emmy for outstanding children's program in 1998, 2002, and 2005, as well as a Peabody Award "for presenting news in a thoughtful and non-condescending manner for both children and adults." In

1993, the series won a Columbia duPont Award, which called the show "a unique contribution to television, produced with imagination, humor and serious purpose." *Nick
News* also received a 1993 Parents' Choice Award, while the Television Critics Association
has recognized Linda Ellerbee for her outstanding achievement in children's programming. Barber and Associates, http://www.barberusa.com/adversit/ellerbee—linda.html
(accessed March 11, 2007).

39 Buckingham, *Making of Citizens*, 58.

40 Kelley Beaucar Vlahos, "Kids News Show to Address Gay Issues," June 5, 2002, http://
www.foxnews.com/story/0,2933,54521,00.html (accessed March 11, 2007).

41 Ibid.

42 Laybourne, "Nickelodeon Experience."

43 Mittell, "Saturday Morning Exile."

44 Ibid., 49.

45 Ibid., 50.

46 Englehardt, "Strawberry Shortcake Strategy."

47 For more on this, see Horwitz, *Irony of Regulatory Reform;* and McChesney, *Rich Media.*

48 Federal Communications Commission, "Children's Educational Television," September
23, 2005, http://www.fcc.gov/cgb/consumerfacts/childtv.html (accessed March 11, 2007).

49 Jordan, Schmitt, and Woodard, "Educational Offerings."

50 Boddy, *Fifties Television.*

51 See Hendershot, *Saturday Morning Censors.*

52 Ibid; Seiter, *Sold Separately.*

53 For a detailed examination of Sesame Street and diversity, see Hendershot, *Saturday
Morning Censors.*

54 Morley, *Television, Audiences, and Cultural Studies.*

55 One of the primary problems with some earlier work on mass media, generated by
scholars ranging from Richard Hoggart to Horkheimer and Adorno, was not simply that
their theories relied upon a notion of the audience member as passive but also that this
reliance necessarily implied a simple reductive relationship between passive and active. In
many of these studies, the audience is positioned as a group, either manipulated by the
media or in need of protection. Because many of these early media studies saw the
audience as impressionable, unformed, and prone to suggestion, it should come as no
surprise that many scholars invoked the figure of the child—literally or as metaphor—as a
way to explain the effect of the media on its audience. For instance, Adorno, in his work
on the culture industry, sees the consciousness of the masses as something that develops
"retrogressively" so that members of consumer media culture are like children: "it is no
coincidence that cynical American film producers are heard to say that their pictures
must take into consideration the level of eleven-year-olds. In doing so they would very
much like to make adults into eleven-year-olds." Infantalization, for Adorno, means that
adults are positioned to conform rather than create, acquiesce rather than resist. This
dichotomy between sophisticated adults and naive children is not unique to Adorno but
has been used historically as a powerful justification for federal regulation of the media. It
also needs to be pointed out that while interventions within cultural studies in the last

twenty years have provided an important challenge to the mass media theories, such as Adorno's, that insist upon the monolithic power of the media over the audience, the notion that the audience is "active" is also one that deserves our frank attention. Horkheimer and Adorno, "Culture Industry."

56 Jenkins, "Professor Jenkins."

57 These moral panics generally concern the presence of pedophiles on the Internet, and the friendship networks are reported in the news media as a particularly rich place for sexual predators to attempt to lure children away.

58 Not surprisingly, media corporations capitalize on this technological knowledge by developing software, video games, and interactive websites where children can demonstrate their savvy. The Nickelodeon website offers television schedules, interactive games, classroom advice, and message boards and is clearly not simply ancillary to the television schedule but rather exists as an entertainment medium in its own right. In September 2005, the website hosted Nickelodeon's "We've Got Your Back" initiative, which is a campaign to help victims of Hurricane Katrina and offers suggestions for how one can help community building.

59 Cook, *Commodification of Childhood.*

60 Nickelodeon, *How to Nickelodeon.*

61 Former Nickelodeon employee, interview by author, January 22, 2004.

62 Viacom, like other media corporations, often restructures its holdings. As of December 2006, Viacom owned these media holdings as well as others, including CMT: Country Music Television and TV Land. In June 2005, Viacom separated into two companies: a new publicly traded company, Viacom, Inc., that consists of the advertising-supported cable networks (including Nickelodeon), Paramount Pictures, and Famous Music (a music publisher); and CBS Corporation, which includes the broadcast television networks CBS and The CW, the pay cable network Showtime, local CBS television stations, and the publishing house Simon and Schuster. See http://www.viacom.com/company—overview.jhtml and http://www.cbscorporation.com/our—company/divisions/cbs—corporation/index.php (both accessed March 11, 2007).

63 Turow, *Breaking Up America.*

64 Dávila, *Latinos, Inc.*

65 See ibid., 10; see also Miller, *Technologies of Truth;* and Canclini, *Consumers and Citizens.*

66 Dávila, *Latinos, Inc.,* 10.

67 Spigel, *Make Room for TV.* For further discussion of the postwar domestic context for television, see Boddy, *Fifties Television.*

68 Frank, *Conquest of Cool.*

69 Turow, *Breaking Up America;* Goldman and Papson, *Sign Wars;* and Schudson, *Advertising.*

70 Turow, *Breaking Up America,* 4.

71 Horkheimer and Adorno, "The Culture Industry."

72 Spigel, *Make Room for TV.*

73 See, for example, among recent popular books, Schor, *Born to Buy;* Linn, *Consuming Kids;* and others.

74 Horkheimer and Adorno's "pseudo-individualism," Marx's "false-consciousness," femi-
    nism's version of false consciousness, etc.

75 The consideration of children as useful changed in late-eighteenth- and early-nineteenth-
    century U.S. society, when laws were developed that eventually prohibited the employ-
    ment of children. These legal changes relied upon a particular understanding of childhood
    as a rationale for implementing a shift in the age requirements for labor. Viviana Zelizer
    argues that during this historical moment, children, newly seen as "corruptible" by social
    forces, began to be protected from the economic world of labor. Children themselves were
    understood as explicitly "noncommercial." This process of shifting the social value of
    children, motivated in large part by changing labor laws so as to prohibit children from
    working for wages outside the home, encouraged what Zelizer calls "the sacralization of
    children," a process whereby adults invest children, and childhood, with sentimental or
    religious meaning. Child labor reform was central to the sacralization of children, and
    child labor reformers positioned children in a new light, where instead of being seen as
    individuals who could secure the future of their parents, they were seen as worthy of their
    parents' sacrifice. Zelizer, *Pricing the Priceless Child*.

76 Ibid., 59.

77 For a more detailed analysis, see Seiter, *Sold Separately*; and Spigel, *Make Room for TV*.

78 Obviously, not all children and their mothers were nestled securely in a domestic space.
    Marketers at this time were directly influential in the creation of a cultural ideal of the
    home, where mothers remained with their children and guided them—morally, intellec-
    tually, spiritually—in childrearing. The commercialization of childhood that occurs at
    this time is part of this ideology. But central to creating domestic space as a lucrative
    commercial avenue was what Stephen Kline calls the "commercialization of childhood."
    Throughout the industrial revolution, as factories were producing more and more goods,
    marketers pursued children as a profitable new market: "The Victorian awakening to the
    preciousness of childhood helped ensure that children's goods would expand along with
    other markets. Culturally, childhood was increasingly characterized by specific behav-
    ioral traits and products. The increasingly vivid image of a separate domain of childhood
    became standard in both the late Victorian arts and product appeals." See Kline, "Making
    of Children's Culture," 102. See also Spigel, *Make Room for TV*.

79 Cook, *Commodification of Childhood*.

80 Seiter, *Sold Separately*, 52.

81 Cohen, *Consumer's Republic*.

82 Ibid.

83 For further discussion of this, see Spigel, *Make Room for TV*; Lipsitz, *Time Passages*;
    Haralovich and Rabinovich, *Television, History, and American Culture*; and others.

84 Palladino, *Teenagers*, 101–2.

85 As the *Seventeen* example demonstrates, this teenage market was even more segmented
    by gender. Angela McRobbie and Susan Douglas, among others, have discussed the ways
    that the methods of encouraging consumption during this era were also uniquely gen-
    dered and began to become bound up in personal identity. Teenage women first began to
    learn about the surveillance of body image through the marketing of products in teen

magazines, both in the features and the advertisements. As the teens aged, sex was also then marketed in a variety of ways to capture on pubescent angst and insecurity. Douglas, *Where the Girls Are;* and McRobbie, *Feminism and Youth Culture.*

86 This is not to imply that marketers think of all consumers in the same way. Indeed, in recent popular culture, there have been companies, such as liquor and car companies, who have been reluctant to see their products associated with hip-hop and rap artists, since this particular U.S. cultural group is often seen as "pathological" consumers, excessively demonstrating wealth and success through extravagant displays of jewelry, expensive cars, and other "bling."

87 We can see this in the contemporary post-9/11 context, when Americans are called upon to go shopping as a patriotic act, to save the economy—and thus "us"—from terrorists.

88 Hendershot, *Saturday Morning Censors,* 217–18.

89 For further discussion of this, see Robbins, *Phantom Public Sphere.*

90 Davies, "*Dear BBC,*" 46.

91 Kulynych, "No Playing," 3.

92 MacKinnon, *Feminist Theory of the State;* Elshtain, *Public Man, Private Woman;* Okin, "Multiculturalism"; Brown, *Manhood and Politics;* and others.

93 Nickelodeon, *How to Nickelodeon.*

94 Linda Simensky, interview by author, February 2004.

95 Morley, *Television, Audiences and Cultural Studies;* Ang, *Desperately Seeking the Audience.*

96 For further discussion of this, see Morley, *Television, Audiences and Cultural Studies;* Buckingham, *Death of Childhood;* and others.

97 Laybourne, "Nickelodeon Experience," 304.

98 Cohn, Marketwatch.

99 Buckingham, *Death of Childhood,* 168.

100 For further discussion of this, see Hebdige, *Subculture;* Fiske, *Reading the Popular;* and McRobbie, *Feminism and Youth Culture.*

101 James, "Confections, Concoctions, and Conceptions," 394–95.

102 Ibid., 404.

103 This point was made by Ellen Seiter in a talk given to the Annenberg School for Communication, University of Southern California, April 2001.

104 Nickelodeon, *How to Nickelodeon.*

2. THE SUCCESS STORY

The epigraph to this chapter is from an interview conducted by the author, February 17, 2004.

1 Mullen, *Rise of Cable Programming.*

2 Although, of course, not all American homes subscribed to cable, and in the early period, relatively few did.

3 Horwitz, *Irony of Regulatory Reform,* 4.

4 There were some critically acclaimed shows produced during the 1970s—*M.A.S.H., The Mary Tyler Moore Show, All in the Family,* to name a few—but these were the exceptions.

For further discussion of "quality television," see Feuer, Kerr, and Vahimagi, MTM; and Staiger, *Blockbuster TV*.

5   Minow and LaMay, *Abandoned in the Wasteland*, 19.

6   Donna Mitroff, interview by author, March 17, 2004.

7   Streeter, "Blue Skies."

8   Gitlin, *Inside Prime Time*; Horwitz, *Irony of Regulatory Reform*; and Sturken and Cartwright, *Practices of Looking*.

9   Hendershot, *Saturday Morning Censors*, 62; and Montgomery, *Target Prime Time*.

10 Williams, *Television*.

11 Ibid.

12 Spigel, *Make Room for TV*.

13 McCarthy, *Ambient Television*. McCarthy discusses the role of television in public or "nondomestic" spaces. The presence of television in bars and taverns, airports, malls, and other "public" spaces does not change the nature of TV as privatized but rather reveals the way that television forges a particular relationship between the public and the private.

14 Horwitz, *Irony of Regulatory Reform*.

15 Minow and LaMay, *Abandoned in the Wasteland*, 68.

16 Streeter, "Blue Skies"; Mullen, *Rise of Cable Programming*.

17 Streeter, "Blue Skies," 222.

18 Mullen, *Rise of Cable Programming*, 1.

19 Czitrom, *Media and the American Mind*; and Pool, *Technologies of Freedom*.

20 Streeter, "Blue Skies"; and Mullen, *Rise of Cable Programming*.

21 Streeter, "Blue Skies."

22 Ibid., 227.

23 Ibid., 228.

24 Spigel and Curtin, *Revolution Wasn't Televised*.

25 Over time, Nickelodeon reconfigured the relationship between advertisers and viewers, and "educational" programming can be interpreted as a kind of consumer pedagogy.

26 Streeter, "Blue Skies," 229.

27 Ibid., 230.

28 Linda Simensky, interview by author, February 17, 2004.

29 Spigel, *Make Room for TV*, 2–3.

30 For more on the Saturday morning exile of children's programming, see Mittell, "Great Saturday Morning Exile."

31 Englehardt, "Strawberry Shortcake Strategy"; and Minow and LaMay, *Abandoned in the Wasteland*.

32 Bodroghkozy, *Groove Tube*; Gitlin, *The Whole World is Watching*; and Spigel and Curtin, *Revolution Wasn't Televised*.

33 Bodroghkozy, *Groove Tube*; and Spigel and Curtin, *Revolution Wasn't Televised*.

34 Gitlin, *Inside Prime Time*; and Newcomb, *Television*.

35 Seiter, *Sold Separately*, 96.

36 Ibid., 97; and Hendershot, *Saturday Morning Censors*.

37 Hendershot, *Saturday Morning Censors*.

38 Ibid.

39 Minow and LeMay, *Abandoned in the Wasteland*, 47.

40 Montgomery, *Target Prime Time*.

41 Hendershot, *Saturday Morning Censors*, 71. See also Seiter, *Sold Separately*.

42 Seiter, *Sold Separately*, 102.

43 Cited in Minow and LeMay, *Abandoned in the Wasteland*, 61.

44 One particularly effective strategy for ACT was their anti-sugar platform. Instead of boycotting sugar-based cereals and candy advertised during children's programming, ACT simply took on "junk food" and the way it was advertised on television. Because these food products were non-nutritious and thus could be harmful to children, ACT argued that ads for junk food worked against the "public interest." Hendershot and Seiter have argued that ACT's position on sugar products, while ostensibly about food and nutrition, was simply part of a larger challenge that children's television (especially those programs that were toy-based) was not tasteful: "across the political spectrum, child TV viewers tend to be problematically figured as unsophisticated, feckless viewers desperately in need of education from inherently more sophisticated adult TV viewers." Hendershot, *Saturday Morning Censors*; and Seiter, *Sold Separately*.

45 Jenkins, "Interview with Geraldine Laybourne," 145–46.

46 In fact, part of ACT's problem with advertising involved not the more obvious commercialization but rather the challenge to this definition of the child as innocent. As Seiter points out, ACT assumed that children do not understand advertising—or at the least, do not understand what the goal of advertising is in terms of selling products. Thus, in this view, children are duped by the manipulative world of advertising. Seiter, *Sold Separately*.

47 McNeal, *The Kids Market*.

48 Ibid, 189.

49 Ibid, 153. As McNeal documents, advertising to kids reached $1 billion in 1990.

50 Seiter, *Sold Separately*, 101.

51 Horwitz, *Irony of Regulatory Reform*; and Minow and LaMay, *Abandoned in the Wasteland*.

52 Montgomery, *Target Prime Time*, 219.

53 Hendershot, *Saturday Morning Censors*, 127.

54 For further discussion of this shift in the kids' television landscape, see Engelhardt, "Strawberry Shortcake Strategy."

55 Simensky, interview, February 17, 2004.

56 Mullen, *Rise of Cable Programming*, 120.

57 Ibid.

58 At this time, in 1981, Nickelodeon gave way at night to Warner's Star Channel/The Movie Channel, because the two networks shared the same transponder. Four years later, in 1985, Nickelodeon began airing *Nick at Nite*, a separate programming block aimed at twenty-five- to forty-nine-year-olds. For further discussion of this, see Mullen, *Rise of Cable Programming*.

59 Ibid.

60 Jenkins, "Interview with Geraldine Laybourne," 136.

61 Pecora, *Business of Children's Entertainment*, 93.

62 Ibid., 93–94.

63 Hennessee, "Cable's Nickelodeon."

64 Ibid.

65 Cited in Minow and LaMay, *Abandoned in the Wasteland*, 61.

66 Harmetz, "Action Group."

67 Hennessee, "Cable's Nickelodeon."

68 Harmetz, "Action Group."

69 Jenkins, "Interview with Geraldine Laybourne," 145.

70 Harmetz, "Action Group."

71 Jenkins, "Interview with Geraldine Laybourne," 145.

72 Harmetz, "Action Group."

73 Brennan, "Kids' Channel."

74 Ibid.

75 Ibid.

76 For further discussion of *Sesame Street*'s use of focus groups, see Hendershot, *Saturday Morning Censors;* and Fisch and Truglio, *"G" Is for Growing*.

77 Bruce Friend, interview by Ellen Seiter and Vicky Mayer, August 13, 1997.

78 Brennan, "Kids' Channel."

79 Zoglin, "Letting Kids," 78.

80 Granville, "Nickelodeon Flexing Muscles."

81 Friend, interview.

82 Donna Mitroff, interview.

83 *Variety,* April 5–11, 1989.

84 Linda Simensky, interview by author, March 4, 2004.

85 Streeter, "Blue Skies"; Mullen, *Rise of Cable Programming;* Pecora, *Business of Children's Entertainment*.

86 Pecora, *Business of Children's Entertainment*.

87 Ibid., 93.

88 Ibid., 33.

89 Lawrie Mifflin, "Following a Tough Act: Nickelodeon Chief Quietly Builds on Celebrated Legacy." *New York Times,* sec. 3, June 17, 1999.

90 Simensky, interview, February 17, 2004.

91 Mitroff, interview.

92 Pecora, *Business of Children's Entertainment*, 95.

93 Mittell, "Great Saturday Morning Exile."

94 Ibid.

95 Brennan, "Kids' Channel."

96 Ibid.

97 Farley, "From Fred and Wilma to Ren and Stimpy."

98 Larsen, "Bottom Line."

99 Ibid., 59.

100 Nickelodeon homepage, http://www.nick.com (accessed February 28, 2005); and Pecora, *Business of Children's Entertainment.*

101 Pecora, *Business of Children's Entertainment,* 95.

102 This doesn't mean that Nickelodeon cartoons were toy-based—Laybourne insisted on creator-driven shows. But as the kids' TV landscape became more competitive, especially with Turner's Cartoon Network, it was less possible to take the kinds of risks with pilot programs that Nickelodeon had enjoyed in the past.

103 Larsen, "Bottom Line."

104 Petrozzello, "Nickelodeon's Herb Scannell."

105 Pecora, *Business of Children's Entertainment.*

106 Petrozzello, "Nickelodeon's Herb Scannell."

107 Mitroff, interview.

108 John Hardman, executive developer, Klasky and Csupo Productions, interview by Ellen Seiter and Vicky Mayer, July 16, 1997.

109 As of December 2006, CBS no longer airs Nick Jr. programs as part of its morning lineup.

110 Pecora, *Business of Children's Entertainment,* 110.

111 Mitroff, interview.

112 Viacom press release.

113 Viacom press release.

114 Viacom press release.

115 Mitroff, interview. It is worth noting that while Geraldine Laybourne is often credited for the launch of Nickelodeon, it was actually Cy Schneider who launched Nickelodeon, and it was under his direction that the channel was devoted to educational, or "broccoli," television. For further discussion of this, see Pecora, "Nickelodeon Grows Up."

116 Zoglin, "Letting Kids," 78.

117 Viacom press release.

3. THE NICKELODEON BRAND

The first epigraph to this chapter is taken from Granville, "Nickelodeon Flexing Muscles." Slaby is a developmental psychologist at Harvard University. The second epigraph to this chapter is taken from Nickelodeon, *How to Nickelodeon.*

1 Nickelodeon, *How to Nickelodeon.*

2 Jenkins, *Children's Culture Reader.*

3 For further discussion of this, see Kearney, *Girls Make Media.*

4 The special was directed by Barak Goodman. See also "The Merchants of Cool: A Report on the Creators and Marketers of Popular Culture for Teenagers," http://www.pbs.org/wgbh/pages/frontline/shows/cool (accessed March 11, 2007).

5 Klein, *No Logo,* 4.

6 Todd Cunningham, interview by Douglas Rushkoff, "Merchants of Cool," http://www.pbs.org/wgbh/pages/frontline/shows/cool/interviews/cunningham.html (accessed March 11, 2007).

7 J., interview by author, July 17, 2004.

8 Nickelodeon, *How to Nickelodeon*, 7.

9 Ibid.

10 Preston and White, "Commodifying Kids."

11 For further discussion of the early-twentieth-century American context of consumerism, see Cohen, *Consumers' Republic*.

12 For further discussion of this, see Cook, *Commodification of Childhood*, and Kline, *Out of the Garden*.

13 Kapur, "Out of Control," 125.

14 Kunkel, "Children and Television Advertising." For a critique of this position, see Seiter, *Sold Separately*, 99.

15 Seiter, *Sold Separately*, 100.

16 I use the term "cluttered" when referring to advertising in reference to Goldman and Papson, *Sign Wars*. For more on this particular research, see Kunkel, "Children and Television Advertising."

17 For an earlier discussion of this, see Atkin, "Children's Toy and Food Commercials." In the current context of childhood obesity in the United States, this argument that children cannot distinguish between ads and programs has not been terribly effective. However, corporations such as McDonalds and Kraft have responded to the current moral panic about obesity in kids by marketing new products apparently designed to address the problem. Nickelodeon, for example, has entered into a partnership with Kraft, "Healthy Kids Now," in a mutual campaign to advertise healthy Kraft foods on the network— clearly, both Kraft and Nickelodeon have a vested interest in this kind of message.

18 Kunkel and Gantz, "Children's Television Advertising," 134–52.

19 Ibid.; see also Kunkel, "Children and Television Advertising."

20 A, interview by author, July 17, 2004.

21 Seiter, *Sold Separately*, 117.

22 Ibid., 115–17.

23 Frank, "Advertising as Cultural Criticism," 382.

24 See, for example, Gladwell, "Coolhunt"; Quart, *Branded;* and Klein, *No Logo*.

25 Gladwell, "Coolhunt," 361.

26 Klein, *No Logo*, 25.

27 In addition to the masquerade of the generational divide, there is another problem with the advertising on Nickelodeon. This utopian world that ads present for children often does not provide a means of accessing this world but instead merely represents this world as an end in itself. Thus, the generational divide that children feel in their daily lives and then see represented in humorous and entertaining forms in advertisements is not actually addressed in these ads as a social problem of significance. In addition, Joseph Turow points out a similar problem in his study of the way in which advertising is "breaking up America." He argues that there are two primary "types" of media that function in U.S. society: society-making media and segment-making media: "segment-making media are those that encourage small slices of society to talk to themselves, while society-making media are those that have the potential to get all those segments to talk to each other"

(*Breaking Up America*, 6). Historically, both society-making media and segment-making media have functioned together, even in overtly commercial settings, to strengthen both individual identity (assured within segment-making media) and collective and national communities, created and maintained through society-making media. Presently, however, advertisers have moved further and further away from society-making media because of the drive to reach ever more narrow and specific niche markets, such that, according to Turow, the United States is losing the potential to have media facilitate "a rich and diverse sense of overarching connectedness: what a vibrant society is all about" (4). The differences, rather than similarities, between consumers are exploited by advertisers in an effort to gain loyalty and to reach new audiences, hence our media practices are more and more segment-making and less and less society-making.

28 A., interview.

29 C., interview by author, July 17, 2004.

30 R., interview by author, July 16, 2002.

31 C., interview.

32 Winski, "'Addicted' to Research."

33 Bruce Friend, interview by Ellen Seiter and Vicki Mayer. August 13, 1997. I am grateful to Seiter and Mayer for providing me with the transcript of this interview.

34 C., interview.

35 Ibid.

36 Ibid.

37 Klein, *No Logo*, 21.

38 Ibid., 16.

39 Interview by author, January 2004.

40 Donna Mitroff, interview by author, March 4, 2004.

41 Interview by author, January 2004.

42 Laybourne, "Nickelodeon Experience," 304.

43 Davidson, *Consumerist Manifesto*, 28.

44 Laybourne, "Nickelodeon Experience," 305.

45 *Nick at Nite* is a separate programming block on Nickelodeon that airs every evening, presenting television sitcoms from the 1960s, 1970s, 1980s, and early 1990s. It airs until the early morning, when Nickelodeon begins again.

46 Alyssa Quart points out that the context for the branding of Nickelodeon is one in which "branding is part of life, marketing and promotion the landscape, instrumental logic of consumerism the primary ideology among youth and teens," in *Branded*, 9.

47 Mitroff, interview.

48 For further discussion of this, see Fisch and Truglio, *"G" Is for Growing*.

49 Nickelodeon's stance against educational television is ironic, given the channel's later production of the extremely successful educational programs *Blues Clues* and *Dora the Explorer*.

50 Nickelodeon, *How to Nickelodeon*, 5.

51 Ibid., 6.

52 Linda Simensky, interview by author, February 17, 2004.

53 *People,* August 23, 1982.

54 Nickelodeon, *How to Nickelodeon,* 11.

55 Simensky, interview.

56 Ibid.

57 Nickelodeon, *How to Nickelodeon,* 20.

58 Ibid.

59 Simensky, interview.

60 Nickelodeon, *How to Nickelodeon,* 21.

61 Kinder, "Home Alone," 85.

62 Tamar Lewin, "Hey There, Dudes, the Kids Have Grabbed a Network," *New York Times,* October 21, 1990.

63 This is similar to the "free speech zones" that are now present in political conventions, college campuses, and other public venues. These are cordoned-off spaces for protesters, apparently so that the protests do not interfere with the structure of the given program. Again, this is a place to "revolt" without having much of an effect.

64 Turow, *Breaking Up America.*

65 Simensky, interview.

66 Nickelodeon, *How to Nickelodeon,* 23.

67 For further discussion of this, see Hendershot, *Nickelodeon Nation.* On this show, which ran from 1986 to 1991 (and was revised as *Double Dare 2000* in 2000–2001), kids were contestants who are asked questions by the host (Marc Summers); if the contestant did not know the answer, s/he could dare the other team to answer it for double the amount of money. The opposing team could "dare back" or double dare, and if the question wasn't answered, the team could take a "Physical Challenge." The physical challenges were the important part of the game, and it was here that slime and gak came into play. For example, "The Wringer" involved one player who jumped through a pair of rollers and down a ramp, which was often coated with either slime or gak. Another infamous physical challenge was the "Sundae Slide," where a player tried to climb up a ramp coated with chocolate syrup and then down a slide into more slime or gak. As one reporter put it: "[*Double Dare*] has paved the way for a new species of programming by presenting what observers consider to be the first game that plays *to* children rather than *down to* children." Rick Sherwood, "A Kids' Show That Dared to be Different," *Los Angeles Times,* December 24, 1987.

68 Nickelodeon, *How to Nickelodeon,* 22.

69 James, "Confections, Concoctions, and Conceptions," 400.

70 Ibid., 402.

71 Mike Thomas, "Kids' Network Replaces Violence with Slime," *San Diego Union Tribune,* September 4, 1990.

72 Buckingham, *Death of Childhood,* 119.

73 Sturken, *Tourists of History.*

74 "Reaching a Nation Nickelodeon-Style." *Selling to Kids,* April 5, 2000.

75 Ibid.

76 Ibid.

77 Mitroff, interview.

78 I am grateful to Ken Wissoker for this reference.

79 Cited in Preston and White, "Commodifying Kids," 10.

80 Preston and White, "Commodifying Kids," 24.

81 Ibid., 25.

82 A., interview.

83 These factors are outlined in Wheeler, *Designing Brand Identity.*

84 Billig, *Banal Nationalism,* 8.

85 Wheeler, *Designing Brand Identity,* 23.

86 Young, "Better Mousetrap?"

87 Simensky, interview.

88 Cyma Zarghami, interview by Vicki Mayer, August 8, 1997. Zarghami became president of Nickelodeon in 2006. I am grateful to Ellen Seiter and Mayer for providing me with the transcript of this interview.

89 Petrozzello, "Nickelodeon's Herb Scannell."

90 Gunther, "This Gang."

91 Lury, "Time and Place," 21.

92 Kunkel, "Children and Television Advertising."

93 Preston and White, "Commodifying Kids."

94 Hendershot, *Nickelodeon Nation.*

95 Ibid., 5.

96 Ibid., 21.

97 Buckingham, *Making of Citizens,* 39.

98 Ibid., 22.

99 Donna Mitroff, interview by author, March 4, 2004.

4. GIRLS RULE!

1 See Douglas, "Girls 'n Spice"; Shugart, Waggoner, and Hallstein, "Mediating Third Wave Feminism"; Driscoll, *Girls;* Kearney, "Producing Girls"; and Baumgardner and Richards, *Manifesta.*

2 Goldman, *Reading Ads Socially;* Sturken and Cartwright, *Practices of Looking.*

3 Pipher, *Reviving Ophelia;* Wiseman, *Queen Bees and Wannabes.*

4 See Seiter, *Sold Separately*

5 Kearney, "Producing Girls."

6 Brunsdon, D'Acci, and Spigel, *Feminist Television Criticism;* and Gerbner et al., "Growing Up with Television."

7 For an industry account of targeting women on television, see Spigel, *Make Room for TV.*

8 Hall, *Representation;* Dávila, *Latinos, Inc.;* Bordo, *Unbearable Weight;* and others.

9 Brunsdon, D'Acci, and Spigel, *Feminist Television Criticism.*

10 Mittell, "Great Saturday Morning Exile."

11 Douglas, *Where the Girls Are,* 29.

12 Ibid.

13 Hendershot, *Saturday Morning Censors*, 5.

14 This is not always the case, of course. For example, *Free to Be . . . You and Me* (which Marlo Thomas produced and for which Carl Reiner and Shel Silverstein were among the notable story writers) was a television program in 1974 which became a "classic" for feminist households desiring to bring up their children to challenge dominant norms of gender and other identity categories. The program featured celebrities such as Harry Belafonte, Michael Jackson, Alan Alda, and Roberta Flack in a series of songs and skits that conveyed "positive messages of self-esteem." Constructed in the feminist language of the time, *Free to Be . . . You and Me* confronted stereotypes with strategies of reversal, so that in the skit "Boy Meets Girl," for instance, two bald babies with no gender-identifying characteristics assume that one is male and one is female based on what each baby likes and thinks is interesting. The assumptions turn out to be wrong, of course, thus illustrating how constraining dominant norms of gender are to thinking and categorizing individuals. In other skits on the show, a boy wants a doll, a girl is competitive and wants to win a race, and the football hero Rosey Grier sings "It's Alright to Cry."

15 Dow, *Prime-Time Feminism*; Brunsdon, *Feminist, Housewife, Soap Opera*; D'Acci, *Defining Women*; and Rowe, *Unruly Women*.

16 See Seiter, *Sold Separately*, for a more thorough discussion of this.

17 I gathered this information from personal interviews with industry executives.

18 Thorne, *Gender Play*.

19 See Seiter, *Sold Separately*.

20 Mitroff, interview.

21 Mitroff, interview.

22 See Douglas, *Where the Girls Are*.

23 Of course, this is not to say that historically empowerment has been impossible to access for youth. However, in this particular cultural context, the empowerment of youth is legitimized through its presence as rhetoric within consumer behavior.

24 Cf. McNeal, *Kids as Customers*; Quart, *Branded*.

25 Nickelodeon press release, 2001.

26 L., interview by author, July 2004.

27 See Miller, *Technologies of Truth*; Canclini, *Consumers and Citizens*; Gross, *Up from Invisibility*; and Dow, "Ellen."

28 Dow, *Prime-Time Feminism*.

29 Fuqua, "PowerPuff Girls."

30 Linda Simensky, interview by author, February 2004.

31 Cf. Kearney, "Producing Girls."

32 Hall, *Representations*; Gray, *Watching Race*; Gross, *Up from Invisibility*; Dow, "Ellen."

33 Gross, *Up from Invisibility*, 253.

34 McRobbie, "Postfeminism and Popular Culture," 5.

35 Ibid., 6.

36 Hogeland, "Against Generational Thinking," 107.

37 McRobbie discusses this shift to a more "lifestyle" type politics in "Postfeminism and Popular Culture."

38 McRobbie, "Postfeminism and Popular Culture," 10–11.

39 Klein, *No Logo.*

40 Baumgardner and Richards, *Manifesta.*

41 Rather, the awareness of feminist accomplishments in the areas of employment, wages, and policy led to a widespread adoption of the adage "I'm not a feminist, but . . ." As Susan Douglas argues, the comma in this statement is hugely significant, marking the contradictions involved in feminist politics: "The comma says that the speaker is ambivalent, that she is torn between a philosophy that seeks to improve her lot in life and a desire not to have to pay too dearly for endorsing that philosophy" (*Where the Girls Are,* 270).

42 Baumgardner and Richards, *Manifesta,* 83.

43 Douglas, *Where the Girls Are,* 293.

44 Goldman, *Reading Ads Socially.*

45 Bellafante, "It's All about Me!" 57.

46 Baumgardner and Richards, *Manifesta;* Findlen, *Listen Up;* and Wolf, *Fire with Fire.*

47 Baumgardner and Richards, *Manifesta,* 80.

48 See Hartsock, *Feminist Standpoint Revisited.*

49 McRobbie, "Notes on Postfeminism and Popular Culture."

50 See Klein, *No Logo;* Gladwell, "Coolhunt"; and Heath and Potter, *Rebel Sell.*

51 See, for example, Gladwell, "Coolhunt"; Klein, *No Logo;* and Quart, *Branded.*

52 Sconce, "Irony," 352.

53 Driscoll, *Girls,* 12.

54 Ibid., 168–69.

55 Ibid., 272.

56 Ibid., 278.

57 John Hardman, interview by Mayer and Seiter, August 1997. Of course, Hardman's argument presumes a traditional notion about women—that they can be either beautiful or smart, but not both. I am grateful to Mayer and Seiter for providing me with a transcript of this interview.

58 Cyma Zarghami, interview by Vicki Mayer, August 1997. I am grateful to Mayer and Ellen Seiter to providing me with a transcript of this interview.

59 J., interview by author, July 2004.

60 Bruce Friend, interview by Vicki Mayer, August 1997. I am grateful to Mayer and Ellen Seiter to providing me with a transcript of this interview.

61 Mitroff, interview.

62 McRobbie, "Young Women."

63 Nickelodeon Press Release, 2000.

64 Hartley, *Uses of Television.*

65 See Kearney, "Producing Girls"; McRobbie, *Feminism and Youth Culture.*

66 Hartley, *Uses of Television,* 184.

67 Hartley, in *Uses of Television,* does not necessarily celebrate the DIY aspect of Clarissa's citizenship; in fact, he argues that the program is indicative of a moment in citizenship where representations of agency have become agency. I am not arguing the "image is

everything" point of view (either as a critique or as an agreement), but rather I situate Clarissa as indicative of the tensions that organize the larger movement of girl power.

68 See Dow, *Prime-Time Feminism.*
69 Zarghami, interview.
70 Interestingly, the subplot of the last episode involved Clarissa's friend Sam, who was rejected at all the colleges to which he applied—except for one, a historically all-female college where he was the first male ever accepted.
71 A., L., and E., interview by author, July 2002.
72 Cooltoons website, http://www.cooltoons2.com/ginger.
73 Ibid.
74 Buckingham, *Death of Childhood,* 186.
75 K., interview by author, July 2002.
76 Jenkins, *Children's Culture Reader,* 32.
77 See Kearney, "Producing Girls."
78 Nickelodeon website, http://www.nick.com.
79 Buckingham, *Death of Childhood,* 187.
80 For more on this resentment, see Seiter and Mayer, "Diversifying Representation."
81 Hardman, interview.
82 Douglas, "Girls 'n Spice," 47–48.
83 Dow, *Prime-Time Feminism.*
84 Ibid., 214.
85 McRobbie, "Young Women."
86 Ibid., 15.
87 Ibid.
88 Douglas, *Where the Girls Are.*

5. CONSUMING RACE ON NICKELODEON

1 "Mattel: Flavas Fashion Dolls." Mattel press release, July 29, 2003. Available online at *Raving Toy Maniac,* http://www.toymania.com/news/messages/3721.shtml (accessed March 11, 2007).
2 Flavas were ultimately not a successful toy, and have been taken off the market. However, a similar line of dolls, called Bratz, continues this "urban" feel and has been successful.
3 Andrejevic, *Reality TV;* Ouellette, "Take Responsibility"; and Grindstaff, *Money Shot.*
4 The show ceased production after its third season was wrapped in the beginning of 2005, but as of December 2006, repeats were still being aired once a week.
5 AZ Central website, http://www.azcentral.com/ent/pop/articles/0805greencard.html (accessed April 24, 2006).
6 See, for example, Wynter, *American Skin;* and Gates and West, *Future of the Race.*
7 Gerard Raiti. "Oh Brother, Where Art Thou? The Absence of African-American Heroes in Animation." *Kidscreen,* January 2005, http://www.kidscreen.com/articles/magazine/20050101/raiti.html (accessed March 11, 2007).
8 Scannell, "Why Not Diversity?"

9 Bourdieu theorized cultural capital as knowledge, or a kind of competence, about styles and genres that are socially valued and that confer prestige upon those who have mastered them. He distinguished between economic capital, which refers to the quantity of material goods and income commanded by an individual, and cultural capital, which refers to a kind of competency—competencies derived from education, familiarity with a legitimized cultural tradition, and modes of consumption. See Bourdieu, *Distinction.*

10 I'm grateful to the manuscript reader from Duke for this clarification.

11 Torres, *Living Color.*

12 Gray, *Watching Race;* Torres, *Living Color;* and Hall, "Spectacle."

13 Bodroghkozy, *Groove Tube,* 3.

14 Ibid.

15 Hendershot, *Saturday Morning Censors.*

16 For a thorough discussion of the pedagogical strategies of *Sesame Street,* see Hendershot, *Saturday Morning Censors.*

17 Indeed, Children's Television Workshop's explicit object was to have parents watch with kids. Hendershot, *Saturday Morning Censors.*

18 See, for example, Bell, Haas, and Sells, *Mouse to Mermaid;* Giroux, *Mouse that Roared;* and Stabile, *Prime Time Animation.*

19 Mittell, "Great Saturday Morning Exile."

20 Ibid.

21 Seiter, *Sold Separately.*

22 Gray, *Watching Race;* and Jhally and Lewis, *"Enlightened" Racism.*

23 Gray, *Watching Race.*

24 Ibid.

25 Ibid., 81–82.

26 As Hall points out in "Spectacle," it does this through the representation of difference as a contradictory dynamic.

27 Gray, *Watching Race.* While Gray recognizes the historical trajectory of these discourses, he also acknowledges that all three practices continue simultaneously.

28 Wynter, *American Skin,* 135.

29 Scannell, "Why Not Diversity?"

30 Gray, *Cultural Moves.* As Gray argues, this proliferation of images does not necessarily connect with a more equitable legal system or a lessening of racist practices in the United States—in fact, the increasing presence of images of African Americans often obscures the ways in which racist society functions.

31 Wynter, *American Skin;* and Smith, "Getting Paid."

32 Smith, "Getting Paid."

33 Ibid., 75.

34 Benjamin, "Work of Art."

35 This does not mean "authentic" ethnicity—i.e., a physical relationship with ethnic identity and history—but rather a more diffused embrace of ethnic identity and the urban.

36 Watts and Orbe, "Spectacular Consumption," 3.

37 John Hardman, interview by Ellen Seiter and Vicki Mayer, July 1997.

38 Ibid.
39 Baudrillard, "Precession of Simulacra."
40 Dávila, *Latinos, Inc.*
41 Ibid.
42 This point was made to me in a conversation with Christopher Holmes Smith.
43 Shank, "Rice to Ice," 259.
44 An example of this can be seen in the annual report of Radio One, a radio organization (with a connected television station) that self-identifies as "The Urban Radio Specialist." Radio One is the largest broadcasting company in the United States that specifically targets African Americans. According to Radio One, it focuses on "programming and urban-oriented music, news, information and talk stations." Radio One sees "urban-formatted" radio stations to have potential market growth for several reasons, including increasing African American population, as well as increasing income levels among African Americans. Because of these factors, there has been subsequent growth in advertising targeting the African American market, as well as a growth in loyal black audiences. What most interests me, however, is that Radio One lists the "Growing Influence of African-American Culture" as one reason that urban media formats make sense in the current media economy. This "influence" is described as the notion that there "continues to be an ongoing 'urbanization' of many facets of American society as evidenced by the influence of African-American culture in the areas of music (for example, hip hop and rap music), film, fashion, sports and urban-oriented television shows and networks. We believe that many companies from a broad range of industries and prominent fashion designers have embraced this urbanization trend in their products as well as their advertiser's messages." Radio One 2005 Annual Report, http://www.radio-one.com (accessed May 2, 2006).
45 Muñoz, "Casting a Wider Net."
46 According to Scannell, "Why Not Diversity?" African American children watched 26.7 hours of television per week, Latino children 21.4 hours, and white children 19.3 hours.
47 Hardman, interview.
48 Chuck Barney, "Kids' Channels Beat Networks to Diversity," *San Diego Union-Tribune*, August 3, 2002.
49 See Lipsitz, *Possessive Investment in Whiteness*; Dyer, "White"; Gotanda, "Critique"; and Kull, *Color-Blind Constitution.*
50 Muñoz, "Casting a Wider Net."
51 Ibid.
52 Scannell, "Why Not Diversity?"
53 Ibid.
54 Ibid.
55 Cyma Zarghami, interview by Ellen Seiter and Vicki Mayer, August 1997. Actually, *Sesame Street* was the first preschool program with African American hosts. This is not the first time that *Sesame Street* is erased by Nickelodeon executives. Indeed, Nickelodeon's use of diversity as branding strategy for both gender and race is part of their marketable claim that they are the first, and often only, *network* to do so, thereby marginalizing how other,

public and thus less brand-oriented, shows on television made the same strides. Recognizing *Sesame Street* would also undercut Nickelodeon's claims to authenticity as well, as part of what makes them genuine is that they were first and thus not following industry trends. I'm grateful to Heather Hendershot for bringing this to my attention.

56 Torres, *Living Color.*

57 Hall, "Spectacle."

58 Muñoz, "Casting a Wider Net."

59 Cabrera, "Adorable Dora."

60 Nakamura, *Visual Cultures.*

61 Cabrera, "Adorable Dora."

62 Dávila, *Latinos, Inc.*

63 This dual function of stereotypes is not unique to *Dora*, of course, but is rather characteristic of stereotyping more generally. For more on this, see Bhabha, "Other Question."

64 Ibid., 89.

65 Cabrera, "Adorable Dora."

66 Ibid.

67 Seiter and Mayer, "Diversifying Representation."

68 Sender, *Business Not Politics*, 3.

69 Bruce Friend, interview by Ellen Seiter and Vicki Mayer, August 1997.

70 Hall, "Spectacle."

71 Zarghami, interview.

72 Klein, *No Logo.*

73 Dávila, *Latinos, Inc.*

74 C., interview by author, July 2002.

75 R., interview by author, July 2002.

76 L., C., K., J., interview by author, July 2002.

77 C., interview.

78 Holly Ocasio Rizzo. "Just Say Sí." *Hispanic Trends Magazine,* October 2004, http://www .hispaniconline.com/trends/2004/oct/cover (accessed March 11, 2007).

79 Ibid.

80 Ibid.

81 Dávila, *Latinos, Inc.*

82 Richard L. Vazquez, "The Brothers Garcia: A Boy's Show." LasCulturas.com. http:// www.lasculturas.com/aa/aa072300a.htm (accessed March 11, 2007).

83 This point was made to me in a conversation with Christopher Holmes Smith.

84 duCille, "Toy Theory," 264.

6. IS NICK FOR KIDS?

The third epigraph to this chapter, a quotation from Alfred Fung, is taken from Beatty, "Something about 'SpongeBob.'"

1 "Nautical Nonsense," editorial, *New York Times,* January 22, 2005.

2 Ibid.

3 Beatty, "Something about 'SpongeBob.'"

4 Hendershot, "Nickelodeon's Nautical Nonsense," 184.

5 Clark, "Commodity Lesbianism"; and Sender, "Selling Sexual Subjectivities."

6 Linda Simensky, interview by author, February 2004.

7 Key figures such as Walt Disney and Ub Iwerks (best known as a collaborator with Disney on such classic animated shorts as *Steamboat Willie* (1928), or Otto Messmer of *Felix the Cat* fame, created cinematic animation that was understood as both an artistic and cultural accomplishment. In fact, Paul Wells specifically connects early animation with modernism; in particular, animation represented the ideological characteristic of modernism to exist in a "state of becoming." As Wells puts it: "This readily relates to the dominant characteristic of metamorphosis in animation where all the events depicted in the graphic space are literally 'acts of becoming,' transitory and formative. Animation is the very language of the Modernist principle, often transcending linguistic necessity and enhancing fine art practice by challenging compositional and representational orthodoxies," Wells, *Animation and America*, 24.

8 This was a gradual process, however. As Mittell and Wells document, in the 1950s, television animation consisted largely of programs that were recycled from film, and they were scattered throughout the television schedule. The audience (primarily a residual film audience) for animation in the 1950s was considered to be both children and adults, and the television schedule reflected this transgenerational appeal: cartoons such as the *Gerald McBoing Boing Show* (1956–58) were occasionally shown during prime time, and there was no discrete designated time slot to program cartoons. Since much of the early televised animation came from film, and thus already had an adult audience, animation was not considered solely the purview of children. The humor involved in early animation was sophisticated and ironic, and the dialogue and the visuals appealed to many different audiences. Mittell, "Great Saturday Morning Exile"; Wells, *Animation and America*.

9 Mittell, "Great Saturday Morning Exile."

10 Boddy, *Fifties Television;* and Spigel, *Make Room for TV*.

11 Boddy, *Fifties Television*, 237.

12 Mittell, "Great Saturday Morning Exile," 49.

13 Ibid., 50.

14 The three-in-one market potential, as discussed in other chapters, indicates that children are conceived of by marketers as actually three different markets: a primary market, where children spend their own money on goods; an influential market, where children often influence their parents' purchasing choices; and a future market, where early brand loyalty is often seen as the ticket to a consumer for life. For further discussion of this, see McNeal, *Kids as Customers*.

15 Mittell, "Great Saturday Morning Exile," 34–35.

16 Simensky, interview.

17 Seiter, *Sold Separately;* and Englehardt, "Strawberry Shortcake Strategy."

18 Seiter, *Sold Separately*.

19 As Seiter points out, toy-based cartoons are not that different from other animated productions, but the assumptions about children needing protection from crass com-

mercialism, among other things, framed the critical debates that surrounded this practice at the time. Seiter, *Sold Separately.*

20 Although, in the late 1990s, Nickelodeon did take on a few toy-based shows (for instance, *Butt Ugly Martians*), these programs were seen as not a "good fit" for the network and were quickly pulled off the air. As Simensky put it: "[Shows like *Butt Ugly Martians*] didn't work for them, and Nick gets rid of the shows that don't work for them. They get rid of them really quickly." Simensky, interview.

21 Simensky, interview.

22 Simensky, "Early Days of Nicktoons," 92.

23 Simensky, interview. Out of the original eight pilots, only three shows seemed to capture the "Nickelodeon voice" as well as appeal to kids: *The Ren & Stimpy Show, Rugrats,* and *Doug.*

24 Simensky, interview.

25 Wells, *Animation and America.*

26 Sturken and Cartwright, *Practices of Looking,* 258; and Wells, *Animation and America.*

27 Wells also argues that animation is uniquely recombinant as an art form, another particularly postmodern characteristic. Recombinancy indicates that contemporary animated programs are based on other forms that have already been established in terms of audience and the market—movies, video games, comics. It is not simply that animated programs are intertextual (where other media texts are referenced within the animated text), but also that animation both reinvents and reinterprets other art forms, such as comics or film. The recombinant trend in animation is also indicative of a larger audience than simply children; adults recognize the various other art forms within the aesthetics of animation and often interpret animated programs through a nostalgic frame. Wells, *Animation and America.*

28 Farley, "Fred and Wilma," 151.

29 Kinder, "Home Alone," 75.

30 John Hardman, interview by Ellen Seiter and Vicki Mayer, July 1997. While Nickelodeon takes the credit for developing programs that appeal to both children and adults, *Sesame Street* had used this strategy for years. I'm grateful to Heather Hendershot for pointing this out to me.

31 Kinder, "Home Alone," 77.

32 Frank, *Conquest of Cool;* Gladwell, "Coolhunt"; Klein, *No Logo;* and Sconce, "Smart Films."

33 Klein, *No Logo,* 78.

34 Ibid.

35 Sender, "Selling Sexual Subjectivities," 172–73.

36 Ibid., 175.

37 S., interview by author, July 2002.

38 A., interview by author, July 2002.

39 R., interview by author, July 2002.

40 Simensky, interview.

41 Bergman, *Camp Grounds,* 5.

42 Ibid.

43 Sontag, "Notes on 'Camp.' "

44 Ibid., 56.

45 Bergman, *Camp Grounds.*

46 Babuscio, "Gay Sensibility," 20.

47 See Bergman for more on this. The "wink" I am referring to indicates a kind of double code. This is well documented in work on gay advertising, for example Sender, *Business Not Politics;* the double code is also commonly found in transgenerational programming. An adult audience, situated historically, can provide the "missing information" and make sense of the social commentary of the show. The younger audience, on the other hand, sees appeal in this and other cartoons precisely because of the narrative codes that adults "don't get." As Herron ("Homer Simpson's Eyes") says, "Cartoons that become powerful and desirable are ones that create an oppositional space for kids to occupy, based on special knowledge and codes that only they understand." This special knowledge and code is precisely the kind of aesthetic convention that is needed to read a representational form as camp, because it is this which allows for a subtextual reading that would perhaps escape the mainstream, intended audience.

48 In other words, as Farley ("Fred and Wilma") points out, the theory of double coding is problematic because it ignores crucial contextual factors. For instance, adults might not like cartoons not because of their child-like character but rather because they are overly familiar. The marketing of cartoons is also rarely directed at adults, so there may also be a simple problem of access and availability. Kids, on the other hand, might like cartoons not because of their inherent naiveté (either their own or the cartoon's) but rather because there are few options for children, or there is a preconceived notion that kids *should* like cartoons.

49 As many have noted, Sontag's refusal to acknowledge the politics of camp also dehistoricizes its strategic function and thus disconnects camp from a subversive subjectivity and practice. Andrew Ross ("Uses of Camp") argues for the necessity of the socio/politico/economic context for camp to emerge in the 1960s. Ross's insistence on the political economy of camp is useful for theorizing a new rendering of camp in the twenty-first century in terms of children's television. Discussing the postwar 1960s culture, Ross argues, "Just as the new presence of the masses in the social and cultural purview of the postwar State had required a shift in the balance of containment of popular democracy, so too, the reorganization of the capital bases of the cultural industries, the new media technology and the new modes of distribution that accompanied that shift necessarily changed the aesthetic face of categories of taste." Ross points to the way in which the style of camp both influences and is influenced by new markets within popular consumer culture. To insist that camp can be part of the popular mainstream is to challenge the idea that camp contains within it a simple double code where one audience reads one possible meaning, and another audience a different one. Indeed, one of the primary problems with a theory of doublecoding is that it relies upon a definite distinction between two taste cultures. If we consider animated programs such as *SpongeBob SquarePants* as contemporary versions of a camp aesthetic, this taste culture boundary is even more

disrupted. Thus a more complicated rendering of the theory of doublecoding is needed in order to situate the place of camp and irony within contemporary media culture (for both children and adults).

50 For further discussion of female impersonators, see Newton, *Mother Camp.*

51 Wells, *Animation and America.*

52 Farley, "Fred and Wilma," 157.

53 Ibid., 159.

54 Langer, "*Ren & Stimpy.*" The subculture of animatophiles is characterized by a high degree of knowledge about animation and animators, a rejection of the infantalization of animation (in other words, a rejection of the idea that all animation is easy to interpret, formulaic filler for children), and most importantly, a dedication to the notion that author-driven animation (as opposed to factory- or mass-produced animation) is characterized by, among other things, the various ways in which the art form subverts dominant taste norms. As Langer points out, "The specialized knowledge of core animatophiles forms a different kind of cultural capital which is defined by its opposition to, or separateness from, the tastes of mainstream culture." *Ren & Stimpy* was precisely the kind of "subversive" animation that animatophiles loved—it was campy and ironic and thus engendered a sophisticated sense of humor, but it was also crude and distasteful.

55 Ibid.

56 Ibid., 168.

57 Ibid., 156.

58 Kinder, "Home Alone"; Langer, "*Ren & Stimpy.*"

59 Langer, "*Ren & Stimpy.*"

60 For further discussion of SpongeBob's unspecific age, see Hendershot, "Nickelodeon's Nautical Nonsense."

61 Simensky, interview.

62 Beatty, "Something about 'SpongeBob.' "

63 Dylan Swizzler, "There's Something about SpongeBob," Double Take, *Planet Out,* October 25, 2002, http://www.planetout.com/news/feature.html?sernum=416 (accessed March 11, 2007).

64 Josh Grossberg, "A 'Sponge'-Worthy Gay Icon?" *E! Online News,* October 8, 2002, http://www.eonline.com/news/article/index.jsp?uuid=6d615ab2-a11b-47d2-b0a2-5b3b6925cb5f (accessed March 11, 2007).

65 Hendershot, "Nickelodeon's Nautical Nonsense," 197. Indeed, when I asked young Nickelodeon fans about the relationship between SpongeBob and Squidward, not a single one mentioned that it could potentially be a sexual relationship—rather, kids said things like, "SpongeBob likes Squidward, but Squidward doesn't like SpongeBob," or "They're neighbors usually and Squidward doesn't really like SpongeBob because he's annoying . . . He usually annoys him in most of the shows, but it's kind of like funny that he annoys him." The kids I interviewed did comment on, however, the campy qualities of the show: "[*SpongeBob* is a good show] because it's really funny, and it's really unrealistic, and all the characters are sort of weird and funny. And so when they're all put together it makes a fun show." Another young fan commented on the originality of *SpongeBob:* "It's a newer TV

series, so people have not run out of—they haven't seen each one like ten times already." M. and C., interviews by author, July 2002.

66 Hendershot argues that *SpongeBob* is one of the least ironic shows on TV; I argue differently, seeing the "straight" earnestness of *SpongeBob* to *be* its ironic edge.

67 Farley, "Fred and Wilma," 160.

68 Ibid., 161.

69 Silverstone, *Why Study the Media?* 64.

70 Ibid.

71 Another seventeen-year-old girl put it this way: "It's like different than all the other shows on Nickelodeon. The humor's a lot different. It's just really really funny. Some of the time on Nickelodeon, they have shows where the humor is so like for younger people that I'm like, 'that's dumb.' But *SpongeBob,* everybody laughs. I know my brother, he's nineteen, and he watches *Spongebob.* And he loves that show." In yet another attempt to define the humor of *SpongeBob,* an eleven-year-old boy put it succinctly, "It's stupidly funny." S. and M., interviews by author, July 2002.

72 Hendershot, "Nickelodeon's Nautical Nonsense," 199.

73 Ibid., 200.

74 Kendall Lyons, "Interview with Butch Hartman." *Animation Insider,* July 24, 2006, http://www.animationinsider.net/article.php?articleID=1088 (accessed March 11, 2007).

75 Ibid.

76 Seiter and Mayer, "Diversifying Representation."

77 R., interview by author, July 2004.

78 This idea comes from Hendershot, who sees Nickelodeon as the "uber-brand."

79 Simensky, interview.

CONCLUSION

1 Charlyn Keating Chisholm, "Nickelodeon Family Suites," About.com, http://hotels.about.com/od/orlando/p/mco—nickelodeon.htm (accessed March 11, 2007).

2 "Nick Study Suggests Best Way to Target Kids," *USA Today,* http://usatoday.com (accessed December 2005).

3 McDowell, "Pitching to Kids."

4 Uricchio, "Television's Next Generation."

5 Ibid.

6 Park, *Consuming Citizenship,* 3.

7 Hendershot, *Nickelodeon Nation.*

8 Ibid., 10.

BIBLIOGRAPHY

Adorno, Theodor W. *The Culture Industry: Selected Essays on Mass Culture.* Edited by J. M. Bernstein. New York: Routledge, 2001.

Allen, Robert C., ed. *Channels of Discourse.* New York: Routledge, 1987.

———. *Channels of Discourse, Reassembled: Television and Contemporary Criticism.* 2nd ed. Chapel Hill: University of North Carolina Press, 1992.

Allen, Robert C., and Annette Hill, eds. *The Television Studies Reader.* New York: Routledge, 2004.

Anderson, Benedict. *Imagined Communities: Reflections on the Origin and Spread of Nationalism.* Revised ed. London: Verso, 1991.

Andrejevic, Mark. *Reality TV: The Work of Being Watched.* Lanham, Md.: Rowman and Littlefield, 2004.

Ang, Ien. *Desperately Seeking the Audience.* London: Routledge, 1991.

Aries, P. *Centuries of Childhood: A Social History of Family Life.* Translated by Robert Baldick. New York: Vintage, 1962.

Atkin, Charles, and Gary Heald. "The Content of Children's Toy and Food Commercials." *Journal of Communication* 27, no. 1 (1977): 107–14.

Austin, Joe, and Michael Nevin Willard. "Introduction: Angels of History, Demons of Culture." *Generations of Youth: Youth Cultures and History in Twentieth-Century America.* New York: New York University Press, 1998.

Babuscio, Jack. "Camp and the Gay Sensibility." In Bergman, *Camp Grounds,* 19–38.

Banet-Weiser, Sarah. *The Most Beautiful Girl in the World: Beauty Pageants and National Identity.* Berkeley: University of California Press, 1999.

Banks, Jack. *Monopoly Television. MTV's Quest to Control the Music.* Boulder, Colo.: Westview, 1996.

Barthes, Roland. *Camera Lucida: Reflections on Photography.* Translated by Richard Howard. New York: Hill and Wang, 1981.

———. *Elements of Semiology.* Translated by Annette Lavers and Colin Smith. New York: Hill and Wang, 1968.

Baudrillard, Jean. "The Precession of Simulacra." *Simulations.* Translated by Paul Foss, Paul Patton, and Philip Beitchman. New York: Semiotext(e), 1983.

Baumgardner, Jennifer, and Amy Richards. *Manifesta: Young Women, Feminism, and the Future.* New York: Farrar, Straus and Giroux, 1999.

Bazalgette, Cary, and David Buckingham, eds. *In Front of the Children: Screen Entertainment and Young Audiences.* London: British Film Institute, 1995.

Beatty, Sally. "There's Something about 'Spongebob' that Whispers 'Gay.' " *Wall Street Journal,* October 8, 2002.

Bell, Elizabeth, Lynda Haas, and Laura Sells, eds. *From Mouse to Mermaid: The Politics of Film, Gender, and Culture.* Bloomington: Indiana University Press, 1995.

Bellafante, Ginia. "It's All about Me!" *Time,* June 29, 1998.

Benjamin, Walter. "The Work of Art in the Age of Mechanical Reproduction." *Illuminations.* Edited by Hannah Arendt. Translated by Harry Zohn. 217–52. New York: Schocken Books, 1968.

Bergman, David, ed. *Camp Grounds: Style and Homosexuality.* Amherst: University of Massachusetts Press, 1994.

Berlant, Lauren. *The Queen of America Goes to Washington City: Essays on Sex and Citizenship.* Durham, N.C.: Duke University Press, 1997.

Berman, Marshall. *The Politics of Authenticity: Radical Individualism and the Emergence of Modern Society,* New York: Macmillan, 1970.

Bettie, Julie. *Women without Class: Girls, Race, and Identity.* Berkeley: University of California Press, 2003.

Bhabha, Homi. *The Location of Culture.* London: Routledge, 2004.

——. "The Other Question: The Stereotype and Colonial Discourse," *Screen* 24, no. 6 (1987): 18–36.

Billig, Michael. *Banal Nationalism.* London: Sage, 1995.

Bird, Elizabeth. *The Audience in Everyday Life: Living in a Media World.* New York: Routledge, 2003.

Boddy, William. *Fifties Television: The Industry and Its Critics.* Urbana: University of Illinois Press, 1990.

Bodroghkozy, Aniko. *Groove Tube: Sixties Television and the Youth Rebellion.* Durham, N.C.: Duke University Press, 2001.

Bogart, Leo. *Over the Edge: How the Pursuit of Youth by Marketers and the Media Has Changed American Culture.* Chicago: Ivan R. Dee, 2005.

Boorstin, Daniel J. *The Image: A Guide to Pseudo-Events in America.* New York: Vintage, 1992.

Bordo, Susan. *Unbearable Weight: Feminism, Western Culture, and the Body.* Berkeley: University of California Press, 1993.

Bourdieu, Pierre. *Distinction: A Social Critique of the Judgment of Taste.* Translated by Richard Nice. Cambridge, Mass.: Harvard University Press. 1984.

——. *The Field of Cultural Production: Essays on Art and Literature.* Edited by Randall Johnson. New York: Columbia University Press, 1993.

——. *On Television.* Translated by Priscilla Parkhurst Ferguson. New York: New Press, 1998.

Brennan, Patricia. "The Kids' Channel that 'Double Dares' to Be Different." *Washington Post,* September 25, 1988.

Brooker, Will, and Deborah Jermyn, eds. *The Audience Studies Reader.* London: Routledge, 2003.

Brown, Wendy. *Manhood and Politics: A Feminist Reading in Political Theory.* Lanham, Md.: Rowman and Littlefield, 1988.

——. *States of Injury: Power and Freedom in Late Modernity.* Princeton, N.J.: Princeton University Press, 1995.

Brunsdon, Charlotte. *The Feminist, the Housewife, and the Soap Opera.* New York: Oxford University Press, 2000.

Brunsdon, Charlotte, Julie D'Acci, and Lynn Spigel, eds. *Feminist Television Criticism: A Reader.* New York: Oxford University Press, 1997.

Bryant, Jennings, and Daniel R. Anderson, eds. *Children's Understanding of Television: Research on Attention and Comprehension.* New York: Academic Press, 1983.

Buckingham, David. *After the Death of Childhood: Growing Up in the Age of Electronic Media.* London: Polity Press, 2000.

———. *The Making of Citizens: Young People, News and Politics.* London: Routledge, 2000.

Cabrera, Yvette. "Adorable Dora Is Opening the Doors of Diversity." *Orange County Register,* September 13, 2002.

Calhoun, Craig J., ed. *Habermas and the Public Sphere.* Cambridge, Mass.: MIT Press, 1992.

Canclini, Nestor García. *Citizens and Consumers.* Minneapolis: University of Minnesota Press, 2001.

Cantor, Joanne. *Mommy, I'm Scared: How TV and Movies Frighten Children and What We Can Do to Protect Them.* New York: Harcourt Brace, 1998.

Clark, Danae. "Commodity Lesbianism." In *The Lesbian and Gay Studies Reader,* edited by Henry Abelove, Michèle Aina Barale, and David M. Halperin, 186–201. New York: Routledge, 1993.

Cohen, Lizabeth. *A Consumers' Republic: The Politics of Mass Consumption in Postwar America.* New York: Knopf, 2003.

Cohn, Edward. "Marketwatch." *American Prospect,* January 31, 2000.

Connell, Robert William. *The Child's Construction of Politics.* Melbourne: Melbourne University Press, 1971.

Cook, Daniel Thomas. *The Commodification of Childhood: The Children's Clothing Industry and the Rise of the Child Consumer.* Durham, N.C.: Duke University Press, 2004.

Couldry, Nick. *Media Rituals: A Critical Approach.* New York: Routledge, 2003.

Creeber, Glen, ed. *The Television Genre Book.* London: British Film Institute, 2001.

Currie, Dawn H. *Girl Talk: Adolescent Magazines and Their Readers.* Toronto: University of Toronto Press, 1999.

Czitrom, Daniel J. *Media and the American Mind: From Morse to McLuhan,* Chapel Hill: University of North Carolina Press, 1982.

D'Acci, Julie. *Defining Women: Television and the Case of "Cagney & Lacey."* Chapel Hill: University of North Carolina Press, 1994.

Davidson, Martin. *The Consumerist Manifesto: Advertising in Postmodern Times.* London: Routledge, 1992.

Davies, Maire Messenger. *"Dear BBC": Children, Television Storytelling and the Public Sphere.* Cambridge: Cambridge University Press, 2001.

Dávila, Arlene. *Latinos, Inc.: The Making and Marketing of a People,* Berkeley: University of California Press, 2001.

Dayan, Daniel, and Elihu Katz. *Media Events: The Live Broadcasting of History.* Cambridge, Mass.: Harvard University Press, 1992.

Debord, Guy. *The Society of the Spectacle.* New York: Zone Books. 1994.

de Certeau, Michel. *The Practice of Everyday Life*. Translated by Steven Rendall. Berkeley: University of California Press, 1988.

Dixon, Bob. *Catching Them Young*. Volume 2: *Political Ideas in Children's Fiction*. London: Pluto Press, 1981.

Douglas, Susan. "Girls 'n Spice: All Things Nice?" In *Mass Politics: The Politics of Popular Culture*, edited by Daniel M. Shea. New York: St. Martin's Press, 1999.

———. *Where the Girls Are: Growing Up Female with the Mass Media*. New York: Times Books, 1994.

Dow, Bonnie J. "Ellen, Television, and the Politics of Gay and Lesbian Visibility." *Critical Studies in Media Communication* 18, no. 2 (2001): 123–40.

———. *Prime-Time Feminism: Television, Media Culture, and the Women's Movement since 1970*. Philadelphia: University of Pennsylvania Press, 1996.

Driscoll, Catherine. *Girls: Feminine Adolescence in Popular Culture and Cultural Theory*, New York: Columbia University Press, 2002.

duCille, Anne. "Toy Theory: Black Barbie and the Deep Play of Difference." In Schor and Holt, *The Consumer Society Reader*, 259–78.

Dyer, Richard. *Only Entertainment*. New York: Routledge, 2002.

———. *White*. New York: Routledge, 1997.

Elmer-Dewitt, Philip. "On a Screen Near You: CyberPorn." *Time*, July 3, 1995.

Elshtain, Jean Bethke. *Public Man, Private Woman: Women in Social and Political Thought*. Princeton, N.J.: Princeton University Press, 1981.

———. *Who Are We? Critical Reflections and Hopeful Possibilities*. Grand Rapids, Mich.: Eerdmans, 2000.

Engelhardt, Tom. "The Strawberry Shortcake Strategy." In Gitlin, *Watching Television*, 68–110.

Ewen, Stuart. *Captains of Consciousness: Advertising and the Social Roots of the Consumer Culture*. New York: Basic Books, 2001.

Farley, Rebecca. "From Fred and Wilma to Ren and Stimpy: What Makes a Cartoon Prime-Time?" In Stabile and Harrison, *Prime Time Animation*, 147–64.

Feuer, Jane, Paul Kerr, and Tise Vahimagi, eds. MTM: *"Quality Television."* London: BFI Publishers, 1984.

Findlen, Barbara, ed. *Listen Up: Voices from the Next Feminist Generation*. Seattle: Seal Press, 1995.

Fisch, Shalom M., and Rosemarie T. Truglio, eds. *"G" is for Growing: Thirty Years of Research on Children and Sesame Street*. Mahwah, N.J.: Lawrence Erlbaum, 2001.

Fiske, John. *Media Matters: Everyday Culture and Political Change*. Minneapolis: University of Minnesota Press, 1996.

———. *Reading the Popular*. London: Routledge, 1991.

Flanagan, Constance A., and Lonnie R. Sherrod. "Youth Political Development: An Introduction." *Journal of Social Issues* 54, no. 3 (1998): 447–56.

Foucault, Michel. *The History of Sexuality: An Introduction*. Translated by Robert Hurley. New York: Vintage, 1978.

Frank, Thomas. "Advertising as Cultural Criticism: Bill Bernbach versus the Mass Society." In Schor and Holt, *The Consumer Society Reader*, 375–94.

———. *The Conquest of Cool: Business Culture, Counterculture, and the Rise of Hip Consumerism.* Chicago: University of Chicago Press, 1997.

Fraser, Nancy. "Rethinking the Public Sphere: A Contribution to the Critique of Actually Existing Democracy." In Calhoun, *Habermas and the Public Sphere,* 109–42.

Friedman, James, ed. *Reality Squared: Televisual Discourse on the Real.* New Brunswick, N.J.: Rutgers University Press, 2002.

Frith, Simon, Andrew Goodwin, and Lawrence Grossberg, eds. *Sound and Vision: The Music Video Reader.* New York: Routledge, 1993.

Fuqua, Joy Van. " 'What Are those Little Girls Made of?' *The Powerpuff Girls* and Consumer Culture." In Stabile and Harrison, *Prime Time Animation,* 205–19.

Gamson, Joshua. *Freaks Talk Back: Tabloid Talk Shows and Sexual Nonconformity.* Chicago: University of Chicago Press, 1998.

Gates, Henry Louis, Jr., and Cornel West. *The Future of the Race.* New York: Knopf, 1996.

Geraghty, Christine, and David Lusted, eds. *The Television Studies Book.* London: Arnold, 1998.

Gerbner, George, Larry Gross, Michael Morgan, Nancy Signorielli, and James Shanahan. "Growing Up with Television: Cultivation Processes." In *Media Effects: Advances in Theory and Research,* edited by Jennings Bryant and Dolf Zillmann, 43–68. Mahwah, N.J.: Lawrence Erlbaum, 2002.

Giroux, Henry A. *The Mouse That Roared: Disney and the End of Innocence.* Lanham, Md.: Rowman and Littlefield, 1999.

———. "Stealing Innocence: The Politics of Child Beauty Pageants." In Jenkins, *The Children's Culture Reader,* 265–82.

Gitlin, Todd. *Inside Prime Time.* Berkeley: University of California Press, 2000.

———. *The Whole World is Watching: Mass Media in the Making and Unmaking of the New Left.* Berkeley: University of California Press, 1981.

———, ed. *Watching Television.* New York: Pantheon Books, 1986.

Gladwell, Malcolm. "The Coolhunt." In Schor and Holt, *The Consumer Society Reader,* 360–74.

Glassner, Barry. *The Culture of Fear: Why Americans Are Afraid of the Wrong Things.* New York: Basic Books, 2000.

Goldman, Robert, and Stephen Papson. *Sign Wars: The Cluttered Landscape of Advertising.* New York: Guilford Publications, 1996.

Goldman, Robert. *Reading Ads Socially.* New York: Routledge, 1992.

Gotanda, Neil. "A Critique of 'Our Constitution is Color-Blind.'" In *Critical Race Theory: The Key Writings That Formed the Movement,* edited by Kimberle Crenshaw, Neil Gotanda, Gary Peller, and Kendall Thomas, 257–75. New York: New Press, 1996.

Gramsci, Antonio. *Prison Notebooks.* New York: Columbia University Press, 1991.

Granville, Kari. "Nickelodeon Flexing Muscles." *Los Angeles Times,* August 28, 1989.

Gray, Herman. *Cultural Moves: African Americans and the Politics of Representation.* Berkeley: University of California Press, 2005.

———. *Watching Race: Television and the Struggle for the Sign of Blackness.* Minneapolis: University of Minnesota Press, 1997.

Greenstein, Fred I. *Children and Politics.* New Haven, Conn.: Yale University Press, 1965.

Grindstaff, Laura. *The Money Shot: Trash, Class, and the Making of TV Talk Shows.* Chicago: University of Chicago Press, 2002.

Gross, Larry. *Up from Invisibility: Lesbians, Gay Men and the Media in America.* New York: Columbia University Press, 2001.

Gunther, Marc. "This Gang Controls Your Kids' Brains." *Fortune,* October 27, 1997.

Habermas, Jurgen. *The Structural Transformation of the Public Sphere: An Inquiry into a Category of Bourgeois Society.* Cambridge, Mass.: MIT Press, 1991.

Hall, Stuart. "Encoding/Decoding." In *The Media Studies Reader,* edited by Paul Harris and Sue Thornham, 51–61. New York: New York University Press, 2000.

——. "Encoding and Decoding in the Television Discourse." Paper for the Council of Europe Colloquy "Training in the Critical Reading of Televisual Language," Leicester, England, September 1973.

——. "The Spectacle of the 'Other.'" In Hall, *Representation,* 223–90.

——, ed. *Representation: Cultural Representations and Signifying Practices.* Thousand Oaks, Calif.: Sage, 1997.

Hall, Stuart, Charles Critcher, Tony Jefferson, John Clarke, and Brian Robert. *Policing the Crisis: Mugging, the State, and Law and Order.* New York: Macmillan, 1979.

Haralovich, Mary Beth, and Lauren Rabinovich, eds. *Television, History, and American Culture: Feminist Critical Essays.* Durham, N.C.: Duke University Press, 1999.

Harmetz, Aljean. "Action Group Aroused by Nickelodeon Ad Plan." *New York Times,* February 14, 1984.

Hartley, John. *Uses of Television.* London: Routledge, 1999.

Hartsock, Nancy C. M. *The Feminist Standpoint Revisited and Other Essays.* Boulder, Colo.: Westview Press, 1998.

Heath, Joseph, and Andrew Potter. *The Rebel Sell: How the Counterculture Became Consumer Culture.* London: Capstone, 2005.

Hebdige, Dick. *Subculture: The Meaning of Style.* London: Routledge, 1979.

Heins, Marjorie. *Not in Front of the Children: "Indecency," Censorship, and the Innocence of Youth.* New York: Hill and Wang, 2001.

Helgesen, Sally. *The Web of Inclusion.* New York: Doubleday, 1995.

Hendershot, Heather. "Nickelodeon's Nautical Nonsense: The Intergenerational Appeal of *SpongeBob Squarepants.*" In Hendershot, *Nickelodeon Nation,* 182–208.

——. *Saturday Morning Censors: Television Regulation before the V-Chip.* Durham, N.C.: Duke University Press, 1998.

——, ed. *Nickelodeon Nation: The History, Politics, and Economics of America's Only TV Channel for Kids.* New York: New York University Press, 2004.

Hennessee, Judith Adler. "Cable's Nickelodeon Wrestles with the Lure of Commercials." *New York Times,* January 2, 1983.

Herron, Jerry. "Homer Simpson's Eyes and the Culture of Late Nostalgia." *Representations* 43 (1993): 1–26.

Higgins, John, ed. *The Raymond Williams Reader.* Oxford: Blackwell, 2001.

Hilmes, Michele. *Radio Voices: American Broadcasting, 1922–1952*. Minneapolis: University of Minnesota Press, 1997.

Hobsbawm, Eric, and Terence Ranger, eds. *The Invention of Tradition*. Cambridge: Cambridge University Press, 1992.

Hogeland, Lisa Marie. "Against Generational Thinking; or, Some Things that 'Third Wave' Feminism Isn't." *Women's Studies in Communication* 24, no. 1 (2001): 107–21.

Horkheimer, Max, and Theodor Adorno. "The Culture Industry: Enlightenment as Mass Deception." *The Dialectic of Enlightenment*. Translated by John Cumming. New York: Continuum, 1972.

Horwitz, Robert B. *The Irony of Regulatory Reform: The Deregulation of American Telecommunications*. New York: Oxford University Press, 1991.

Hunt, Darnell. *O. J. Simpson: Facts and Fictions: News Rituals in the Construction of Reality*. Cambridge: Cambridge University Press, 1999.

James, Allison. "Confections, Concoctions, and Conceptions." In Jenkins, *The Children's Culture Reader*, 394–405.

James, Allison, and Alan Prout, eds. *Constructing and Reconstructing Childhood: Contemporary Issues in the Sociological Study of Childhood*. Washington, D.C.: Falmer Press, 1997.

Jameson, Fredric. *Postmodernism; or, The Cultural Logic of Late Capitalism*. London: Verso, 1991.

Jenkins, Henry, ed. *The Children's Culture Reader*. New York: New York University Press, 1998.

——. "Interview with Geraldine Laybourne." In Hendershot, *Nickelodeon Nation*, 134–53.

——. "Professor Jenkins Goes to Washington." *Harper's Magazine*, July 1999.

Jhally, Sut, and Justin Lewis. *"Enlightened" Racism: The Cosby Show, Audiences, and the Myth of the American Dream*. Boulder, Colo.: Westview Press, 1992.

Jones, Jeffrey P. *Entertaining Politics: New Political Television and Civic Culture*. Lanham, Md.: Rowman and Littlefield, 2004.

Jordan, Amy, Kelly L. Schmitt, and Emory H. Woodard, IV. "Developmental Implications of Commercial Broadcasters' Educational Offerings." *Journal of Applied Developmental Psychology* 22, no. 1 (2001): 87–101.

Kantrowitz, Barbara, and Pat Wingert. "The Truth about Tweens." *Newsweek*, October 18, 1999.

Kaplan, E. Ann. *Rocking around the Clock: Music Television, Postmodernism and Consumer Culture*. London: Methuen, 1987.

Kapur, Jyotsna. "Out of Control: Television and the Transformation of Childhood in Late Capitalism." In Kinder, *Kids' Media Culture*, 122–37.

Katz, Jon. "The Rights of Kids in a Digital Age." *Wired*, July 1996.

Katz, Richard. "Media Titans, Ad Buyers Fight Over the Kids." *Variety*, January 26–February 1, 1998.

Kearney, Mary Celeste. *Girls Make Media*. New York: Routledge, forthcoming.

——. "Producing Girls: Rethinking the Study of Female Youth Culture." In *Delinquents and Debutantes: Twentieth Century American Girls' Cultures*, edited by Sherrie A. Inness, 285–310. New York: New York University Press, 1998.

Kellner, Douglas. *Media Spectacle*. New York: Routledge, 2003.

Kincaid, James. "Producing Erotic Children." In Jenkins, *The Children's Culture Reader*, 241–53.

Kinder, Marsha. "Home Alone in the 90s: Generational War and Transgenerational Address in American Movies, Television and Presidential Politics." In Bazalgette and Buckingham, *In Front of the Children.*

——, ed. *Kids' Media Culture*. Durham, N.C.: Duke University Press, 1999.

Klein, Naomi. *No Logo: No Space, No Choice, No Jobs*. New York: Picador, 2002.

Kline, Stephen. "The Making of Children's Culture." In Jenkins, *The Children's Culture Reader*, 95–109.

——. *Out of the Garden: Toys, TV, and Children's Culture in the Age of Marketing*. London: Verso, 1995.

Kondo, Dorrine. *About Face: Performing Race in Fashion and Theater*. New York: Routledge, 1997.

Kull, Andrew. *The Color-Blind Constitution*. Cambridge, Mass.: Harvard University Press, 1992.

Kulynych, Jessica. "No Playing in the Public Sphere: Democratic Theory and the Exclusion of Children." *Social Theory and Practice* 27, no. 2 (2001): 231–65.

Kunkel, Dale. "Children and Television Advertising." In Singer and Singer, *Handbook of Children and the Media*, 375–94.

Kunkel, Dale, and Walter Gantz. "Children's Television Advertising in the Multichannel Environment." *Journal of Communication* 42, no. 3 (1992): 134–52.

Langer, Mark. "*Ren & Stimpy:* Fan Culture and Corporate Strategy." In Hendershot, *Nickelodeon Nation*, 155–81.

Larsen, Allen. "Re-Drawing the Bottom Line." In Stabile and Harrison, *Prime Time Animation*, 55–73.

Lasn, Kalle. *Culture Jam: The Uncooling of America*. New York: Eagle Brook, 1999.

Laybourne, Geraldine. "The Nickelodeon Experience." In *Children and Television: Images in a Changing Socio-cultural World,* edited by Gordon L. Berry and Joy Keiko Asamen, 303–7. London: Sage, 1993.

Linn, Susan E. *Consuming Kids: The Hostile Takeover of Childhood*. New York: New Press, 2004.

Lipsitz, George. *Dangerous Crossroads: Popular Music, Postmodernism and the Poetics of Place.* London: Verso, 1994.

——. *The Possessive Investment in Whiteness: How White People Profit from Identity Politics.* Philadelphia: Temple University Press, 1998.

——. *Time Passages: Collective Memory and American Popular Culture*. Minneapolis: University of Minnesota Press, 1990.

Livingstone, Sonia. *Young People and New Media: Childhood and the Changing Media Environment.* London: Sage, 2002.

Locke, John. *Two Treatises on Government and A Letter Concerning Toleration,* New Haven, Conn.: Yale University Press, 2003.

Lott, Eric. *Love and Theft: Blackface Minstrelsy and the American Working Class.* New York: Oxford University Press, 1995.

Lury, Karen. "A Time and Place for Everything: Children's Channels." In *Small Screens: Television for Children*, edited by David Buckingham. London: Leicester University Press, 2002.

Lyotard, Jean-François. *The Postmodern Condition: A Report on Knowledge*. Translated by Geoff Bennington and Brian Massumi. Minneapolis: University of Minnesota Press, 1979.

MacKinnon, Catharine. *Toward a Feminist Theory of the State*. Cambridge, Mass.: Harvard University Press, 1991.

Mankekar, Purnima. *Screening Culture, Viewing Politics: An Ethnography of Television, Womanhood, and Nation in Postcolonial India*. Durham, N.C.: Duke University Press, 1999.

Marvin, Carolyn. *When Old Technologies Were New: Thinking about Electric Communication in the Late Nineteenth Century*. London: Oxford University Press, 1990.

Marvin, Carolyn, and David W. Ingle. *Blood Sacrifice and the Nation: Myth, Ritual and the American Flag*. Cambridge: Cambridge University Press, 1998.

McCarthy, Anna. *Ambient Television: Visual Culture and Public Space*. Durham, N.C.: Duke University Press, 2001.

McChesney, Robert. *Rich Media, Poor Democracy: Communication Politics in Dubious Times*. New York: New Press, 2000.

McDowell, Jeanne. "Pitching to Kids." *Time*, August 15, 2005.

McNeal, James U. *The Kids Market: Myths and Realities*. New York: Paramount Market Publishing, 1999.

——. *Kids as Customers: A Handbook of Marketing to Children*. New York: Lexington Books, 1992.

McRobbie, Angela. *Feminism and Youth Culture*. Boston: Unwin Hyman, 1991.

——. *Feminism and Youth Culture*. 2nd ed. New York: Routledge, 2000.

——. "Notes on Postfeminism and Popular Culture: Bridget Jones and the New Gender Regime." In *All about the Girl: Culture, Power, and Identity*, edited by Anita Harris, 3–14. New York: Routledge, 2004.

——. "Young Women and Consumer-Citizenship: The Danger of Too Much Pleasure." In *Postfeminist Disorders: Gender, Culture, and Social Change*. London: Sage, forthcoming.

Miller, Toby. "Introducing Cultural Citizenship." *Social Text* 19, no. 4 (2001): 1–5.

——. *Technologies of Truth: Cultural Citizenship and the Popular Media*. Minneapolis: University of Minnesota Press, 1998.

——. *The Well-Tempered Self: Citizenship, Culture, and the Postmodern Subject*. Baltimore: Johns Hopkins University Press, 1993.

Miller, Toby, and Alec McHoul. *Popular Culture and Everyday Life*. Thousand Oaks, Calif.: Sage, 1998.

Milner, Murray, Jr. *Freaks, Geeks, and Cool Kids: American Teenagers, Schools, and the Culture of Consumption*. New York: Routledge, 2004.

Minow, Newton, and Craig LaMay. *Abandoned in the Wasteland: Children, Television, and the First Amendment*. New York: Hill and Wang, 1995.

Mittell, Jason. *Genre and Television: From Cop Shows to Cartoons in American Culture*. New York: Routledge, 2004.

——. "The Great Saturday Morning Exile." In Stabile and Harrison, *Prime Time Animation*, 33–54.

Montgomery, Kathryn. *Target Prime Time: Advocacy Groups and the Struggle over Entertainment Television.* New York: Oxford University Press, 1989.

Morley, David. *Television, Audiences and Cultural Studies,* London: Routledge, 1993.

Morley, David, and Kuan-Hsing Chen, eds. *Stuart Hall: Critical Dialogues in Cultural Studies.* London: Routledge, 1996.

Mullen, Megan. *The Rise of Cable Programming in the United States: Revolution or Evolution?* Austin: University of Texas Press, 2003.

Muñoz, Cecilia. "Casting a Wider Net," report from National Council of La Raza, http://www.nclr.org (accessed December 2004).

Nakamura, Lisa. *Visual Cultures of the Internet.* Minneapolis: University of Minnesota Press, forthcoming.

Newcomb, Horace. *Television: The Critical View.* Oxford: Oxford University Press, 2001.

Newton, Esther. *Mother Camp: Female Impersonators in America.* Chicago: University of Chicago Press, 1972.

Nickelodeon. *How to Nickelodeon* (Corporate Employee Handbook). New York: MTV Networks, 1992.

Okin, Susan Moller. "Is Multiculturalism Bad for Women?" In *Is Multiculturalism Bad for Women?,* edited by Susan Moller Okin, Joshua Cohen, Matthew Howard, and Martha C. Nussbaum. Princeton, N.J.: Princeton University Press, 1999.

Ouellette, Laurie. " 'Take Responsibility for Yourself' ": Judge Judy and the Neoliberal Citizen." In *Reality TV: Remaking Television Culture,* edited by Susan Murray and Laurie Ouellette, 231–50. New York: New York University, 2004.

Palladino, Grace. *Teenagers: An American History.* New York: Basic Books, 1997.

Park, Lisa Sun-Hee. *Consuming Citizenship: Children of Asian Immigrant Entrepreneurs.* Palo Alto, Calif.: Stanford University Press, 2005.

Pecora, Norma. *The Business of Children's Entertainment.* New York: Guilford Press, 1997.

——. "Nickelodeon Grows Up: The Economic Evolution of a Network." In Hendershot, *Nickelodeon Nation,* 15–44.

Petrozzello, Donna. "Nickelodeon's Herb Scannell: In Toon with Kids." *Broadcasting & Cable,* February 2, 1998, 28–31.

Pipher, Mary. *Reviving Ophelia: Saving the Selves of Adolescent Girls.* New York: Ballantine Books. 1995.

Polan, Dana. *Power and Paranoia: History, Narrative, and the American Cinema, 1940–1950.* New York: Columbia University Press, 1986.

——. "The Public's Fear; or, Media as Monster in Habermas, Negt, and Kluge." In Robbins, *The Phantom Public Sphere,* 33–41.

Pool, Ithiel de Sola. *Technologies of Freedom.* Cambridge, Mass.: Harvard University Press, 1984.

Press, Andrea L. *Women Watching Television: Gender, Class, and Generation in the American Television Experience.* Philadelphia: University of Pennsylvania Press, 1991.

Preston, Elizabeth Hall, and Cindy L. White. "Commodifying Kids: Branded Identities and the Selling of Adspace on Kids Networks." *Communication Quarterly* 52, no. 2 (Spring 2004): 115–28.

——. "The Spaces of Children's Programming." *Critical Studies in Media Communication* 22, no. 3 (2005): 239–61.

Quart, Alyssa. *Branded: The Buying and Selling of Teenagers.* New York: Perseus, 2003.

Robbins, Bruce. *The Phantom Public Sphere.* Minneapolis: University of Minnesota Press, 1993.

Roediger, David. *Towards the Abolition of Whiteness: Essays on Race, Politics, and Working Class History.* London: Verso, 1994.

——. *The Wages of Whiteness: Race and the Making of the American Working Class.* London: Verso, 1991.

Rogin, Michael. *Blackface, White Noise: Jewish Immigrants in the Hollywood Melting Pot.* Berkeley: University of California Press, 1996.

Ross, Andrew. *No Respect: Intellectuals and Popular Culture.* New York: Routledge, 1989.

——. "Uses of Camp." In Bergman, *Camp Grounds,* 54–77.

Rousseau, Jean-Jacques. *Emile; or, On Education.* Translated by Allan Bloom. New York: Basic Books, 1979.

Rowe, Kathleen. *The Unruly Woman: Gender and the Genres of Laughter.* Austin: University of Texas Press, 1995.

Sammond, Nicholas. *Babes in Tomorrowland: Walt Disney and the Making of the American Child, 1930–1960.* Durham, N.C.: Duke University Press, 2005.

Sanchez, George. *Becoming Mexican American: Ethnicity, Culture, and Identity in Chicano Los Angeles, 1900–1945.* New York: Oxford University Press, 1993.

Scannell, Herb. "Why Not Diversity?" In *Children Now Newsletter,* Summer 2002, http://www.childrennow.org/assets/pdf/issues—media—medianow—2002.pdf (accessed March 11, 2007).

Schiller, Dan. *Objectivity and the News: The Public and the Rise of Commercial Journalism.* Philadelphia: University of Pennsylvania Press, 1981.

Schor, Juliet. *Born to Buy: The Commercialized Child and the New Consumer Culture.* New York: Scribner, 2004.

Schor, Juliet B., and Douglas B. Holt. *The Consumer Society Reader.* New York: New Press, 2000.

Schudson, Michael. *Advertising, the Uneasy Persuasion: Its Dubious Impact on American Society.* New York: Basic Books, 1984.

——. *Discovering the News: A Social History of American Newspapers.* New York: Basic Books, 1980.

——. *The Good Citizen: A History of American Civic Life.* Cambridge, Mass.: Harvard University Press, 1999.

Sconce, Jeffrey. "Irony, Nihilism, and the American 'Smart' Film." *Screen* 43, no. 3 (2003): 349–69.

Seiter, Ellen. "Children's Desires/Mothers' Dilemmas: The Social Contexts of Consumption." In Jenkins, *The Children's Culture Reader,* 297–317.

——. *The Internet Playground: Children's Access, Entertainment, and Mis-Education.* New York: Peter Lang, 2005.

——. *Sold Separately: Parents and Children in Consumer Culture.* New Brunswick N.J.: Rutgers University Press, 1995.

Seiter, Ellen, and Vicki Mayer. "Diversifying Representation in Children's TV: Nickelodeon's Model." In Hendershot, *Nickelodeon Nation,* 120–33.

Sender, Katherine. *Business, Not Politics: The Making of the Gay Market.* New York: Columbia University Press, 2004.

——. "Selling Sexual Subjectivities: Audiences Respond to Gay Window Advertising." *Critical Studies in Mass Communication* 16, no. 2 (1999): 172–96.

Shank, Barry. "From Rice to Ice: The Face of Race in Rock and Pop." In *The Cambridge Companion to Pop and Rock,* edited by Simon Frith, Will Straw, and John Street, 256–59. Cambridge: Cambridge University Press, 2001.

Shohat, Ella, and Robert Stam. *Unthinking Eurocentrism: Multiculturalism and the Media.* London: Routledge, 1994.

Shugart, Helene A., Catherine Egley Waggoner, and D. Lynn O'Brien Hallstein. "Mediating Third Wave Feminism: Appropriation as Postmodern Media Practice." *Critical Studies in Media Communication* 18, no. 2 (2001): 194–210.

Silverstone, Roger. *Why Study the Media?* London: Sage, 1999.

Simensky, Linda. "The Early Days of Nicktoons." In Hendershot, *Nickelodeon Nation,* 87–107.

Singer, Dorothy G., and Jerome L. Singer, eds. *Handbook of Children and the Media.* Thousand Oaks, Calif.: Sage, 2001.

Smith, Christopher Holmes. " 'I Don't Like to Dream about Getting Paid': Representations of Social Mobility and the Emergence of the Hip-Hop Mogul." *Social Text* 21, no. 4 (2003): 69–97.

Smith, Suzanne E. *Dancing in the Street: Motown and the Cultural Politics of Detroit.* Cambridge, Mass.: Harvard University Press, 2001.

Sontag, Susan. "Notes on 'Camp.' " *Against Interpretation and Other Essays.* New York: Picador, 1961.

Spigel, Lynn. *Make Room for TV: Television and the Family Ideal in Postwar America.* Chicago: University of Chicago Press, 1992.

——. "Seducing the Innocent: Childhood and Television in Postwar America." In Jenkins, *The Children's Culture Reader,* 110–35.

——. *Welcome to the Dreamhouse: Popular Media and Postwar Suburbs.* Durham, N.C.: Duke University Press, 2001.

Spigel, Lynn, and Michael Curtin, eds. *The Revolution Wasn't Televised: Sixties Television and Social Conflict.* New York: Routledge, 1997.

Stabile, Carol A., and Mark Harrison, eds. *Prime Time Animation: Television Animation and American Culture.* London: Routledge, 2003.

Staiger, Janet. *Blockbuster TV: Must-See Sitcoms in the Network Era.* New York: New York University Press, 2001.

Stewart, Susan. *On Longing: Narratives of the Miniature, the Gigantic, the Souvenir, the Collection.* Durham, N.C.: Duke University Press, 1993.

Streeter, Tom. "Blue Skies and Strange Bedfellows: The Discourse of Cable Television." In Spigel and Curtin, *The Revolution Wasn't Televised*, 221–242.

Sturken, Marita. *Tourists of History: Memory, Consumerism, and Kitsch in American Culture from Oklahoma City to Ground Zero.* Durham, N.C.: Duke University Press, forthcoming.

Sturken, Marita, and Lisa Cartwright. *Practices of Looking: An Introduction to Visual Culture.* New York: Oxford University Press, 2001.

Thorne, Barrie. *Gender Play: Girls and Boys in School.* New Brunswick, N.J.: Rutgers University Press, 1993.

Torres, Sasha, ed. *Living Color: Race and Television in the United States.* Durham, N.C.: Duke University Press, 1998.

Turow, Joesph. *Breaking Up America: Advertisers and the New Media World.* Chicago: University of Chicago Press, 1997.

Uricchio, William. "Television's Next Generation: Technology/Interface Culture/Flow." In *Television after TV: Essays on Medium in Transition,* edited by Lynn Spigel and Jan Olsson. Durham, N.C.: Duke University Press, 2004.

van Zoonen, Leisbet. *Entertaining the Citizen: When Politics and Popular Culture Converge.* Lanham, Md.: Rowman and Littlefield, 2004.

Watts, Eric King, and Mark P. Orbe. "The Spectacular Consumption of 'True' African American Culture: 'Whassup' with the Budweiser Guys?" *Critical Studies in Media Communication* 19, no. 1 (2002): 1–20.

Wells, Paul. *Animation and America.* New Brunswick, N.J.: Rutgers University Press, 2002.

Wheeler, Alina. *Designing Brand Identity: A Complete Guide to Creating, Building, and Maintaining Strong Brands.* New York: Wiley, 2003.

Williams, Raymond. *The Sociology of Culture.* New York: Schocken, 1987.

———. *Television: Technology and Cultural Form.* 2nd ed. New York: Routledge, 1990.

Winski, Joseph. " 'Addicted' to Research, Nick Shows Strong Kids' Lure." *Advertising Age,* February 10, 1992.

Wiseman, Rosalind. *Queen Bees and Wannabes: Helping Your Daughter Survive Cliques, Gossip, Boyfriends and Other Realities of Adolescence.* New York: Crown, 2002.

Wolf, Naomi. *Fire with Fire: The New Female Power and How to Use It.* New York: Fawcett Books, 1994.

Wynter, Leon E. *American Skin: Pop Culture, Big Business, and the End of White America.* New York: Crown, 2002.

Young, Josh. "A Better Mousetrap?" *Entertainment Weekly,* December 4, 1998.

Zelizer, Viviana A. *Pricing the Priceless Child: The Changing Social Value of Children.* Princeton, N.J.: Princeton University Press, 1994.

Zoglin, Richard. "Letting Kids Just Be Kids." *Time,* December 26, 1988.

brownness, 155, 158

Buckingham, David, 13, 14, 33, 101, 134, 137

Budweiser commercials, 156

Buena Vista Motion Picture Group, 163

Buffy the Vampire Slayer, 202

Bugs Bunny, 184

Bushman, David, 112

Bust, 115

Butler, Judith, 204

Butt Ugly Martians, 241n20

Cable News Network (CNN), 45

cable TV: animation and corporate culture, 62–68; broadcast TV and, 18, 30, 38, 41, 42, 45, 62, 65, 66; deregulation (1980s) and children's TV, 50–52; industry structure of, 5, 18, 30, 43; Laybourne era and, 52–56; media reform of broadcast networks and, 45–49; Nick and commercial child, 49–50; Nick and Viacom, 60–62; Nick as neighborhood, 57–60; overview of, 38–40; as utopia, 41–45, 77, 78

California, 143, 156

camp style: controversy over *Ren & Stimpy* and, 193–97; of *The Fairly OddParents*, 205–10; irony/double coding and, 187–93; of Kricfalusi, 197–99; mainstreaming of, 242–43n49; Nick animation and, 185–87; overview of, 178–82; politics of, 36, 37; *SpongeBob SquarePants* and, 199–205

Canclini, Nestor García, 9, 20

Cancun, 175

capital, cultural. *See* cultural capital

capitalism, 45, 46

Captain Kangaroo, 99

Care Bears, 76, 193, 194

Cartoon Network: adult cartoons on, 187; Nick vs., 64, 72, 96–97, 98, 209–10; toys and, 185, 229n102

cartoons: animatophiles and, 181, 187, 199, 243n54; camp/irony and double coding in, 186–87, 188, 190, 192; cinematic style

of, 16, 149, 183, 187; cost of, 63–64; as creator-driven, 185–86; gender/sexuality and, 184; innocence of, 184, 187; marketing/merchandising and, 46, 61, 185, 186; philosophy of, 185–86; politics/violence/censorship and, 184; race and, 108, 149, 150; Saturday morning exile and, 16, 45, 65, 183, 184, 186; styles of, 180–81, 187–88, 207–10; transgenerational appeal of, 63, 184–88. *See also* animation

Catholicism, 176

CATV (Community Antenna Television), 42

CBS Corporation, 60, 65, 67, 223n62

celebrities, 10–11, 189, 234n14

censorship, 47, 183

cereal, 76, 204

Charren, Peggy, 16, 47, 49, 56, 72, 84

chase and flight dynamic, 78–79

Chicano nationalist movements, 157–58

Chichen Itza (Mexico), 174, 175

child audience: as active/passive, 18, 99, 113; advertisers appealing to cynicism/skepticism of, 78; as being in Nick, 213; broadcast TV required to serve, 16; coolness and, 22, 23, 82; diversity and, 145; early loyalty of, 72; economic value of, 183; empowerment of, 15, 59, 69, 70; imagined, and cartoons, 187; as impressionable, 76; meaning of childhood and, 59; news as inappropriate for, 13; respect for, 102; school-age vs. adolescent vs. tween, 102; sophistication/naïveté of, 16, 20, 49, 58, 80, 183, 188; targeting of, 21, 46, 64

childhood: commercialization of, 224n78; cultural definition of, 59; culture of, 4, 34, 101; economic configuration of, 75; as modern invention, 24; victimization and, 91

children: access to power of, 25; active participation with media of, 4, 35, 70; addressed as mature adults, 188; in ads, 77, 95; adult audience similar to, 222–23n55; adults vs., 34, 75, 76, 88, 184; adver-

Sarah Banet-Weiser is an associate professor in the
Annenberg School for Communication at the University
of Southern California. She is the author of *The Most
Beautiful Girl in the World: Beauty Pageants and National
Identity* (1999), and a co-editor of *Cable Visions:
Television Beyond Broadcasting* (2007).

Library of Congress Cataloging-in-Publication Data
Banet-Weiser, Sarah, 1966–
Kids rule! : Nickelodeon and consumer citizenship /
Sarah Banet-Weiser.
p. cm. — (Console-ing passions)
Includes bibliographical references and index.
ISBN-13: 978-0-8223-3976-2 (cloth : alk. paper)
ISBN-13: 978-0-8223-3993-9 (pbk. : alk. paper)
1. Nickelodeon (Television network) 2. Television
programs for children—United States. 3. Child
consumers—United States. I. Title.
PN1992.92.N55B36 2007
791.450973—dc22   2007014054